A Soldier's Son

An American Boyhood During World War II

A Soldier's Son
An American Boyhood During World War II

John E. Hodgkins

Foreword by Bill Roorbach

DOWN EAST BOOKS

CAMDEN, MAINE

Printed at Versa Press, East Peoria, Illinois

5   4   3   2   1

Designed by Harrah Lord, Yellow House Studio

Down East Books
Camden, Maine
Distributed to the trade by
National Book Network, Inc.
Book Orders 800-685-7962
www.downeastbooks.com

ISBN-10: 0-89272-716-0
ISBN-13: 978-0-89272-716-2

Library of Congress Cataloging-in-Publication Data
Hodgkins, John E.
  A soldier's son : an American boyhood during World War II / John E. Hodgkins.
    p. cm.
  ISBN 0-89272-716-0 (alk. paper)
  1. Hodgkins, John E. 2. Hodgkins, John E.—Family. 3. World War, 1939-1945—Children—
Maine—Temple. 4. World War, 1939-1945—Maine—Temple. 5. World War, 1939-1945—Personal
narratives, American. 6. Children—Maine—Biography. 7. World War, 1939-1945—Campaigns—
Western Front. I. Title.
  D810.C4H56 2006
  974.1'72—dc22
                                        2006001646

Contents

FOREWORD

T emple, Maine, is still the "Town that Ends the Road," as poet and former resident Theodore Enslin put it in a long and rather bleak poem of the same name. Maine Route 43 does indeed end just past the pleasing shambles of the current village, just past the wrecks of old mills, just past the town store (barely holding on as a branch post office and antique store, and still called Hodgkins Store), just past a sharp curve and a hump in the road—old rusty skidder lurking in the woods—ends without ambiguity: the heavy black state pavement switches suddenly to the faded town pavement, the beautifully painted double yellow lines simply stop. The road itself continues up the intervale (as bottom land is called around here), crossing a small bridge for Mitchell Brook, then carrying on, always alongside Temple Stream, past defunct farms, past a well-kept settler cemetery, past houses old and new, past an old red schoolhouse (now the Temple Historical Society building), past the former Congregational Church (now the Temple Stream Theatre), up a slight incline another mile or so to the end of pavement. The road goes on, increasingly rutted, finally all but unpassable, clear to Avon over the plateau between Mount Blue and Day Mountain. But we'll stop where the pavement ends, park the car by a small field of well-tended balsam fir Christmas trees.

Back up the hill to the left is a fine, old Federal style house, beautifully restored, painted white, which I know from my reading is the Oakes house or Mitchell house, depending on how far back memory reaches, the house where once Theodore Enslin lived, now John and Beth Hodgkins's house. And this is where my wife, Juliet, and I have gone to get our yearly Christmas tree from the first years we lived downstream. It's a charming place in December as at other times, buried in the first snows, the hill of the driveway icy with the trails of trees felled and dragged by cheerful families, the sound of carols half-heard, half-imagined, the very sound of angels singing. Or is that wind in the old sugar maples? We grab a bow saw off its peg at the barn, shuffle up the tractor road to the farthest field of trees in all sizes, something for every living room.

This one?

No—that one!

A happy hour of indecision, then a job of sawing the perfect fragrant Tannenbaum, feeling sweetly a couple. Dusk falling, snow sifting down, a warm light in the Hodgkins house, smell of birch logs burning. We drag that one best tree hundreds of yards down the hill, stop to write a very small check. We know whom to make it out to. But it's years before we actually meet the Hodgkinses, nearly ten.

Our daughter's two by that time. Elysia's sad we will cut a tree. But we do. She wails: we have killed it. At the house, as I write my annual check, the front door opens and Mr. Hodgkins is in the light. He seems very serious, with clear, intelligent eyes. "Would she like a cookie?" he asks kindly.

That stops the wailing. Elysia's a cookie monster.

We shake hands, trade names.

John grins. "I know you," he says. And goes on to say that he's writing a book about his childhood and youth in this valley and has used *Writing Life Stories*, a book of mine, to help. We live barely three miles apart. I'm working on a book about Temple Stream, as it happens, which flows down below John's lower field (and in his childhood memories as well) and later through the fields below my house.

I grin too. I want to know what the village was like before the war.

I want to know which farms were still in operation, which of the schools. I want to know if John used to play in the stream. We have a lot to talk about, do so in few words. John's got photos of the intervale in the old days.

Juliet was in a hurry till she saw those photos, but now she's captured, and we proceed frame by frame down the stairwell hallway as down the corridors of a museum, inspecting those old images. Elysia has a fresh cookie. John's wife, Beth, appears from back in the kitchen. She's as reserved as he and at the same time as warm, that light of intelligence in the eyes, a certain wry glint. There are a lot of visitors this time of year and you don't necessarily want to encourage every single one of them, says her face. But she sees Elysia and that takes care of that and after introductions we're all nodding at one another and nibbling at cookies and comparing notes in as few words as possible. Beth finds a book of her granddaughter's, *Papa, Please Get the Moon For Me*, and we all look at that, that rickety ladder all the way to heaven, and Elysia loves it and our tree is waiting outside and it's a Christmas tableau.

In the next several tree seasons we'll visit again, work toward friendship, learn more about these people incrementally: John Hodgkins met Beth Gamage—who was teaching school downeast in Wiscasset—on a blind date set up by mutual friends, 1964. And not just any blind date but the quintessential blind date of the times: a Peter, Paul, and Mary concert down in Portland. Something clicked between "Puff the Magic Dragon" and "Blowing in the Wind," it seems, for John and Beth were married in 1965.

Presently, they settled in Yarmouth, just north of Portland. John studied toward his master's degree in civil engineering from the University of Maine at Orono, where eventually he'd teach courses in that subject as an adjunct professor while working for the Maine Department of Transportation. In 1966, daughter Bethel was born; in 1967, Jack; and finally in 1970, Bill. Bethel studied civil engineering at

Cornell, now owns an engineering firm, has four sons. Jack went to Cornell too, now works in real estate finance, with interests in affordable housing and historic preservation. He has two girls and a boy. Bill is an inspector of bridge construction for the Maine Department of Transportation.

Count the grandchildren: seven.

In late 1979, John and Beth bought the old Oakes house as a retreat, spent weekends and vacations working on it, planted the first Christmas trees, added them to the yearly project and tradition of maple sugaring, the farming of trees something more than a hobby, something less than a living, good satisfying work back in the heart of John's home world, not so much a full circle as a spiral upwards, and upwards again. They're retired now and can spend months at a time in Temple, and it's just good to know such folks are at the end of the road, that what once seemed bleak is once again imbued with life.

It's good to know, too, that John has finished his book. And what a book it is—the lost world of the war years, a world of pain as well as growth, all brought to life with a sharp eye, sharp memory, and no flinching. Hodgkins's Temple is a place where a neighbor's makeshift cider mill is all the entertainment a boy might need, where a cord and a half of borrowed firewood marks the difference between freezing and surviving, where the exotic sauna of Finnish neighbors becomes a comical social magnet. There are few more complicated characters in literature than young Johnny's Aunt Marion, few more heroic than his mother, Clarice, few more bedeviled than Pa as he heads off to World War II, leaving his family and a good many failures behind. And there are very few memoirists with the economy of language, clarity of memory, sense of humor, stoic charm, and plain honesty of John Hodgkins. He's written a hell of a good book.

And here it is.

—Bill Roorbach

PROLOGUE

O ne day during the summer before my father died, he set two
cardboard boxes and a locked strongbox on my kitchen floor.
"These are yours," he said and handed me a key.

I suspected the boxes contained the accumulated memories of his
earlier life. For years I had known, in a roundabout way, of the existence
of a war diary, but I had not seen it and had no inkling that he owned
a collection of keepsakes. "I'll care for them," I told him.

After my father died, I opened the boxes and found World War II
memorabilia: letters from my mother, letters from me, letters from
friends and relatives, training camp newspapers, transport ship
newsletters, copies of *Yank, The Army Weekly*, and letters and postcards
he had written home. There were unit patches, service ribbons, medals,
and souvenir shreds of German army uniforms stored in these boxes.
Train tickets, telegrams, copies of military orders, collections of newspaper clippings, and a sprinkling of photographs told of his comings
and goings during the war years. His war diary began with an entry on
the day he left England for France and ended when he boarded a train
in Trenton, New Jersey, for home. There's a story here someplace, I
thought, and I put the boxes aside.

I was eight years old in 1943 when my father was drafted into the
army of World War II. He was not a war hero—far from it—but he did
not shirk his duty as some said he could have. Thirty-three years old
with a wife and three small children, he did not seek deferment. His

friends—young, strong, single, and without family responsibilities—were going, and he felt honor bound to follow.

He never told me stories of the war. But as the years after his death slid by, I felt strongly that his story, whatever it was, should be written. When I was ready, I read again the contents of those old boxes, my father's diary, and his letters from Germany. My mother's letters written from our lonely refuge in Temple, Maine, told of her overpowering difficulties: lack of firewood, money, and transportation; temptation; and conflict with relatives. I read period issues of our local newspaper, *The Franklin Journal*. As I read, memories came rushing back: my father's absence, frigid days and nights, farming our half-acre place, the doings of folks about town, friendships, and loneliness.

I read book after book about the war in Europe and those times by such compelling authors as General Omar N. Bradley, Stephen Ambrose, Doris Kearns Goodwin, Private Raymond Gantter, Russell F. Weigley, Captain Charles Leach, Stanley P. Hirshon, Winston Churchill, Tom Brokaw, and Marion Hargrove. Beth, my wife of thirty-five years, traveled to Europe with me, and we tracked my father's experiences as he told them in his diary. I joined the 8th Armored Division Association and exhausted the information on its Web site and in its newsletters. I diagrammed the floor plan of my boyhood home, sketched the plot of land we lived on, and talked with people who lived in Temple at that time. I studied old-photo backgrounds with a magnifying glass. I constructed notebooks and went to school to learn the rudiments of writing a memoir.

I am grateful for the interest, suggestions, and encouragement that have come my way from the many people who have watched over this four-year project. My sisters, Nancy and Patty, who lived those long-ago days with me, have furnished considerable help reviving my memory. Beth, who spent countless mornings alone while I secluded myself at my keyboard, has been an avid reader and insistent advocate of clarity in my storytelling. "If I can't understand what you're saying, who can?" she asked. Digressions in punctuation and grammar have been graciously and competently pointed out by linguistic aficionados Stewart Goodwin and Lynn Ross.

A Soldier's Son: An American Boyhood During World War II is the truth as I know it: what I recall, what I saw, what I heard, what I read, what I felt in my heart, and what I have learned. Dialogue represents what was said or written and is not intended to be literally correct. It comes from letters and news items as well as from conversations I overheard or engaged in. World War II soldiers found it nearly impossible to communicate with their comrades without liberal—often excessive—reliance on what is referred to as the f-word. Harvard-educated Private Raymond Gantter wrote in *Roll Me Over*, his memoir of experiences as an infantryman in World War II, that he once listened in on a poker game, and the three players used the f-word thirty-four times in two minutes. Like Gantter, I chose not to use it, which, of course, relegates dialogue between soldiers to the unrealistic. Thus, you may wish to frequently—and silently—insert the word into these conversations.

The writing of *A Soldier's Son* has been an inspiring, heart-stirring, soulful, and, yes, wistful journey for me. I have labored long over this work, not out of remorse or anger—I have come to terms with the past—but out of a boy's yearning to hear of his father's adventures. And in my attempt to resurrect his stories, I discovered in those old boxes that I, too, had a story to tell.

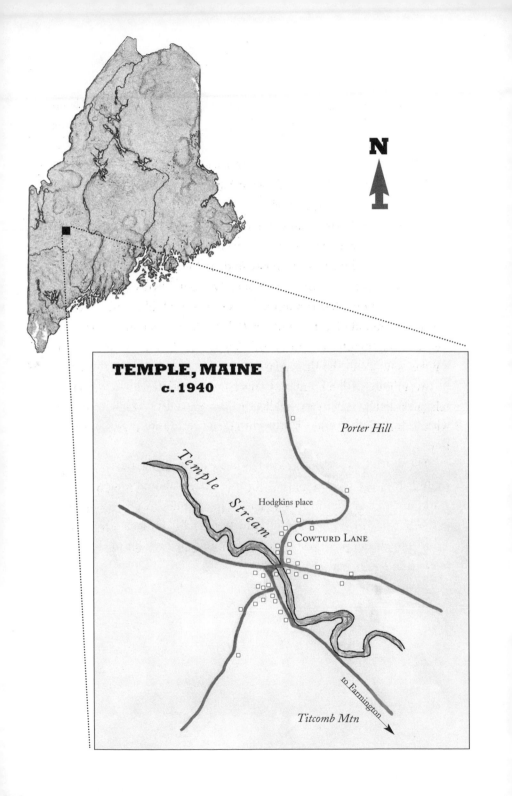

N

TEMPLE, MAINE
c. 1940

Porter Hill

Temple Stream

Hodgkins place

Cowturd Lane

to Farmington

Titcomb Mtn

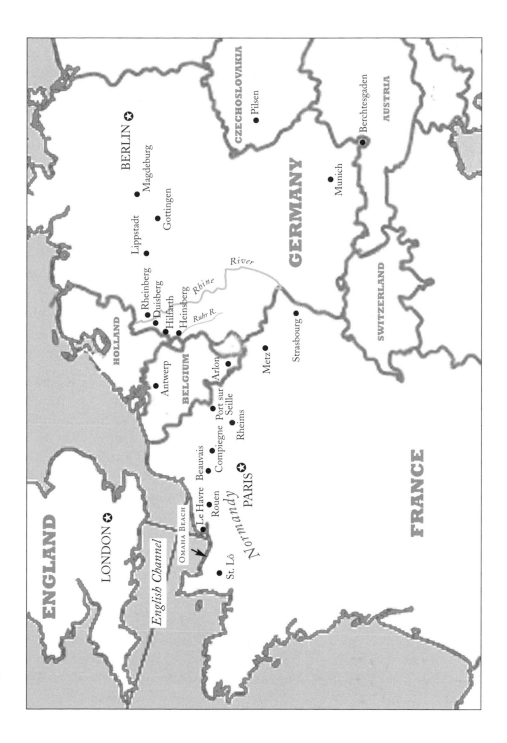

Chapter One
TEMPLE 1943

*I'll tell you all the yarns you want to hear about the old days in
Temple. Ayeh. Pure bullshit, too. . . . Did you know there was
a whorehouse in this town? Famous one, yeah. . . . Your ears
perkin' up? Ha ha! . . . Never was such a thing. . . . This was
a town of churches and Grange Halls and little schools. Ayeh.
No whorehouses . . .*

—George Dennison, *Temple*

Ma should have gone home to modish Kennebunk after she
graduated from Farmington Normal School. Instead she
came to Temple and, after a few not-so-innocent years as the village
schoolmarm, married my father. Now, some eight years later, she tends
a sparse country kitchen and three wanting youngsters. Pa looks after
two cows, a heifer, a hog, and a dozen chickens in the barn and walks
to the general store at supper time to fetch his link to the outside world,
the *Lewiston Evening Journal,* which arrives on the 5:00 P.M. mail stage.

We're stranded here. Outside of the kitchen window, winter
presses on the land like a cold flatiron. Snow stretches at eye level to
the pasture gate and beyond, unbroken except for the curved ends of
big-wheel cultivator handles poking through the surface like twin
periscopes. The snow lies deep against our house. Drifts are banked

against the pasture fence. The bare apple trees lining the lane are veiled in white. Beyond, the land is indistinguishable from the pale wintry sky. I could as well be in Greenland as in this little Maine foothill town of snow-plugged roads and idle loggers.

Outside of the front door, the road is unplowed and has been since early December when Pa, a half a bottle of Carstairs whiskey in his stomach, put the top up on the roadster and tried to drive to nearby Farmington once more before winter locked us in. But winter had arrived, and Pa abandoned the roadster midway between our house and the village bridge in a storm that piled snow so deep folks measured it with hoe handles. The car sits there now, under a blanket of snow, a bizarre bulge in the road, like a man hiding under a bedsheet with his ass in the air. Our neighbors, who live up the hill a mile beyond us, detour their horse and sleigh around the lump in the road on their way to the general store. Nancy, my reticent and pensive younger sister, and I walk in the horse path on our way to the Village School and back. We don't speak about the roadster. It sits there as a symbol of the struggle that winter brings to our part of the world. Patty, the youngest, yet perhaps the most curious and chattery, asks "Where did he go? When is he coming back? Why is the car in the road?" Patty doesn't walk to school with us, not yet. Patty stays home with Ma.

The loggers, too, sit in their parlors and eye the snow outside of their windows, and Pa, who trucks their logs to the mills, waits. He reads the *Lewiston Evening Journal* and listens to the Emerson; World War II permeates the news. Daily the newspaper's headlines report the actions in Tripoli and Tunisia, Guadalcanal and New Guinea, and Gabriel Heater shouts above the static out of the Emerson the actions of *Generalissimo* this and *Generalfeldmarschall* that. It all seems far away from this snug kitchen, but soldiers and sailors home on leave walk the roads and lanes of Temple, and they linger in the general store to tell their stories.

Twilight closes around me. I hanker for the shelter of the heated cookstove, but I struggle into a coat, reach up inside the cuffs to pull my shirtsleeves down, put on a hat and mittens, and go to the shed. I must fill a hungry woodbox. I open the cover and take tomorrow's stove wood from the stacks and toss it in the box. Ma, in the kitchen, opens a small door in the kitchen wall and takes out a few sticks for the stove. Nancy laughs at me out through the opening, "Better hurry. It's getting emptier, not fuller," she chuckles. "You'll be there all night."

I don't like dusk in winter. It frightens me. I'm lonesome, and I scurry to fill the woodbox and go back to the warmth of the stove.

Later Pa comes in from the stable carrying a pitcher of warm cow's milk. I turn to look at him and he asks me how about it, is the woodbox full? It's done, I say. He sets the pitcher on the table and goes back out. I try to ignore him, but he says for me to follow, and I reach for my coat again. Ma, who preserves garden vegetables and shops for food supplies with ration coupons, sends Nancy to the cellar for potatoes and carrots and takes flour and sugar from the food cupboard for biscuits and a custard pie—Pa's favorite. I go to the barn.

In the barn, steam rises from the fresh cow shit in the gutter. The cows stand quietly in their stalls and munch on their cud. Pa tells me what to do. "Rake both stalls clean, then spread some sawdust for the cows to sleep on."

There is no talk between us otherwise. We work in silence, interrupted only by an occasional burp or blat from a cow. I want to ask about the roadster in the road, but I'm not sure of his mood. So I wait. Perhaps he will show me a smile, or tell a story, or take an interest in my schoolwork. Then I will ask him.

In my earliest memory of my father, about 1939, I see him at his workbench upstairs in the barn. He stands back-to in blue-denim overalls, and his shoulders slouch forward over the bench. He is cleaning a rusty wrench, or some other tool he has found in the road. Except for his hands, he is motionless. He doesn't whistle or hum or speak to me. He just stands there, his face invisible, and rubs the rust from an old, thrown-away wrench.

Pa's adult beginnings had been spent in the Great Depression, in what must have been a soulful experience for a man who relied on laboring for a living. Like many of that time, he was a saver. We lived a folklore of recycling. He found space to store balls of foil and string, boxes of metal cans and glass bottles, piles of nondescript scrap metal and tied newspaper bundles, stacks of worn-out rubber tires and car batteries, and remnants of abandoned automobiles strewed behind the shed. He expected me, then, to contribute string, aluminum foil, gum wrappers, and old magazines and comic books to his recycling piles, just as he does now, in addition to the barn chores he has doled out to me.

Pa met Ma, then a full-time teacher at the Village School, in 1930. She fell hopelessly in love with his carefree demeanor, and four years later—four months before I was born—they married. Later, when I had grown old enough to discover nine months were necessary to produce a child, I thought I had been a miracle or at least a prodigy. Pa must have thought so too. He left my learning to someone else.

According to Aunt Marion, his hypercritical sister, if he hadn't married Ma, he could have been successful. I think she meant he could have been more like her, an aggressive and sometimes egocentric accumulator of position, possessions, and portfolio of accounts receivable from favors and gifts she had bestowed on others. Consequently, she considered Pa inferior to his assertive and important siblings, who saw little value in an intelligent person working with his hands for a living. Nevertheless, I admired his work. He used adult-sized "toys," and I could see the results: woodpiles, haystacks, graveled roads, and cleaned fields. Ma, brought up under the strict guidance of scrupulous parents who had denied her the simple pleasures of a movie or a dance, saw romanticism in Pa's work, and she was attracted to it; his siblings were not. Many times Pa felt unwanted or unappreciated in the family circle.

Pa's cronies at the West Farmington Fire Company welcomed him into their frequent poker games. It was the only club he belonged to. He spent many hours there and a measurable amount of money that he must have considered dues. He took me there once when I was five years old or so. Perhaps he thought he could show me a real man's side of life, but it's more likely that he didn't want to miss the game. My memory is dim: men's faces hidden in blue cigarette smoke, and talk in words I didn't understand. His pals invited him to stay, motioning to an empty straight-backed chair, "Sit down, El. We've got room for another one. Five and ten." Pa sat lightly and placed a pile of coins on the table. Cards were dealt quickly. "What brings you out, El? You babysittin' today?"

"Babysitting? No," Pa said. "We've been over to Blackie's for a haircut. Don't he look good?" Pa stared at his cards. "C'mon. Hit me. Hit me *easy*—Oh, shee-it!" Someone chuckled and swigged from a bottle.

Blackie was the barber of choice for Pa's crowd. We had waited in the barbershop while Blackie snipped and shaved and told stories, mostly about drinking and women and fishing. A favored customer would take a short break from storytelling and go into Blackie's men's room just long enough to take a couple swigs from a bottle stashed there, then come back ready to tell a story of his own. I had watched and listened carefully. Pa had exposed me to an education not many five-year-old boys get. Blackie, in his white barber's smock, perched me on a board he had placed across the arms of his barber chair, cranked me as high as he could, and clipped and snipped until Pa said Ma would like it, then he doused my hair with Wildroot or Lucky Tiger tonic and slicked it down. All the while, I listened to Blackie's wisecracks and watched the scene behind me in the wall-long mirror. Men would come in who didn't need haircuts, just a visit to Blackie's bathroom. Men would come in to tell a story, and Blackie would always tell a better one, like the time he had sex with a woman twice in twenty minutes and drank a pint of whiskey in between.

"Ain't the kid a little too young to be going to Blackie's?" someone asked.

"Nah. It's good for him to hear some mantalk once in a while. He spends too much time with his mother." Pa fingers his cards, looking for the ace he doesn't have. "Jeez-*us*," he mutters, then goes on. "You shoulda seen him when Apple come in. Apple had one of those eyepiece things, a kaleedascope or sumthin', that you look into and see a different naked woman every time. Said his son sent it to him from San Diego. He passes that around the room, and Johnny eyes it all around, and I think good gawd Apple's gonna show it to him . . . but he didn't."

"Gonna be just like his old man ain't he, a chip off the old block," someone said.

"Gawd, I hope not. Whose deal is it, anyway?"

A cloud of cigarette smoke hung low over the table. They passed a bottle from one to another. They spoke in two-word sentences. No more stories. Stone-faced men engaged in serious business. When Pa's stack of change was gone, we left. I never went back, nor did I want to, but Pa, drawn to the unfulfilled promises of easy income and loyal friendships, went there often and played away a pile of nickels and dimes.

Now, on a January night in the barn, cows fidget in their stalls while steam rises above fresh cow shit in the gutter. I rake the stalls with a garden hoe and spread hay chaff and sawdust for the cows to sleep on. Pa shovels the dung out of a small window to a growing manure pile in the back. "They need hay, too," he says, and I go up to the loft in the dark and pitch hay down through a trap door. And I wait.

Finally, when the work is about done, I dare to ask him about the roadster. Pa has been an expert at keeping the roadster running. The inner tubes are a mosaic of patches. He has replaced broken spring leaves with ones found in the auto graveyard out back. He covers the radiator with a blanket on cold nights, as though the roadster were one of Kike's plow horses down the road, and, when the battery is dead, he cranks the engine with a crooked socket wrench through a small hole in the front grill. Gas rationing has restricted pleasure driving, but Pa has tried kerosene and siphoned gasoline from his truck to take us riding. He has made it work, except for the December snowstorm.

Now I want to go to the movies and the soda shop in Farmington, like my friends do, but the roadster is in the snowdrift. "Can't we get our car out of the way so the tractor can plow the road?" I ask.

"I asked the damned arses to plow around it, but they say they can't," Pa answers. "Plow's been broke down or stuck most of the winter anyway."

"Why can't we shovel a path to it and bring it home?"

"Wise up, boy. It's been there over two months. We could never get it moving. I'm gonna leave it there 'til the snow melts."

Pa thinks he's punishing town officials for not plowing the road. Actually he's punishing me. "Gene Autry is in a movie at the State. I want to go," I say.

"Your Auntie May will take you. Talk to her. Or your mother will take you on the mail stage."

I get the message. It's always the same. Either I don't need to, or someone else can do it instead of him. He takes me only to places he wants to go, like the West Farmington Fire Company. I stick to my work.

Pa was dominant in our self-reliant rural family, and I knew it. I didn't question or avoid his authority. I submitted to it. He steered my formal education, and my social and cultural upbringing, except for Blackie's, to the teachers at the Village School, to Ma, and to my Aunt Marion. His place at the head of the family, it seemed to me, did not include teaching me or training me in the ways of life. What I learned from Pa, I learned by watching. His infrequent personal attempts to strike a blow at my ignorance were limited to a single phrase, "Wise up, boy," and my occasional attempts to find comfort in his presence were repulsed.

Around home Pa had to have his way. I saw no partnership between him and Ma. It seemed he had vowed to charm her, adore her, and bully her, and she had promised to love him, respect him, and suffer his iniquities. Their match bordered on turbulence, undercut by uncertainty. On the one hand, they socialized together, partying with friends—mostly our Finnish neighbors—drinking beer, dancing, making love, enjoying each other, seldom respecting the culture of their families. On the other hand, like the north ends of two magnets—she a predictable clinger and he a mysterious, unpredictable, psychic-driven loner—they often repelled each other. But Ma, a small, delicate, fragile, and introverted woman, the product of a puritanical upbringing of church, home, and duty, took no chances with disagreement. She was fiercely attracted to the free-spirited, risk-taking, independent country boy and wanted to please him. Nonetheless, as hard as she tried not to be, she was scared.

At the supper table, Pa talks of loggers and deep snow, and the hunting and fishing gear in the new L.L. Bean catalog, and then he mentions it. "I heard Weikko got his notice today. Has to go to Portland on Tuesday for a physical." Pa taps his fingers on the table. "I expect it'll be Vilio next."

Men have been disappearing from Temple for a year, to army training camps and navy bases, and to the war zones across the oceans. "Elliott, all your friends will be gone," Ma says. "You'll be the only one left. What if you have to go? What will I do? I don't know how to take care of this place. I'm worried."

"I'll hafta get someone to take care of the cows and the pig and so forth, you know what I mean . . . if I leave. Probably I could handle it that way," Pa answers.

"But there's still a lot more to do, like the firewood and the gardens and taking care of the house. I've never done anything like that alone. And your family doesn't like me."

"They don't? Why don't they like you?"

"I'm sure they think I'm not good enough for you."

"How do you know that?"

"Just the way they act. They think I'm holding you back and keeping you from making something of yourself, from being a successful businessman like your brothers."

"That's bullshit, Clarice, and you know it."

"No, I don't know it. You know darn well they won't lift a finger to help me. I don't know what I'll do if you go. I'm scared."

"We'll see what happens," he says. "Maybe I won't have to go. After all, I'm thirty-three years old, and we have three kids born before the war even started."

Ma has already told Nancy and Patty and me she wants to go to Kennebunk if he leaves, but she hasn't mentioned that to Pa yet. She doesn't dare. She chooses to live with uncertainty rather than wrangle.

After supper, in a scene being repeated all over town, Pa pushes away from the table and lights a cigarette. He leans forward slightly, puts his hands on his knees as if to get up, and looks at Ma. "I'm going to the store. You want anything?"

Ma heads for the dishpan with a dirty plate in each hand. "No. I don't need anything, but find out how Bertha is. I heard she was taken to the hospital."

I ask Pa to take me with him. He asks Ma. She smiles and says okay. I smile too. Evenings at the store are usually just for the men.

In 1943, Temple was a Grange Hall, dance hall, and one-room schoolhouse town of conservative politics, independent living, and neighborly assistance; a village of tin roofs, a telephone switchboard in someone's parlor, and a post office in the corner of the general store. The recent past had been far less generous economically than the pre-Depression days of sawmills and high employment, which had sustained the town's former prosperity. Now only faint remnants of the mills and bunkhouses on Temple Stream remained, the saws and machinery had gone silent and been auctioned, and the town lacked cash. Some folks were still logging, but most of the town's two hundred fifty or so people, less those who had gone soldiering or to work in defense plants, existed mainly on small family farms with little more than a cow, a pig, a heifer, a few chickens, and a large vegetable garden.

Townsfolk exchanged the current news and local information at the general store and post office, more so even than eavesdropping on their hand-cranked, party-line telephones. Opened for business in 1895, and passed to the next generation in 1940, the store had served up the essential needs of a small town—groceries and fresh meats, beer, fuel, hardware, durable goods, and the opportunity to chat with friends and neighbors—for nearly fifty years.

Pa and I walked there in the darkness. A countryman, Pa was not a country walker. He didn't gangle or sway or swing his arms or stir up the air. He walked erect and stepped straight ahead without a sound, his arms at his sides, his jumbo-sized hands moving only slightly, like a sea anchor, to stabilize his gait. We followed the beaten trail around the roadster, now just a dark hulk looming in the pathway ahead, and strode over the bridge. I regarded that nighttime walk to the store with Pa as a treat, not because there would be ice cream in the freezer, or soda in the cooler, or candy in the glassed-in counter, but because there would be rich conversation around the woodstove. Men would talk about the war and their lives.

A single outside bulb lit the entrance. A hand-cranked kerosene pump stood like a sentinel at the far end of the platform, surrounded by the faint odor of spilled fuel hanging in the cold and still night air. Although Uncle Austin, Pa's younger brother, had owned the store for three years, the sign over the door still read Clarence F. Hodgkins General Store.

Clarence F. Hodgkins was my paternal grandfather and, I thought, the most prominent person ever in the public life of Temple, even more so than a mayor, had one existed. Known about town as C.F., he was a countryman. He moved slowly and drawled his words in a country manner, and every day he wore a necktie and a tattered fedora and smoked a nicotine-stained pipe. But he held citified jobs. He opened the general store in 1895, and in the following years served as superintendent of schools, town treasurer, and Temple's tax collector. He had been postmaster since 1905 and moderator of town meetings for the past forty years. Everyone in town knew, admired, and appreciated him. Most were indebted to him.

At his store, Grandpa C.F. had obliged all the folks in town. In forty-five years as the owner, which included the period of the Great Depression, he had filled a file drawer with credit slips for goods he had sold to people who could not pay. Those uncollected accounts, often the source of a scolding from Grandma Luna and his daughter (my Aunt Marion) who accused him of being duped by his own trustfulness, were discarded when he sold the store to Uncle Austin in 1940.

Grandpa C.F. pidgeonholes the daily mail in his corner post office at the general store.

A peaceful and unassuming man, he had no taste for conflict or argument. Instead he absorbed and deflected the objectionable, shared what he had with needy townsfolk, and lived in harmony with his world.

I considered Grandpa C.F. to be a recreational farmer before I knew such progressives existed. He kept a remarkable garden that included muskmelons and watermelons, he raised turkeys for food, and he produced maple syrup. In the spring, I watched him collect sap from tin cans he had hung on sugar maple trees at Aunt Marion's and Uncle Austin's, then boil the sticky-sweet liquid in a flat pan on a hot woodstove. When sap was plentiful, he spent all day in his old, weather-beaten garage stoking the fire, tending the steamy liquid with a ladle and a scoop, and telling stories to whoever came along. At the end of the day, when his speech was whiskey-slurred and his behavior erratic and the liquid in the pan looked just right to him, he strained

the syrup through a piece of stained flannel, tasted it, and with fum-
bling fingers, poured it into an empty whiskey bottle and tightened on
the screw cap.

Keeping Grandpa C.F. sober was a challenge taken on by Grandma
Luna and Aunt Marion that they failed to achieve. He outsmarted
them every time. Mixed drinks were not his specialty, so he had no
paraphernalia or ritual that gave him away. He'd just reach for the bottle in the pocket of a bulky sweater or coat or in a bureau drawer or in
a grain bag outside his turkey pen and swig straight whiskey. In the
spring he drank amidst the smoke and steam and syrup-making equipment in his garage and filled his empty bottles with fresh maple syrup.
During the summer he fished Temple Stream and carried a stubby of
Genesee ale in his boot, and when he trolled for salmon at Varnum
Pond, he carried a pint in his tackle box. In the cold of winter, he
swigged in his bedroom. He found ways to drink in obscurity, or so he
thought. But his drinking was obvious in burned syrup pans, fish that
got away, and empty bottles strewed under the bedroom window after
the snowmelt, evidence that he had taken up the challenge offered by
Grandma and Aunt Marion. But they were being unknowingly—until
it was too late—victimized by their own righteous ways. Instead of
keeping Grandpa C.F. sober, they kept him drinking.

In spite of their warnings that alcohol would kill his brain cells, he
was preeminent at checkers. Year after year he put down the challenge
by Harold Staples, a farmer who lounged near the woodstove on winter evenings, and kept his local ranking as number one. Later he would
teach me the game. He was merciless. We played daily for months—
probably a hundred games before I won—the beloved old man and the
student. He punished my mistakes by capturing multiple checkers in a
single move and repeatedly established an impregnable defense to bar
me from kings' row. He showed me no compassion, but he taught me
checkers—and perseverance.

He won't be here tonight, but I will recall his calm voice from behind the candy counter as my sisters and I—with a single penny among us—had often looked through its glass front, first at the two-for-a-penny candy, then up at him, and then back at the twofers. "Special sale t'day," he would say. "Three fer a penny."

Pa and I climb the steps to the platform, and I follow him into the dimness of the store's interior. Men in manure-laden boots and smelling of dried sweat sit and stand around a warm woodstove, out of focus in the vague cloud of pipe smoke and the bluish haze of roll-your-own cigarettes. Here and there on the floor at their feet lay snow shovels, gum-rubber boots, a child's sled, and several axes, all for sale, testimony to the severe Temple winter outside. Pa moves close to the fire and unbuttons his mackinaw. "Too cold to snow, ain't it?"

"I say we got some comin' by the sound a' the train whistle in West Farmington, but we don' need it. Plow's still stuck from the last one."

"Anyone heard from Larry since he left?"

"No. But I see Dick is home again."

"So's Oiva," Pa says.

They take turns and talk of work and neighbors and sickness and soldiers, or soldiers-soon-to-be, and their own future. I look through the dimness at shelves suspended beyond the stove into the darkness, shelves that display the necessaries of small-town life: work gloves, shoes, pack boots, canning jars, minnow buckets, turpentine, hunting hats, a mailbox, patent medicines, lamp chimneys, baking soda, and other country-store riches.

Uncle Austin leaves the cash register and joins the conversation. No one there wants to buy the treasures I stare at.

Pa asks about his friend Harold Waltonen.

"He's still at Fort Devens. Should be shipping out soon," Uncle Austin says.

They talk of friends in distant places. I listen carefully. They say that more will go, including some here around the woodstove this winter night, and they will be gone a long time. I am captivated by war talk. I have admired soldiers on leave in their new uniforms as they walk past me on the road, or tell stories at the general store, or appear at our house. I have read headlines in the newspaper, stared intently at the *Movietone News* at the State, and been to a military movie when Ma would let me. Patriotism filled the town. Folks displayed flags, and service stars hung in the windows of soldiers' homes. The war was far away and likely would not reach here, but men in town were going, and I didn't know whether or not Pa would go. I knew that he might, but he was older and had kids, and no one knew how many men would be needed or how long the war would last.

The men around the woodstove continue to talk in the semidarkness. They pity the death of local farmer Charles Cony. "That heart attack took him jus' like that. Don't know what his wife'll do now."

They gripe about rationing. "Someone said they was gonna ration fuel oil. Imagine that. On nights like this. Pro'bly firewood'll be next!"

Pa stands next to the white-tail deer he shot with his 16-gauge shotgun.

"They got a ceilin' price on it now. Costs ten bucks a cord if you hafta buy it."

They debate the government. "Lawrence gonna run for selectman agin? I'll vote for 'im. He's one a the few around town who don't have an ax to grind."

They spin humorous tales. "An' then the dang fool went and tried to put the sickle bar on upside down. Hah!"

Other nights they applauded prizefights on the radio, grumbled about the Boston Red Sox, debated national politics, and described how they'd killed a deer.

It's a conversation that has endured for generations.

After an hour, some rise from their soda-case seats and start to leave. Pa pays Uncle Austin a dime for a pack of Camels, then he looks at me and says, "How about it?"

It's warm beside the woodstove, but we tighten our coats around us and go into the cold night. "Did you find out anything about Bertha?" I ask him.

"No," he says.

My kinship with my father was respectful and bordered on fear. I knew not to complain or disagree and to only question him gently. Although I often wondered at or was disappointed with what he did or said, I knew not to pursue matters he obviously had ended. We walked home together in the freezing night, and I listened to my boots crunch on the snow.

Chapter Two
LITTLE ADOLPH

Only a tiny percentage of them wanted to be there, but only a small percentage of these men failed to do their duty.
　　　　　　　　　　—Stephen Ambrose, *Citizen Soldiers*

O ne Sunday in early spring, Pa's friends Vilio and Elmer come to the house, each carrying a bag filled with a quart of Krueger or a few stubbies of Genesee ale. They stand in the dooryard, first in the bright sun, then in the shade of the barn door, bags sheltered under their arms, making lazy talk with Pa. Next door, cantankerous Old Carr spades his garden. Pa says Kike, a local teamster, will come up the road later with his horse and plow and turn over both of our gardens. Elmer says his peas are up. Soon the men move again, this time to the kitchen, and sit around the dinner table. I know they will talk about the war. I ask Pa if I can stay. He nods, and I sit on the kitchen counter, legs dangling over the edge. I listen carefully to every word, in wonder of the events taking place in the world, uncertain if the war will affect me.

On other Sundays they have been relaxed, but not today. Sipping out of their bags, they talk hollow at first, uneasy, not nervous but fidgety. Pa goes down cellar and fills a pitcher from a wooden barrel of last year's apple cider, fermented enough now to be a possible cure for

Two of Pa's friends show off their new uniforms in the driveway in the spring of 1943.

cancer, and sets it on the kitchen table. Water drips from the sink faucet into a white-enameled pail. The morning fire is cold.

Someone produces a deck of cards. They break matchsticks: plain halves are a nickel, sulfur-headed ends a dime. Pa fills a glass. Elmer deals and bets a sulfur head to open. Vilio follows. Pa folds, takes a Camel from his shirt pocket, taps one end of it on his watch crystal, puts it in his mouth, and lights the other end with a sulfur-headed dime.

"Fred needs to fix that damned road into Wilder," Pa says. "I damned near snapped a driveshaft gettin' a load of pulpwood outa there last week. Told him I wasn't goin' back 'til he did somethin' about the road. He don't pay nothin' anyway."

Vilio rakes in the pot of broken matches. "Can't," he says. "The mill don't pay him nothin'." He deals the next hand. "How can we fix somethin' if it does break? Can't get new parts. We're all workin' for nothin' anyway. We gotta find parts in El's junkyard out there and fix it ourselves, or it don't get fixed."

My heels start to bang against the cupboard doors, impatient for something more exciting. Pa tells me to quiet down.

Pa mentions the war first. "John get his draft notice yet?" He asks. The others shift in their chairs.

"John who?"

"John who! Hell, you know. Lives up on Gallup Road."

"I heard he did," Elmer says. "Goes to Portland Tuesday for his physical. I expect to hear from the draft board myself soon. Before it's done, we'll all be over there, 'cept mebbe for El here. He's got kids," pointing toward me on the counter no longer banging my heels, just listening.

Not one says he wants to go; not one admits he's afraid—and they all agree that they want to get Little Adolph, as they call him.

"You stayin' in shape?" Pa asks Elmer. Elmer, a short and stocky bull of a man, smiles and nods.

"Little Adolph will get his. Right up his . . ."

"Yeah, and I'd like to be the one to give it to the sunnavabitch."

Pa reaches for his glass of cider, sips, and sets it down. "Maybe we'll all be over there to give it to the little bastard," he says.

"Did you hear 'bout that Pierce fellow there? Wa'nt that awful?"

I think Vilio, a man who shuns frivolous notions, has come today to ask just that question. The room goes quiet.

"Aah, he never knew what hit him."

"I bet he did."

"No one will ever know." They sip from their bags and blow cigarette smoke into the kitchen air.

Vilio asks another question. "So what do we do?"

"Do?" Elmer shakes his head and tosses in his cards. "Ain't nothin' to do but wait. So deal."

In a few minutes, Vilio has won most of the broken matches, and the game breaks up. What happens next is so clear it's like I am still there. Pa, out of sulfur heads, gets up, goes into the bedroom, and comes back with a .30-caliber Remington rifle he has shot deer with the past three years. He hands it to Vilio and asks him how it feels. Vilio balances it in his hands, opens and closes the chamber, holds it to his shoulder, and squints down the open sights at an imaginary target right there in our small kitchen. Pa and Elmer sip beer and cider and wait for a turn. My heels start to bang against the counter again. I'm nervous, but Pa doesn't notice. The rifle looks dangerous to me. I know if it can kill a deer it can kill a man. I leave the counter and slide around the kitchen to stay behind where they point it.

Elmer lifts it to his shoulder and squints along the barrel, "Right there. That's it," he says. "I could hit a beer bottle a hundred yards away with this thing."

Vilio guffaws. "The hell you could."

Elmer gets serious. "El, you got any ammo? I wanna show you guys how to shoot this thing."

I follow them outside, beyond the shed and the lower garden, to the stream bank where the old autos lay, where broken headlights stare out of the skeletons of rusty sedans like the hollow eyes of human skulls. I stop at the McIntosh apple tree, afraid to go farther, and stand in the shade of its blossomed branches and watch.

Someone puts the open end of an oil can down over the top of a fence post. One after the other, they fire at it, first standing, then kneeling, and finally prone on the damp earth. The can pops and shakes each time a slug tears into it, and it finally falls to the ground in shreds. I hear the men shout with pride, "See that! See that!" They are comfortable and skilled with rifles, and they know that survival at war, their very lives, will depend on that skill. Thus, they practice. I watch, first in awe, then in fear.

I try to imagine what it will be like with Pa gone. I sense he wants to go. Ma is terrified, but I want to see him walking around town in his uniform, like the other men and to listen to his stories. I don't think about him getting hurt or dying. I want to be proud of him. He doesn't talk about it. Usually someone else—Ma or Aunt Marion or a friend like Vilio—speaks for him, that he won't have to go because he has kids. But he waits. And he stands in the auto graveyard on a Sunday with his friends and fires his deer rifle at a tin can. He knows. He knows he has to be part of it.

Chapter Three
A RIDE IN THE ROADSTER

Farmers [need] to check each quarter on the Certification of
War Necessity to determine if they have gasoline enough to
carry on their farming operations for the year 1943.
                    —*The Franklin Journal,* January 1943

F olks around the village call our road Cowturd Lane. The smell
of manure, fresh from cows walking in the road on their way
to Uncle Austin's barn and back, hangs in the air like swamp gas. The
stench is worse in spring when the cows' diet changes from dried barn
hay to green pasture grass. The smell is so bad sometimes that Nancy,
old enough to know it's not normal to have to step around cow turds
on the way to school and wise enough not to speak a naughty word
aloud, is repulsed. "Aargh! It's aaawful." Repulsed, too, is Mrs. Mosher,
our neighbor across the road, who calls the county sheriff from time to
time to demand that the road be cleaned.

Smells identified the seasons in Temple. The breezes delivered reports of the town's industry. During summer the aroma of freshly
mown hay drifted through the village from nearby fields. Come fall
the smells of pickled cucumbers, canned mincemeat, boiled vegetables, and stewed fruits floated outside of the country kitchens. Later
in the year, pungent, acrid woodsmoke hung quietly over the town in

Cowturd Lane in Temple. Old Carr can be seen working in his garden. Behind him is our place. c 1940 (Temple Historical Society)

the cold winter air. Then, in the spring, manure turned our noses— manure in the road, manure in piles outside the village barns, manure in the gardens. Today, as the early summer sun warms the earth with promise of a lazy and tranquil Sunday, the stench of manure hangs heavily in the air.

Pa backs the roadster out of the barn, sets the hand brake, and opens the door. "Get in," he says to us. "We're going for a ride."

Pa was a truck driver. In his two-axle, dual-tired Ford, he coaxed heavy loads of logs and pulpwood off Temple's mountains and forded the Sandy River with the dump body rounded with river gravel. I sometimes sat beside him in white-knuckled fright as he tortured the engine, horrified as the truck lurched and creaked over surfaces absent of any evidence of a road. He'd read the gauges. "You hafta read gauges if you're gonna know how to drive a truck," he'd say. And then he'd work his truck to its limit. His yearly income of fourteen hundred dollars was enough to keep the truck gassed and oiled, take care of his taxes, and pay frequent visits to the West Farmington Fire Company and the liquor store. But there was never enough money, it seemed, to take us to a ball game or a movie or a museum someplace. We go where he wants to go.

On his day off, we go for a ride.

"Where we going, Daddy?"

"You'll see."

"Do we have any gas?" Ma asks. "I didn't think we had any gas in the car."

"'Course we have. Haven't you seen what I've been doing?"

Earlier I had watched him stick a long rubber hose into the truck's gas tank and suck on it to siphon gas into a tin can on the ground. He had steadied the hose in the can with one hand, spit and sprayed gas from his mouth into the air, coughed, wheezed, spit several more times, then rinsed his mouth with a swig of Genesee ale. When the can had filled, he yanked the hose from the truck's tank and poured the gas into the roadster.

"I always got plenty of gas," he says.

Patty crawls into the front seat. "Let's go. I want to go. Hurry up. Where we going, Daddy?"

He doesn't answer.

So much of our life occurs in this motley arrangement of seats and steering wheel that I think of the roadster as another room in the house. At various times of the year, Pa furnishes it with a telescoping fishing pole under the front seat or a shotgun or rifle perched against the floor near his right hand. Empty grain

The roadster. c. 1941

43

bags, bathing suits, a softball and glove, and scraps of cloth are in the rumble seat. And he always has a pint of whiskey or a few stubbies of beer tucked under the front seat or in the cubby hole. We spend more time together here than at the supper table.

Nancy and I scale the tinny rear fender and yank open the rumble seat. We stand on its musty cushion, and Pa says to sit down. He pushes his thumb against the shiny chrome starter button sticking out of the dashboard, and the engine comes to life. He engages the long, curvy shifting stick, eases the clutch, and guides the open-top roadster through the village center and out of town. We ride north up the Temple Stream valley—what we call the intervale—through open farmland, by wineglass elms, and past fields of new, green grass. We pass Moses Mitchell's place, where his old Plymouth sedan sits in front of the barn. Two bales of hay, bought yesterday in West Farmington, stick out of the Plymouth's trunk, and his cows wait for it in the barn. At the Hamlin farm, the pastureland is fenced along a row of maples, cows graze on the new grass, and a dozen twenty-gallon milk cans sit in the back of a pickup truck next to the barn. We roll on, between fields bordered by bushy fence lines, past Howard Mitchell's cider mill, which sits idle on the stream bank, toward pink and yellow hills of maple, birch, and beech trees that rise beyond the fields.

Pa drives as fast as he dares. Pebbles rattle against the fenders, and a cloud of dust curls up behind us and hangs there. Potholes jolt us, and patches of washboard road shake us like Ma shakes a dust mop. Patty snugs up to Ma. Nancy and I stand in the rumble seat and brace ourselves against the rush of air. Our eyes water, our faces stretch, and our speech slurs. We try to talk, "*Halo-o-o. Cain yuu tee ennytin?*" Ma leans over and accuses Pa of showing off. He scoffs, and she straightens up and says, "Elliott, you're going too fast."

"How do you know?" he asks.

"Patty's scared."

He looks down at Patty and laughs and says "Aren't you Daddy's girl? You're not scared, are you?"

Patty hugs Ma and says yes she is.

We pass the Intervale School. The bell tower is silent and the playground empty. We pass a church, its one-hundred-year-old wagon shed sagging under the weight of its own timbers, and farther on a softball field where I have watched Pa play during other summers. Pa slows the roadster, and we begin to climb. We leave the cleared, well-kept valley and enter the hills; hills that have reclaimed the early farms; hills dotted with overgrown barnyards and abandoned apple orchards and rusty mowing machines.

We pass Burt Mitchell's place, where bushes are taking over the orchards and white pines and maples dominate the hillsides. Pa turns right and crosses Temple Stream on a worn-and-weathered plank bridge, and climbs out of the valley through eroded wheel ruts and over rocks that have been heaved up by winter frosts. The road steepens, Pa downshifts into first gear, and the roadster crawls upward. We pass between stone walls hidden in the undergrowth, and Pa points to the left, beyond one of the walls, and says, "I helped Phil cut hay down there last year, in the lower field next to the stream. It's a hellish place to get a truck in and out of. I doubt if he'll do it this year."

The road levels, and Pa turns right, passes through an opening in the stone wall, and stops in a field next to an abandoned building. The house shows broken windows and a rotted roof. The door hangs by a single hinge. A pile of rotted boards marks the location of a collapsed shed. Rusty cans, broken bottles, a few bricks, and pieces of rusty iron are strewn here and there. Blackberry bushes smother the front of the house. I look at Nancy and ask her who would want to come here. She guesses Pa would.

"This place is spooky," says Patty. "It's old."

"This is the old Merrill farm," Pa explains. "Merrill settled here years ago, cleared the land, and, like the other farmers 'round here, tried to eke out a living in these hills. He failed, and so did most of the others."

I look in a window. No one has lived here for a long time.

"They grew apple trees. Sold the apples to Burt Mitchell down the hill who shipped them all over." Pa takes a stubby from under the seat of the roadster, snaps off the cap, and tosses it on the ground. "Let's go look at his apple orchard."

In the back we find an old field, clogged now with small bushes, the apple trees standing in rows as Merrill planted them, overgrown into a complicated web of unlopped branches.

Patty, four years old and what seems to her like a long way from home, stands in knee-high grass. "Why do we want to come here? Are there snakes here? I'm scared of snakes." Again, but louder and more emphatic, "*Are there snakes here?*" She looks at me. "*John*, are there snakes here?"

I don't know, and I say so. She grabs Ma's hand.

Pa swigs on his stubby and says, "Jeezus, look at the apples. Guess we can come back in the fall and get enough for a barrel of cider, and Ma can make us a pie, too."

I know now why we came. Pa is taking inventory.

Ma takes Patty, who is still looking for snakes, by the hand and leads us back to the roadster. The way is narrow, and we walk single file. She finds a blanket in the rumble seat, spreads it on a sunny spot in front of the house, and sits. Pa pokes around in the ruins for scrap metal or an old tire he can add to his stack. I ask him how long ago Merrill moved away from here. He doesn't know. I ask him if Merrill had any kids. He doesn't know. He throws open the car doors and says it's time to leave. Ma, who has relaxed in the sunshine, says she wants to stay and for Pa to get her a beer. He says no, not now.

The road worsens. We cross a swamp, and Pa eases the roadster through muddy ruts. Grass and rocks and cobbles rub on the bottom and sound like an orchestra tuning up. Nancy says it's darn poor music. We jolt over a washed-out culvert and past a run-down farmhouse and the ruins of a barn. Chokecherry and wild raspberry grow close to the shed, and more apple trees stand at the far end of the barn. Pa says old man Huntington still lives here in the summer. He grows lettuce and carrots and beets and Swiss chard and moves north to a place in Phillips in winter. I ask Pa whether he turned right or left out of his driveway to get to Phillips, and he said he didn't know. Either way he would travel in deep ruts, as we are today. At the top of a rise, we enter a clearing. Pa stops.

The road divides here. The right fork continues farther up and disappears into the shade of a hardwood forest; the left fork goes past a three-story farmhouse and between fields enclosed by weathered walls of fieldstone and decorated with dandelions, buttercups, and daisies. Beyond lies a forest of poplar, birch, and maple trees, their new leaves soft pastels of pink and yellow and green rising to blue mountains of spruce and fir profiled against the sky, a scene like one on Aunt Marion's picture calendar.

A man stands in the farmyard surrounded by a rusted sickle-bar mowing machine, a dump rake, and two small wagons. Pa stops the car in the road, gets out with his beer, and walks across the yard to the man. He sets the bottle on a broken board, offers the man a cigarette, takes another one from the pack and taps the end of it on a silver-colored Zippo lighter. He cups his hands around the flame, lights both cigarettes, and retrieves his beer. They talk while we wait.

Patty stands up. "Who's that man? What's he doing here? Can I get out? Why don't we leave?"

"Can I go pick a bouquet?" Nancy asks.

Ma exhales a puff of cigarette smoke and says, "When your father gets back you can ask him. Stay in the car. It won't be long."

"But I want to get out now."

When Pa's cigarette burns down too short to hold in his fingers, he snuffs it on a rock and returns to the car. "Ready to go?" he asks.

"Nancy wants to pick flowers," Ma says. "Who was that man?"

"I don't know. Harold somebody. Says he's going to cut the hay here for his horses. Said he was just looking the place over."

"I bet he is!" Ma frowns and turns to look at the man. "People in this town don't just look things over. Besides, there doesn't look like much hay here to me. What's he looking over anyway? Is he looking for something to take?"

"Clarice, you don't understand." If Pa knows an answer, he expects us to know, too, so he doesn't answer directly. His attitude stresses Ma and gives him a feeling of superiority. Many times I've had to guess at what was right, and many times I've guessed wrong, and many times he has said, "Wise up, boy." So I stopped asking questions and try to figure out what is right myself. But Ma, a schoolteacher, fills the air between them with questions, and Pa, instead of offering an explanation, accuses her of being dumb. She doesn't object.

"I probably don't understand, but sometimes I wish I did." Ma is careful. "I just think there's something strange here, but it doesn't matter."

"Can I pick some flowers?" Nancy asks again.

"Not now," Pa answers. "We have to go."

Ma wants to stay and admire the scenery, and she asks him to let her sit awhile in the sun. Pa says no; he has someplace he wants to go.

He lets the roadster coast between the weathered stone walls that border the fields, into the woods, and then steeper through eroded ruts. We pass over the stream again, now half the size of where we crossed it earlier. Pa pushes the roadster's starter button and turns back toward the village. It's cool under the canopy of maples and beeches, and I wish we were still on the hill in the sun.

Patty wishes we were home. "Can we go home now? I'm hungry. I want to go home."

Ma ponders the man in the farmyard. Pa is occupied with the roadster. At the junction with Conant Road, we enter the sunshine again, and Pa turns and winks at Patty and says he wants to go home, too, but no one else does. Then he swerves off the road into the stream and stops midway in the flowing water.

At that moment, it goes silent inside the roadster. Outside, the stream tumbles and swirls around us. Patty looks out at the water and yells, "Daddy!"

"What?" That's all he says.

"Daddy! Don't do this! I'm scared!" She looks at Ma. "Mommy, tell him to stop."

Ma smiles. "It's just your father. It's okay."

Pa says, "I have stopped. See." He holds up his hands.

I lean out over the rear fender and look at the water, clear as the sky, the stream bottom distinct in bands of cobbles, gravel, and sand, like a picture in an encyclopedia. I turn to Nancy "Looks okay to me."

Pa hears me. "It is okay. Take off your shoes. The water's not deep. We're gonna wash the car." And he clambers backward into the rumble seat to find rags and sponges. "Here," he says, as he hands them to Nancy and me. "Go to work."

I step barefooted onto the cobbled stream bottom. Nancy follows. Ma grabs a stubby from under the seat, takes Patty's hand, and struggles, one arm extended to keep her balance, across the cobbles to shore. Pa, Nancy, and I wash the car on the rock-strewn streambed in water so cold I can't feel the pain.

Ma watches, perched on a huge boulder in the sun with the stubby of Genesee in one hand and the end of a cigarette between the tips of two fingers of the other. "Nancy, watch out," she says. "The bottom is rough."

Nancy screws her face into a testy scowl. "I *know* Moth-herr, I've almost fallen twice already. I *know*."

Ma, inclined to let us grow up by ourselves, ordinarily makes little maternal sacrifice, but occasionally she is compelled to perform some motherly duty, even while drinking a Genesee ale. "Well, just be careful, that's all."

When we finish, Pa backs the roadster out of the stream and leaves it in the sun to dry. Patty jumps up to get in, but Pa says, "I've got one more thing to do here before we leave."

She slumps back down on the rock, "What is it now, Daddy?"

"I'm going to catch a fish. I know right where there're two of 'em." He reaches under the front seat and pulls out his telescoping rod and a Prince Albert tobacco can. He extends the fishing rod to about half its length and attaches a reel, then he looks at me and says, "C'mon Johnny, I'll show you where they are." He opens another Genesee, walks up narrow and rutted Conant Road a hundred yards or so, stops, and looks into the bushes next to the road.

"I think this is the place," he says. "C'mon." He threads the rod through the thick brush, holding the branches aside with one arm and pushing the rod ahead of him with the other, and steps through the growth to a small brook and a falls splashing over a ledge. I follow him.

I shouldn't have gone with him. Maybe I thought it would be different this time. Maybe I thought he'd let me fish. Maybe I'd even catch one. I don't know why I went along, but I did, and I learned that I should have stayed on the bank with Ma.

He sets the stubby on a rock, opens the Prince Albert can, and takes out a worm suspended between his thumb and forefinger. "Half an angleworm is enough for these fish," he says and cuts the worm in two with his thumbnail and threads half onto his hook. "They're not big fish here, but we'll fix this up so it looks good to 'em." He attaches a small silver spinner to the line about ten inches above the worm, pauses for a swallow of Genesee, and admires his work. "The fish won't care about the spinner; it might even scare them, but when they see this worm chasing it, they'll go for the worm. Watch."

He creeps to the stream bank above the falls, casts the worm into the pool below, and lets the current carry it downstream. At the end of the pool, he tightens the line and begins to pull the worm back upstream. Then the trouble starts. Suddenly he yanks the rod, and a hooked fish flies out of the water and over Pa's head. It comes loose from the hook and sails end over end through the branches above my head and into the underbrush behind me.

Pa looks back at me. "Did you see where it went? That one's for you.

Go find it while I catch another one."

Who, me? I'd seen all of that fish I wanted to while it somersaulted over my head into the underbrush. Why should I have to search for it, crawling on the ground with branches whipping at my face and black-berry bushes scratching my arms?

I turn and hear the fish flopping wildly in the dry leaves. I crouch under willow shrubs, push prickly branches out of my way, and strug-gle through the thick scrub to where I can see the desperate trout flap-ping around in its frantic search for water. I'm not anxious to grapple with the slippery, eel-like thing, but I have my orders. I crouch in the branches of a small evergreen and watch it flop, waiting for my chance to lunge for it in the dry leaves and duff. I miss. On my hands and knees now, I stalk it and slap a hand at it just a split second after it flops someplace else, and do it again, and again, like slapping at a fly on the kitchen table. I wonder if this is my fishing lesson. I know Pa's an ex-pert, but is this some new technique he's teaching me, or what? Why isn't he doing this? The fish is now camouflaged by dried leaf pieces and pine needles and disappears into the duff. An occasional twitch reveals its location. Finally, after what seems like eternity, the chase ends. I seize the desperate creature with both hands and hold it against the ground. I yell to Pa, "I got it!"

"Okay," he says.

Okay? What do I do now? I can't move my hands, or the thing will get away. How long does it take a fish to die? I hope I don't have to pee first. "Come get it," I yell, "or it'll get away again."

I don't move until he arrives, picks up the fish, and breaks its neck. "There, I guess we got him, didn't we."

He had caught one more fish while I suffered in the undergrowth. He slides them both onto a forked stick for me to carry, then collapses his fishing rod and picks a small bouquet of painted trillium from the streamside. He retrieves his beer, and we walk to the car. We had been gone less than a half hour.

He gives the flowers to Ma and shows the two fish to Nancy and

Patty and boasts, "See the fish I caught."

He caught? I climb into the rumble seat and wait to leave.

Farther downstream we leave the forest and pass Burt Mitchell's place. In another mile, Pa turns the roadster left onto an unpaved road with grass growing between the wheel paths. We recross Temple Stream and climb out of the valley again. We pass a small pond where Pa downshifts into second gear and drives uphill for nearly a mile before coming to a house. He veers into an open yard and stops in front of a weather-beaten bungalow. A mongrel dog jumps off the porch and barks. A small, wrinkled woman, who has aged too soon, sits in a chair on the porch and calls to the dog, "Come back here, you. Right now!"

Hilma Koski is one of the original Finnish immigrants to Temple. She and Lauri came here thirty or so years ago with twenty-some other Finns as loggers to work in Temple's forests. They married and raised two sons. Weikko, wearing a soldier's uniform, and Vilio stand in the driveway next to an old Plymouth with its side panel raised and stare at the engine.

Pa greets the two men. "Halloo, there."

"Hey, El."

He walks over and grips Weikko's hand. "How've you been? How long you home for?"

Weikko is young, not yet twenty, and until the army called had never been away from Temple. "Not long this time," he says. "One more week is all." He shakes his head and goes on. "But I don't think the army's for me. Too damned humongous. Too fussy. I'll pro'bly be shipped across when I get back, but I don't know where to."

Pa talks to Weikko about army life, and I wonder when Pa will go, or if he will. I ask Nancy, does she think Pa will go in the army. She says she doesn't think he will. She says no one has to go who has kids to care for. Then she looks at me. "You want him to go, don't you?" she asks.

I draw my initials in the dirt with a stick and think. If I say yes, I'll feel guilty for wanting Ma and us to manage the place alone without him. But I know how I feel. If I say no, I will be lying. I want the excitement and pride of him being in an army uniform. I want him to be part of it. I want to be proud of him; I will be the only kid in Temple whose father is in the war. I want to see him walking across town in his uniform, like the other soldiers. I want the blue star to hang in our window. I want to feel good about my father instead of always being put down by him. Am I asking for too much, to have a father who makes me proud to be his kid? I throw away the stick and look at Nancy. "I don't know . . . I wish . . ."

"Maybe we could go to Kennebunk and live with Grammy Watson. And go to school there. And to the beach in summer."

Kennebunk is not for me, I tell her. No one in Kennebunk will know me, or know that Pa is in the army, or that he wears gold buttons on his uniform and fires big guns at the Germans. I don't want to live in Kennebunk and have to go to fourth grade with twenty-five other kids. "John who?" they'd say.

Lauri Koski, a small and wiry man with the callused hands of a laborer, returns to the yard from pitching hay and scrubbing stalls in the barn. He joins the three men around the Plymouth.

As he does, Pa turns and reaches for a Camel. "Hey, Lauri."

"Hello, El. Good you come. Vat you bring to drink?"

Pa shrugs. "I'm dry."

Vel, you are a hellava guy. I go get."

Pa looks at Weikko, "Out with the kids today. Behavin' myself."

Weikko scratches his chin. "Long night last night. I'm taking it easy today myself."

Lauri comes up from his cellar with a two-quart pitcher of home-brewed beer. The men give up on the Plymouth and sit in the shade of the porch with Hilma and Ma. Hilma opens a package of Finnish hardtack bread and passes it around. Patty looks at me, a question in her eyes. I'm hungry but know it's useless to tell Ma I want to go home, so I take some. Patty does too.

Vilio chuckles and asks Pa if he's been making any money.

I think he means at poker, but Pa takes a sip of Lauri's home brew, lights a Camel, and says, "Don't know about you, but I haven't had much work lately. Hauled a few loads of fertilizer for the Union, but that's been it. I 'spect to hear from Fred about some hardwood he has ready, but I don't know when. I'm runnin' out. If I don't get somethin' soon, I'm gonna take the T off the truckin' sign on the side of my truck and paint an F on there in its place. See if that helps." He smiles and waits for Vilio to guffaw, which he does, a loud belly laugh that turns Weikko's hungover head around. Pa goes on. "No gas around either. I tried kerosene in the car here, but it don't work. I had to swig some gas from the truck to get up here today. But it'll all come out in the wash, I guess. Boy! This is good brew, Lauri."

Lauri smiles and says it should be; it's two months old from a wooden barrel.

"I see in the paper," Pa says, "that Elmer got a job at the woolen mill, and Earle's up in Eustis all week working in a sawmill. Don't know why they'd want to go so far; mebbe to get extra gas for havin' a job outta town." Pa is quick to criticize anyone who breaks the rules but proud to get away with the same things himself. He smiles and points to the roadster sitting in the yard. "Take us, we don't have gas—no more pleasure driving." Ma is quiet and lets him talk. "Nobody has cash either. It was a long winter. Jakie the Jew was around my place last week. Said he'd come from Fairbanks and was on his way to New Sharon. I hadn't seen him for a month, so I sold him a half-dozen batteries I'd picked up someplace and some tinfoil I'd been savin' for him. He hung around 'til dinnertime, but he didn't look to me like he needed much food. I didn't offer to feed him, so he paid me and left. That and truckin' a couple loads of fertilizer is all I've had since last fall. And all we got to look forward to now is goin' in the army. At least they'll pay us, won't they, Weikko?"

"Not enough, El. But they feed ya and give ya a place to sleep if ya don't mind sleepin' with a hundred other guys."

"Any WACs where you are?"

"Yeah. But the brass gets 'em all."

Pa and Vilio look at each other. Vilio says they'd probably get some more in before Pa had to go. Pa doesn't say any more. We leave when the pitcher is empty and glide back down the hill.

Patty asks if we're going home. Nancy is quiet, thinking I suppose. Ma says she wants to ride up to see her schoolteacher friend Anna. Pa says no. He says he wants to go up Gallup Road to look at the log yard. Ma says Anna has been unhappy, something about her husband Norman, and she wants to see her, but Pa says he's going to stay away from them. Instead of turning around, he presses down on the gas pedal. Neither of them hears me say I want to go home. Ma says to Pa, "Don't go so fast; it will still be there when you get there."

He looks at her. "You want to drive?"

"You know I can't drive. You won't teach me. You just criticize me." She has tried several times but can't seem to manage both feet and both hands at the same time. I have seen her struggle with trying: the roadster jerks and jumps and coughs, she shifts to another gear and it balks and stalls, and she gives up. No instructions from Pa. No coaxing. No compliments.

"Of course you can drive. You just don't think you can," he says, taking both hands off the wheel. "Here. Try it."

"Elliott!"

"You can drive anytime you want." I can hear the mockery, the ridicule, in Pa's voice. I know he won't stop.

"I wouldn't know where to go."

"Just follow the signs," he says. He crosses Hen Mitchell Brook and turns onto Gallup Road. Dust kicks up behind us and rolls into the open rumble seat. Nancy and I duck under the cubby.

"There aren't any signs," Ma says. "Besides, I just want you to slow down. Patty's scared."

He jams on the brakes. "Is this slow enough? Tell you what, Clarice.

I won't drive anymore." He grabs the key out of the ignition and tosses it at her. It flies out of the car into the underbrush beside the road.

"Daddy, don't!" Patty yells.

We sit there, stunned, hearing only the sound of the brook. After a few moments, Ma says he shouldn't have thrown the key, that she didn't mean to get him upset, and that she is sorry. He calms down, and we look for the key in the ditch.

Pa eases the roadster up Gallup Road about two miles, crossing the brook three times on worn plank bridges. The road narrows and appears more desolate. Pa drives past a faded farmhouse where several large maple trees stand behind an eroded ditch. Farther up, at the edge of the road, sits the yellowed Gallup house and a weather-beaten shingled barn next to it. Beyond the Gallup place, we enter a hardwood forest, and the road worsens. Pa downshifts and traverses a rocky slope. Nancy leans forward and asks, "Where does this road go, Daddy?"

"It used to go over by Center Hill and then to Wilton," he says, "but now it goes where all the other roads in Temple go, nowhere." He stops, squints out over the narrow hood to the road ahead, and says, "Fred's been cuttin' pulp all winter up on Derby Mountain. I'm hopin' to start trucking it out next week, and I wanted to get up to the yard and see what they had out. Hang on."

He presses the shift lever forward into first gear and eases the clutch. The roadster crawls upward over eroded ruts and around heaved-up boulders in a re-creation of a historic wagon trip over Center Hill to Wilton. For the next half mile, he shifts, clutches, brakes, and shifts again, then turns onto a logging road. The road opens into a logging yard cut into the forest under the slope of Derby Mountain. I look out from the rumble seat at a clearing full of logs, trees cut with crosscut saw and ax by Temple loggers, dragged here by horse teams, and then bucked into four-foot lengths. Pa says they are hardwood logs for the mills. They sit in stacks around the perimeter of the yard—rows and rows of beech, rock maple, birch, ash, and oak—waiting, he tells us, for him to lift and toss them onto his truck with a hand hook.

Pa, calm now, explains. "There's yards like this all over Temple. About four thousand cords a year are taken to the mills as far away as Rumford, and some even to railroad cars in West Farmington. These are Temple's only jobs, cutting and trucking timber to the mills. Not many people in town have jobs not connected to these logs."

"Didn't you say that Earle's in Eustis in a sawmill?" Ma asks, referring to a local logger who no longer goes into the woods.

"Yeah. And he's probably sawin' logs from Temple."

"But some other people work out of town too, like Earle," Ma says, then tells Pa that Lucille, one of her former students in the Village School, is welding ships together in South Portland. "I read it in *The Franklin Journal.*"

"An out-of-town job is news in Temple," Pa says.

"At least you've got work with the truck to pay our bills. For God's sake, what will happen if you have to leave? What will I ever do?"

"The government will pay you, probably more than the thousand or so I make, and you won't have to do nothin'."

"Except worry and fret," Ma says.

"Can we get out of the car?" Patty asks.

He looks around some more, taps the end of another Camel on his Zippo, lights it, and answers, "No. Not now. I've seen what I wanted to see. Mother wants to go home. How about it?"

Ma smiles at him. "I'll cook your fish—if you'll clean them first."

"Johnny will. He caught one of 'em."

Pa takes us down out of the hills toward home. The two bales of hay still stick out of Moses Mitchell's Plymouth. The general store is closed now, and the morning sun has moved behind the barn and no longer shines into Ma's kitchen. I don't clean the fish. Pa takes them to the barn, and Ma takes charge of supper.

She goes to the woodbox for alder. "Johnny, we need wood. Better do it now before your father comes in with the fish." She turns to the cookstove, drips a little kerosene over the alder, and lights a fire. "Nancy, you can set the table. Wash the oilcloth first. Your father will have a plate and fork, the rest of us bowls and spoons. When you're done, you can get a loaf of bread and the mustard out of the cupboard. And we need glasses on the table, too." She reaches under the counter for a can of Campbell's tomato soup, wrestles with a can opener, and speaks to me through the woodbox door. "Johnny, when you come in, bring the package of bologna from the icebox."

Pa brings in the fish, and she sends him out to the icebox for milk. She fries the two fish in corn meal and puts the frying pan to the side to keep them warm. She heats the soup in a pot and makes bologna sandwiches. She stands on a worn linoleum floor, surrounded by a plain wooden table covered with oilcloth, a cookstove, an oilcloth-covered counter, a storage cupboard, an iron sink with water dripping into an enameled pail, and a small door in the wall to the woodbox. She works fast, and soon supper is ready.

Pa eats one fish and shares the other with Ma. Offered a bite, Patty turns up her nose. "I can't eat that," she says. She turns her eyes toward me.

I had had enough of that fish in the thicket next to the brook. "I can't either," I say.

"Good day, wasnt it?" says Pa.

Chapter Four

THE ARMY CALLS

This is the first lottery I ever won in my life.
—First U.S. Army draftee, October 1941

S now sits on the windowsill. A motley pattern of ice crystals has crept up the bedroom windowpane in the night. Above the frost, the December sky outside is black. It's cold, and I can see my breath. I shiver and dress in the dimness of a single bulb.

Downstairs there is no comfort on the hot-air register, and the bitter kitchen floor numbs my feet. Ma, her small and frail frame barely five feet tall and one hundred pounds, stands next to the Glenwood stove holding a burnt match in one hand. A wisp of smoke curls out of the firebox, soon followed by the roar of flames, the only sound in this cold and barren gathering place. Patty shivers in a chair next to the stove and waits for the promised warmth. Nancy and I take breakfast bowls from the cupboard and warm them with our hands. No one speaks. No one questions the silence. No one has to.

Ma's one undeniable and irrepressible craving is to be with my father. She loves him totally, and she has since she came to Temple twelve years ago. She is helpless without him. She doesn't drive the car; she has no aptitude or love for the care of animals or house repairs; she relies wholly on Pa for most rural necessaries—transportation, a wood supply, removing snow, and bartering with the locals.

She stands now across the worn linoleum, next to the wood-burning cookstove, a plain and tattered robe tight around her thin waist, her bony face cast in shadows of yellowish light. She stirs hot water and stares out the icy window. Her mouth is drawn taut; her eyes are blank. The smell of burnt toast drifts up from the stovetop. She looks, then lays the spoon aside. The toast falls to the floor. "Oh, darn," she says to no one, then picks up the toast and returns it to the hot iron. "Well, you can just scrape it off."

"Is the water hot yet?" Nancy asks. No answer. She says again, "Is the water hot yet, *Mother?*"

Ma then pours steaming water over the chocolate powder waiting in her cup. "We need milk, too," Nancy adds.

"It's in the icebox. Johnny can get it." She goes back to the stove and assembles the coffee percolator with desperate and shaky fingers.

In the bedroom, I hear Pa cough and hack and then go to the cellar to build a fire. Ma goes to the bedroom and comes back with a fresh handkerchief, wipes her eyes, adds a stick of birch to the fire, and stands there.

She is engulfed by fear. It pulls at her, drawing her away from thoughtfulness and comfort and security. The news had appeared in *The Franklin Journal* in November. Nineteen fathers had been drafted into the army, the first fathers from Franklin County. Ma's fear has kept us from talking about it. Two days ago, we had gone with Pa to Aunt Marion's where his family and a few friends had gathered. They played cards and nibbled at a cake decorated with "Good Luck Elliott" and wished him a safe return.

Ma now faces the day. "Eat your breakfast, kids. You need to leave soon."

I gulp. A father leaving for war, I think, should be reason enough to miss a little school. "But can't we stay until he leaves?"

"No," Ma says. "It's school for you. You both can say good-bye now."

"But Patty will see him leave," I plead.

"She doesn't have school to go to. You do. Please hurry up."

Pa appears in the kitchen in T-shirt, trousers, and slippers, unshaven and suffering the effects of too much Smirnoffs and too little sleep. He fills a mug with steamy coffee and sits heavily at the table. He coughs twice, then lights a Camel and says, "Mind your mother now." He sips coffee and fiddles with his cigarette, then calmly issues instructions to Nancy and me, his hoarse words hanging in the anguished space of our little kitchen. I remember the crux of them. "Help your mother . . . keep the woodbox filled . . . feed your pig . . . you're big enough to shovel snow . . . and be good."

Ma, listless at the stove, rubs her red eyes, stifles a sniffle, and stirs the hot water to which she has added oatmeal. She listens to his every word and stares at his every move. Patty dangles her feet from a straight-backed chair and shivers. Nancy and I gawk at Pa, seemingly a stranger, who is talking at us.

Blue cigarette haze and a two-day beard blur his face. One hand fidgets with a cigarette, and the other surrounds his coffee cup. He continues his scratchy words. "Take care of yourselves . . . write to me so I can see what you're learning in school . . . I'll be back someday . . . just remember that."

Pa had not volunteered to go, but when his draft notice arrived he did not object. I think he even welcomed the opportunity. He shows no anxiety and seems proud that he has been called. He has avoided the criticism of being conspicuously in town with so many others gone to war.

He continues, "Don't worry about me. I'll be okay."

Of course he will be okay; a million soldiers will be helping him. But, I wonder, who will help us? Although skeptical about us being able to cope, I am proud that Pa will serve. I am awestruck by the men I see in uniform walking around town or at the store, and now Pa will soon be one of them.

Ma says it's time for us to go. Pa gives us both a hug and issues his final orders, "Be good," he says. We plead again to stay.

"Now go," Ma says. "It's getting late." She helps us into our coats and pushes us out the door. Nothing, not forty inches of snowfall, not the loss of electricity, not subzero temperature, and now not even war, can keep us from school.

Outside, gray sky shows overhead and fresh snow swirls around us. I pull my hood strings tight and slide my jacket front over my chin. I have said good-bye, and now I hurry to join my schoolmates, not because I'm late, but because I want to tell them my father is in the army. "C'mon, Nancy. Hurry up."

She looks at me. "You wanted him to go, didn't you?"

Unwilling to disagree with Nancy and unsure if I should reveal my real feelings, I hesitate, then murmur, "I . . . I, uh, think so."

"He didn't have to go, you know. He could have gotten out of it. What are we going to do now?"

"I know. I know," I say. But I also know how I feel, how proud I am of Pa. Is it asking too much to have a father I can admire and be proud of? Pa hasn't given me much reason to be proud of him, but now I am the only kid in school, except for Nancy, who has a father fighting the war.

"Mom's going to have a hard time," she says. "There's no one to help her, and she doesn't know much about the place."

"Someone will help, or we can," I say.

"I don't know. I don't know. Mom's scared. I'm scared, too, sometimes, 'cause I don't know what's going to happen."

Nancy is right. But I'm determined not to let reality interfere with my moment of excitement. I'm too keyed up to think about what might happen to us later.

We arrive at the little schoolhouse late, hang our coats in the hallway, and take our seats with the others. The room is quiet. Mrs. Stolt, proper and punctual, is choosing leaders for prayer and the Pledge of Allegiance. There is no one to talk to. Who can I tell? Who will listen? I am not brave enough to make an announcement, so I wait and keep the news to myself until I have a chance to talk to someone. My opportunity comes at recess. I tell my fourth-grade classmates that Pa has gone, but it doesn't seem like such big news to them. They shrug it off. And so do upperclassmen Leo and Myron and Albert and Calvin. Oh well, I think, they probably know anyway. Finally, desperate for someone to take notice of my news, I write a note on my math work sheet before I pass it to Mrs. Stolt. On the top front, where she will not miss seeing it, I print the words, "My father went into the army today." She doesn't acknowledge my note. She probably knows, too.

I walk home with Nancy for lunch. Ma is alone.

Chapter Five
CHILLED POTATOES

Didja ever see a little house without nobody in it? Didja ever
try to play a game with just yourself to win it? Didja ever
smell a flower that just didn't have no smell? Or know the
swellest secret and not have no one to tell?

— Ma, December 1943

F illed with pain and fear, Ma cried often in those first days
without Pa. She cried quietly in the evenings. She sobbed with
Grandpa C.F., who hugged her tightly, at the sight of Pa's plaid shirt
and dress trousers he had worn when he left and mailed back to her. She
started a letter to him but couldn't finish it. A postcard arrived, and she
read it ten times. He had arrived safely at the Fort Devens,
Massachusetts induction center, but he was too busy to write more.

Ma missed Pa awfully, and she didn't know when he would return,
except that it would be a long time. Her anguish, like influenza, spread
to Nancy and Patty and me. When I saw the suffering on Ma's face,
my heart filled with tenderness for her but not for him. Instead, I
proudly pictured him training to fire bazookas at tanks, or to launch
artillery shells at targets miles away. I pictured him home on leave,
showing off his uniform with the stripes sewn on his long army over-
coat like other soldiers in town.

Patty had no image of where he was or why he was gone. "Where did Daddy go, Mommy?"

"He's gone away to the army," Ma answered.

"When is he coming home?"

Ma sniffed and wiped an eye. "I don't know."

"He is coming back. Isn't he?"

"Yes. He'll come back." Ma said. And Patty would start the questions again.

Ma poured her heart out in her first letter. She longed for him. She cried for him. She wrote that if she tried to discipline us, we cried, too. She wrote that Patty kept asking when he was coming home, and that Nancy nagged for a letter from him. She wrote that the days were bad but the nights were worse. She screamed at night in her sleep, she wrote. She missed him and she loved him and she wanted him home to care for her.

Pa had insisted that Ma stay in Temple while he was away at war, and she had agreed, but right away she was sorry. Our eight-room house sat covered with snow on the edge of the village. Each day it struggled to fend off the frigid December air—we were low on furnace wood, and the house couldn't hold out the cold. At Thanksgiving time, a wind-driven thirty-inch snowstorm had clogged Temple's roads and kept loggers at home. Ma didn't know, nor did anyone, when the roads would be passable again. She feared that we would be without furnace wood.

And she hurt. Ma wasn't ready to live alone in this—to her—unkind place. Mornings she rose out of bed early to keep busy, and she was cold. Or she stayed in bed longer to keep warm, and thoughts of Pa kept her awake. When she did sleep, her nightmares woke her, screaming. One night she fought the Germans. Another night, she said, someone reached from under the sink and grabbed her legs while she washed dishes. Still another night, a murderer came into her nightmare and chased her across the pasture.

Pa's family, except for Grandpa C.F., showed no interest in us, and

I worried that no one but Grandpa cared that Ma was alone and afraid. But what could I do? Although I did not suppose I was man of the house—I was eight years old—I tended to my barn chores promptly, and I filled the woodbox in the evening. Sometimes Ma, who heated the kitchen with stovewood, emptied the woodbox early, and I filled it right after school. On weekends I often filled it twice, morning and evening. I cleaned the cow stalls, spread hay chaff for them to lie on, and pitched hay down from the loft for their supper, all before Ted, our milkman, came to shovel out the manure and milk the cows.

Pa had hired Ted to milk, but he soon quit our job for another. Ma, frantic, asked Kike, a neighbor who mostly tended horses, to milk the cows in exchange for milk and butter.

"Kin I take extra milk home to sell?" Kike asked.

"No," Ma said. "You can take all you and Bertha need for yourselves, and butter, too. But I want the extra left here."

"Waal then, I dunno if I want to do it," he told her.

"But, Raymond," as Ma called him, "I need help. Won't you try it for a while?"

"Waal. I'll see what I kin do." But Ma caught him selling our milk and told him not to come back. She then pleaded with Ted, and he came again to milk our cows.

I also pitched hay down to a new calf and cleaned its stall and fed it grain and talked to it. I told her what Pa might be doing, and she nuzzled me and asked for more grain.

The hungriest creature in the place was a dirtied white hog that spent the winter in flimsy quarters in a corner of the shed. I didn't call it by any name; I knew it would appear on the supper table some night in the spring. Ma would stir up a meal for it, and I slopped it into his trough after supper. Ma said I should show the hog respect when I got near his pen, but he knew I was there to feed him, I told her, and I didn't feel threatened. A dozen haggard chickens spent the winter in the shed, too, behind a chicken-wire fence near the privy. They ate the least. I fed them a mixture of corn and chicken feed from a bag Pa had brought from the Farmers Union, and they flapped their wings and cackled thank you. I knew the animals looked forward to seeing me each day. I helped them cope without Pa. I wished Pa's family, who kept to themselves, could have done the same for Ma. But the snub had not surprised Ma, she said; she had predicted it. So she looked after the place the best she could and waited for something to happen.

One Saturday morning, Fern Knowles comes to see Ma. Fern married Elmer Knowles, a local logger, a short while back and stops in from time to time to keep Ma up to date on her doings and to hear Ma's views on matters in town. She tosses her coat aside and pulls out a chair from the table. "Gawd," she says, "I gotta take the weight off these feet. You gotta cup of coffee?"

"What's going on?" Ma asks as she empties the pot into Fern's cup.

Fern's round face smiles at me sitting on the sideboard, "Hey, kid. How are ya?"

I don't answer. She sips her coffee, sets her cup on the oilcloth, and looks at Ma.

"Well, Clarice, the old boy is suing me for divorce. He wants a hundred dollars, and I have to pay fifty more so he can get the hundred!"

"Pay fifty?" Ma asks.

"Yeah. Chrissakes, I gotta hire a lawyer. He's suing me."

"What's the hundred for?"

"Alimony! He wants me to pay alimony for chrissakes."

Ma knows that Fern has not let marriage interfere with her former life as a single woman. "Fern, does he know?"

"It looks that way, don't it? Why else would he be tryin' to dump me? He accuses me of seeing my old friends, and, get this, Clarice, he says I'm using your haymow."

"Now that's not right, and you know it."

"Yeah, but he's watching the place. I know that, too."

Ma looks up from the ironing board. "Wait a minute, Fern. I know you—but I know Elmer, too. Maybe he's got a girlfriend."

"What! Do you think so? Why that sonofabitch!"

"I don't know that he does, Fern, but that's it; you never really know."

Fern jumps to her feet and stomps back and forth across the faded linoleum. "Elmer says you and I are having parties here, but he can't find any witnesses. I know he asked one man to be a witness for him, but he's not going to. Maybe he's just blowing out a smokescreen. Wouldn't that be somethin'? Him foolin' around. Guess I'd have to go some to catch up to him."

"Fern, if you need a place to stay, there's room here. Really, I think you should move in with us. I need company, and you could be a big help. You need someone to talk to, too. Move in."

When Fern came to live with us, the mood of the household changed. Pa's absence still victimized us, but Ma's constant and hellish loneliness disappeared, and we began to cope with our predicament. Fern had grown up in the country and knew the country lifestyle: food from gardens and animals, heat from firewood, and make do with what you have. At our house, she took charge of sawing and splitting wood, driving the car, arranging our meager social life, and advising Ma on how to handle her affairs. She acted with confidence and spoke with conviction. Ma listened to her, and so did Nancy and Patty and I. "No, you can't," she'd say. "You go to bed—now—or the bear'll come over the mountain and gitcha!"

She proved to be a blessing. But as stimulating and helpful as Fern was, Ma's most serious problem not only remained unsolved but worsened.

Fern could not solve the emerging conflict with Pa's family, nor did she try. Instead, her presence in our house aggravated it. Aunt Marion, a haughty and assertive woman who carried herself with a lift of her chin that underscored her self-righteous personality, viewed Fern as an immoral interference in Ma's responsibilities to Pa and to her care of his kids. She believed that Ma and Fern were jointly courting moral decadence and complained that Fern's presence would tempt Ma to take up all-night partying and other disreputable activity and wreck Ma's standing in the community. And she treated Ma like cat turd.

Aunt Marion had never liked Ma. In Aunt Marion's view, Ma had forsaken her teaching job, become dependent, drank beer and smoked cigarettes, hobnobbed with shady friends, and loved Pa. Aunt Marion, to the contrary, was a self-reliant and independent full-time teacher supervisor who attended church regularly, was repulsed by alcohol and tobacco, and trucked with relatively upscale folks. Ma had tried to be cordial and show an interest in Pa's family, and now, in Pa's absence, she needed them. But instead of coming together, the schism widened.

Aunt Marion was known in town as an extremely well-intentioned and charitable person who often gave time, money, advice, and gifts to others. But she expected payback for the giving. She expected her generosity to earn supporters and allies and admiration. She expected folks not only to like her and respect her but to agree with her. But in Ma's case, Aunt Marion's good deeds, as Fern sardonically called them, were many times hurtful.

One day in mid-December after Pa had left for Fort Devens, Aunt Marion calls Ma and invites her to ride to Farmington. "I won't be gone long if you'd like to come along," she says.

"It's slippery isn't it?" Ma asks. "Do you think we can make it all right?"

"Why, of course! I have snow tires. Who would think such a thing? Of course I can make it."

"I'd like to go, "Ma answers. "I'll be ready when you get here."

"Is Johnny doing anything?" Aunt Marion asks. "Why don't you bring him along."

I knew she favored me. I didn't know why, nor did I know why she didn't include my sisters, but I went along.

On the ride to Farmington, forceful Aunt Marion and reticent Ma join in polite conversation, like two people who don't know each other very well but, prompted by each other's presence, feel obliged to talk. I stare out the steamy window at the snowbanks and listen. Aunt Marion speaks first. "How are the kiddies?"

"They're fine. Nancy has a little cold, but it's getting better. School vacation will be good for her. Perhaps she can rest. They're all exhausted."

Aunt Marion presses her glasses against the bridge of her nose and lifts her chin slightly. "Perhaps we can find something for them today, a little gift that will help them feel better," she says, figuratively tucking my sisters into her pocket.

Ma objects. "You needn't do that. They have too much already."

"We'll see. Have you heard from Elliott lately?" Aunt Marion knows first when we hear from Pa. She is at the post office when Grandpa C.F. sorts the mail, and a letter from a soldier, particularly Pa, is news around the woodstove before even Ma knows it.

"Not for a while now. He wrote a week ago that he was expecting orders to a new camp and not to write until he sent the address. It'll probably be a few more days."

"Oh? That's funny." Aunt Marion says funny when she thinks she's been slighted. "I wonder why he didn't tell me. I hope he's getting my letters."

"I'm sure if he isn't, he will eventually."

Aunt Marion's chin goes out a little farther. "Well, I'm sorry he didn't tell me."

"I'm going to have to wait to send his Christmas gift," Ma says. "I hoped to get him a subscription to *The Franklin Journal* today, but I don't know where to send it, so I guess I'll do it another time."

"I've already done that."

Ma turns sharply. "You have? Why? Why did you do that? I told you I was going to send it to him. It's something I know he wants and I can afford."

"Well I thought it would be easier for you if I did it."

"I told you it was my Christmas gift to him. Now I don't know what I'll do."

I swell with compassion for my mother. I want to relieve her pain, but there is nothing I can do or say that will help; the spiteful damage cannot be undone. The air between them turns cold and silent.

Aunt Marion has, since I have known her, competed for achievement and recognition. She has demanded attention and gotten it. She has competed with Ben Staples, a Temple gardener, for the earliest pea harvest; with Uncle Austin for the newest model automobile; with county volunteers for the highest war-bond sales; and with her neighbors for the latest efficiency in home heating. And now, unable to connect with Ma in any meaningful way, she competes with her for my father's gratitude.

Shoppers crowd the downtown sidewalks in Farmington. Aunt Marion, her coat wrapped tight around her, scurries from store to store to select the gifts on her list. She then ushers us to Ferrari's men's shop where she picks out a winter coat for me. "Here," she says to Ma. "This can be for him for Christmas. From you and Elliott."

"Oh no," Ma answers. "You needn't do that."

"But I want to. I want the kiddies to have a happy Christmas. Maybe I can make up a little bit for their father not being here."

Aunt Marion aggravated my mother. She took away Ma's plans to give, and more so, wedged herself into my mother's relationship with my father. Ma was given no chance.

When Pa first wrote Ma from his new camp, Aunt Marion brought the letter to her from the post office. "A letter from Elliott came for you today," she said. "He's at Fort Bragg in North Carolina."

"Oh?"

"Let's open it and see what he has to say."

"Well, I kind of think," Ma stammered, "that I should finish my ironing."

Aunt Marion sat down at the kitchen table. "That's okay. I'll wait a few minutes."

Ma, her face painfully red, ironed another dress, then sagged into a chair to read to Aunt Marion. Later, she blurted out the story to Fern.

"She knows when I get a letter, Fern, and she rushes right over with it and stands there until I read it so I won't know anything she doesn't know. Darn her! Doesn't she understand they're my letters and I might not want to tell her everything that's in them?"

"Damned right she understands. And she's makin' goddam sure she finds out what's in 'em. And when Elliott says he wants you to send him somethin', she fixes it so he can thank her instead of you. And you let her do it."

"What am I supposed to do, tell the old . . . the old *bee* . . . to mind her own business?"

"I think that's a damn good idea. If it wuz me, I'd tell her right where the bear shit in the buckwheat. You're damn right I would. I jus' think she's tryin' to get Elliott on her side. She's up to somethin', Clarice."

Ma was hurt, but not ready to confront Aunt Marion over Pa's letters. She would try to get along, even if she had to concede to mistreatment along the way. "We'll see what happens, Fern."

As I listened, I imagined Ma challenging Aunt Marion. I knew they would both yell for an instant, and then there would be tears. I could see Ma sobbing and Aunt Marion turning her stern face and stomping away and vowing never to speak to Ma again. And I knew there would be repercussions. Pa would be troubled and rant at Ma and maybe at Aunt Marion. I sighed with relief that Ma wanted harmony, and that she yearned for Aunt Marion to understand and stop hurting her.

As Christmas approached, Ma's metabolism went into low gear. She turned pallid and looked empty. Her futile attempts to cope with Aunt Marion and to acquire gifts for Pa and us had disheartened her. In the past, Christmas had been an exhilarating time for me. Although

I had received few gifts—usually boots, a shirt, and perhaps a toy tractor—I had savored the school celebration, the sledding and skating
with friends, and the anticipation of Santa Claus. Now melancholy
hung over Ma like fog. I questioned whether we could create the
Christmas spirit. I knew Ma would seek to duplicate past Christmases,
but I feared she would fall short at filling Pa's absence. Nonetheless,
more than one replacement for Pa would emerge.

The first is Eddie Fontaine who works for Uncle Austin and is the
local odd-jobber, carpenter, wood chopper, and mechanic who seems
capable of doing anything. He has volunteered to kill a chicken for our
Christmas dinner.

He comes, one day, to the kitchen door carrying a small ax and a
piece of rope in his leathery hands. "W'ich one did you want, ma'am?"

"They're in the coop in the shed, Eddie. Pick the fattest."

"I'll need a pan of boilin' water, ma'am."

I assume the ax is bad news for a chicken, and Patty does, too.
"What's he going to do, Mommy?"

"Fix a rooster for Christmas dinner," she says. "You don't have to
watch."

Soon I hear squawking and cackling and fluttery commotion from
beyond the kitchen door, and I put on my coat and go there. Nancy and
Patty go in the other direction. Eddie has caught the biggest rooster
from the coop in the corner and now holds it tucked under his arm, its
wings and heaving body pinned tight against his faded and torn blue-
denim frock. The bird's desperate eyes scream for escape. Eddie gently
strokes its back and head with his gloved right hand and speaks, "Thar.
Thar. Everthin's gonna be all right. Jist calm down now." The coop is
silent, seemingly in reverent thanks for respite from Christmas dinner.
A chopping block sits in the center of the floor. The ax stands slantwise
against the block.

Eddie leans forward slightly, the terrified chicken tight under his
left arm, takes a step to balance his stocky frame, and maneuvers the

rooster's head and neck over the block. He reaches for the ax. "Thar, thar now," he says again. "Everthin's gonna be all right."

Uneasy, I back away but continue to stare. Eddie takes a deep breath and raises the ax high over his head. I hear a muffled squawk. Eddie grunts and drives the ax toward the block.

It is not a clean cut. The head hangs by a piece of skin. Eddie strikes again, and I notice his denim sleeve spattered red. The carcass twitches, then collapses. Eddie shouts to Ma, "I need the hot water now, ma'am." Ma steps out of the kitchen door with the steaming water, and Eddie dunks the chicken into the pot. He looks at me and explains, "Dis loosen de feather so they pull. Want to help?"

"No!" I say. Pulling rooster feathers is not for me. I retreat to the safety of the kitchen. Soon Eddie comes in with a mostly plucked rooster still oozing warm blood from its neck.

"Here 'tis, ma'am. I di'nt get all de pin, but I get most. You need to singe off the small feather I don't get."

"Eddie, can you do another one? I really need two. And get one for you and Nellie if you'd like."

I do 'nother one, ma'am, but I don't need one for me." He looks down at me. "You comin', too?" He goes to the shed to stalk another bird.

I have seen enough. I join my two sisters in the parlor. "We're having chicken for Christmas dinner," I announce.

"What did Eddie bring the rope for?" Patty asks.

"I don't know. He didn't use it."

"Was it an awful sight?"

"He's doing another one if you want to watch."

"Not me," Nancy says. "I have schoolwork to get done before vacation."

On the first vacation day, Ma, Nancy, and Patty leave with Aunt Marion to Christmas shop. Fern stays behind. She doesn't do Christmas shopping, not much anyway. But she will celebrate

Christmas with us and boost us up when things don't go as she thinks they should.

"John," Fern says to me after everyone has left, "where in hell are we gonna get a Christmas tree?"

"I know where there's one," I say to her.

"You do? Where the hell is it?"

"There's one growing along the wall out in the lane. Daddy showed it to me in the summer. Said it would make a good one this year."

"Well, jeez. Why don't you take his saw, the little one, and go get it. Chrissakes, we need a tree here."

Fern has shown me a way to fill in for Pa. I slide on his snowshoes, wrap the cowhide straps twice around my ankles, and buckle them tight. I take his saw from the shed and tramp over the snow to the pasture gate, then along the lane where snow clings to bent birches and snowdrifts sidle against the stone wall. I recall where Pa and I hiked in September looking for apples and signs of partridge or deer, and I retrace our steps. Past the orchard where we picked northern spy apples for the barrel in the root cellar, I find the fir as we left it, its branches full of bushy growth and its tip long and straight. I push the snow away from its trunk, hold the saw below the lower whorl of branches as I had seen Pa do other Christmases, and saw until it falls into the snow. I drag it toward home, following a trace of wood smoke that hangs in the winter air.

Fern greets me. "Boy, you found a nice tree."

"Daddy picked it out. Do you think it's okay?"

Fern eyes it and acclaims it fitting for the parlor. "Of course it's okay," she says.

Eddie came and cut the end square with Pa's bucksaw, showed me how to nail a piece of board on the bottom, and helped me lift it through the house to the front room, where we stood it by the bay window. Later, when Nancy and Patty returned, we strung colored bulbs, hung old, wrinkled tinsel and glass ornaments we had saved from previous Christmases, and draped a homemade paper garland among the branches. With just a few days left, we were ready for Santa Claus.

On Christmas Eve, Aunt Marion arrives. She says she wants to help us hang our stockings.

Ma, exhausted, turns pale at the sight of her but tries to be pleasant. "Come in. Sorry the place is so messy. I've been roasting roosters and wrapping gifts, and I'm anxious for bed, but I'll do the dishes tomorrow. I'll get the stockings now, and we'll sit in the living room. Fern's built a nice, warm fire in the fireplace. She snowshoed up to C.F.'s old shed this afternoon and found a few sticks of wood. Come and sit." Ma fetches the stockings, the biggest we have, the long gray-cotton leggings we hated to wear, and Aunt Marion tacks them into the wooden mantle and lets them hang down in front of the fire.

"There," she says as she steps back to admire her work, "Santa will fill those right up when he gets here."

"Have a seat, Marion," Fern says. "You ready for Christmas?"

"Oh, yes, but I hope it's happy for the kiddies. It's a shame their father's not here. I hope I can help make up the difference."

Fern then takes a few moments to deliver a Christmas message to Aunt Marion. "We're tired out here," she says. "It's been a long month since Elliott left. Snow, cold, no wood, no money, kids and animals to care for. I don't know when we'll get straightened around again."

Aunt Marion raises her chin, and her mouth goes tight. "Oh, I know. We've all had it harder with him gone. Everyone wishes he were here. I've been right out straight, too, but the kiddies need a happy Christmas."

"We coulda used more help," Fern says. "It's been rough on Clarice to scratch for wood and stuff. And then you discombobulated her plans to get a present for Elliott and a toboggan for the kids. And it's her that's missing Elliott the most. She don't feel good, Marion. She's the one that needs a happy Christmas."

"Well, I should say! After all I've done."

Fern goes on. "Done what? Yes, the kids will soon be dreaming of Santa Claus, but it's been hard for them, too."

I listen, fearful of the tension. Aunt Marion will pout and sulk and shun Ma, and I will be shamed. I can see Christmas going down the sink.

"I know," Aunt Marion says as she buttons her coat. "We all do what we can. Mother and I will be up in the morning. We promised Elliott."

"Good night, Marion. Merry Christmas," Ma says.

After Aunt Marion leaves, Ma, who had been silent, looks at Fern and says, "Fern, you shouldn't have been so tough on her. She means well."

"Yeah, but it don't always turn out good. I had to tell her. She's too stuck on herself."

"But that's the way she is."

"I know, an' it ain't right. Chrissakes, she wouldn't let you get a present for Elliott or one for your kids. What kind of a Boy Scout good deed is that? What the hell right does she have to tell you not to buy your kids a toboggan? 'Cause it's dangerous? Dangerous, my ass. Hell, Johnny knocked four teeth out of his mouth last year slidin' on his sled in the road. That's what I call dangerous. They hafta sit up straight in a toboggan, and they likely won't be in the road neither. Besides, the kids begged for a toboggan. You shoulda told her right then where the bear shit in the buckwheat. Damn right you shoulda."

Ma sighed. "We're all going to bed, Fern. Don't wake me up in the morning. I want to sleep."

"Don't wake me neither. Let the kids do it."

The next morning, Christmas packages wrapped in red and green tissue paper sat under the tree. The homely cotton stockings were packed full of surprises, and a Christmas wreath hung on the wall above the fireplace. Fern relit the fire, and the aroma of fresh balsam hung in the air. Ma came out of the bedroom rubbing her sleep-worn eyes and whispered, "Merry Christmas, kids. My, my. Look at the presents." But she lacked the spirit. I could see it.

I emptied my stocking and found a Big Little Book, new mittens, and, at the bottom, an orange. Nancy, Patty, and I opened gifts together. We tore tissue paper from a cradle, a dart game, some paper dolls, a tabletop bowling alley, a new coat for me and dresses for Nancy and Patty—more gifts than ever before. But afterward the setting seemed hollow, quiet, the house empty.

Later, Aunt Marion brought Grandma Luna, who wore a long winter coat and a fur collar tucked around her neck and didn't smile all the time she was there, to see our Christmas tree. I supposed she was busy taking smug pleasure at the absence of a toboggan for Nancy and Patty and me under the tree. Aunt Marion was neither friendly nor discourteous. She played the role of Pa again. She put the cradle and the bowling alley together under the watchful eye of Fern, who offered her unsolicited advice.

"Not that way!" Fern butted in. "You have to put the rails in first, before the other end piece. Gawd almighty! Anybody would know that."

Grandpa C.F. came alone to see us after we had eaten the roasted chicken. He appeared smoking a pipe and wearing earmuffs under his fedora, "I've been wearing these around the house this week so's I can't hear the advice I been gettin'," he said. He set them on the kitchen table and smiled, "But I don't need 'em here, except when Fern gets to spoutin' off. Merry Christmas to you all," he winked.

"Listen, sourpuss," Fern grinned. "I notice you listen pretty close to what I say and sometimes want me to say more than I should. Well, I ain't gettin' into any trouble today, so there. Merry Christmas."

Grandpa C.F. and I played darts, and I beat him. He laughed and said that he saw two dartboards. "You should be used to that by now," Fern told him, and he laughed again. Later, after he had put his earmuffs on and left, Fern said he brightened her whole day.

We didn't expect Pa to call on Christmas, and he didn't. Ma wrote him Christmas night that being both father and mother to three children during the holidays was hard, that she was struggling with his relatives, that the shopping and the decorating had been no fun without him, and that several people had rallied to fill his shoes—Eddie, Fern, Aunt Marion, even me. Ma was relieved when Christmas ended.

One day, after Christmas, Fern took all of us to Madrid in the roadster. She said she had to find her coat. In Madrid, she turned onto a narrow, snowy, tree-lined road and drove slowly into the woods to a logging camp with a snow-covered roof, tar-papered sides, and tiny windows. Men worked all day in the woods with crosscut saws and axes and teams of horses. At night in the camp, they ate meals, played cards, and whittled by candlelight, then got out of their bunks at 5:00 A.M. and went back into the woods to saw and yard logs.

We stayed at the camp for supper. Women who lived here while their men worked in the forest roasted pork and baked beans, bread, and apple pies. We all ate together at a long wooden table. Fern, in long johns, baggy slacks, and a sweatshirt, was at home here. She knew the language and sassed the loggers and told stories just like they did. "I went to Lowell's Market in West Farmin'ton the other day," she said, "and asked Mr. Lowell if he had any beef to deliver personally, and boy kin he deliver it!"

We stayed late. We stuffed ourselves with food and inspected the wooden squirrels and birds the loggers had whittled out of limbs and stood next to the hot stove as long as we could. We watched the loggers play cards—pinochle, Fern called it—and then went back into the cold and home. It was more fun than Christmas. People were happy and teased each other and didn't bicker.

But Ma continued to worry. She had so little faith that she believed she would never see Pa again and would be alone forever. Frightened, she asked Fern to take her in the roadster to a fortune-teller in

Fairbanks. Fern tried to talk her out of it, saying that fortune-tellers were all baloney; if soothsayers didn't have watches, she said, they wouldn't know the time of day. But Ma prevailed. "I just have to know. I can't go on without knowing whether he will be okay or not," she wailed.

So on a dark winter day, while I waited in the cold rumble seat with my sisters and thumped my feet together to keep my toes warm, Fern and Ma watched a clairvoyant gaze into a crystal ball and fiddle with some tarot cards and voice astrological queries and match vague clues with Ma's troubled answers.

Not a word was spoken on the way home, but once we were in the kitchen Ma wailed at Fern, "I told you so. I told you so."

"You told me what, Clarice?"

"I told you I wouldn't see him again," she sobbed. "I just knew it."

"Chrissakes, Clarice. She told you he'd be home again. And she didn't say how bad he'd be hurt. Just that he'd be on crutches. He might be in good shape. Anyway, I bet she got Elliott mixed up with somebody else, prob'bly Elliott Roosevelt. He's in the army, too, you know."

Soon after, Fern dressed in pleated skirt and sweater and dress shoes and took us to the State in Farmington to see *Lassie Come Home,* a story of a father who lost his job and loved his family so much that to buy food he sold his son's dog to a faraway duke. Lassie escaped from the duke and labored through a strange and perilous land for eight hundred miles without shelter or food, except for a morsel or two by a few kind folks along the way, and risked her life to go back to the boy she loved. I cried. Ma cried. Nancy and Patty cried. Fern bought us all popcorn and sobbed too. Fern had taken us there to cheer Ma, she said, but I thought we went there to sit in the heated theater. Our firewood supply at home had declined to a few sticks, and the furnace had gone cold—except on the most frigid days.

We had started the winter without furnace wood. Pa had left us with only the remainder of last year's stack in the cellar and a promise that his brother Austin—who owned woodlots in the Temple outback and kept a crew cutting much of the time, except when the roads were clogged with snow—would bring us more. Meanwhile, Ma learned to conserve and not use much wood. She did not have a furnace fire during the day: Nancy and I would trudge home from school in midafternoon and find Patty and Ma huddled by the kitchen stove. Fern would set a fire in the furnace and heat the house for suppertime, then we'd go to bed to keep warm.

Eddie came at Christmastime and sawed the few oversized chunks that were scattered around the cellar. "You have 'bout 'nough for 'nother week," he told Ma.

Ma called Uncle Austin, "What can you tell me about the wood? Eddie says I've only a week left."

Uncle Austin seldom said no to anyone. "I'll get some for you pretty soon. They say the plow'll be fixed in a day or two."

A few days later, Ma counted five sticks in the cellar and called Uncle Austin again.

"Maybe Phil has some out at the Merrill farm," he said. "I ought to call him. If he don't have any, I can get some pretty soon."

By this time, Ma didn't trust Uncle Austin. She called Pa's brother in Farmington. "Phil, I'm looking for wood. We're nearly out. Can you help?"

"Well, maybe," he said. "I should have a cord at the Burt Mitchell place. If the snow's not too deep, maybe Wayne can get it with Elliott's truck."

Ma seemed to be getting nowhere. Fern grew impatient and put on boots and fit them to Pa's snowshoes. "I'm goin' across to that old shed over there to see what I can find."

"Fern, the snow's too deep."

"No, it ain't. Besides, I gotta see if there's any wood over there."

I watched her go. She dragged a sled behind her and tramped in the tracks I had made to get the Christmas tree. Soon she returned, out of breath, her face red and covered with sweat beads. But she had found a sled-full of dried firewood.

"I gotta saw . . . whew," she wiped the sweat from her brow, "saw up these long ones so's they'll fit. C'mon out and toss 'em down cellar for me, will ya, Clarice? I gotta chop outside. There ain't enough room down cellar to swing an ax. You can toss it down after I cut it up." They worked until dusk. Fern bucked the long sticks into two and split the ones she could, and when she could catch her breath she swore like a pirate. Ma tossed the fitted pieces down the bulkhead steps. When they finished, Fern let out a deep breath and dusted her hands together. "There," she said. "That oughta hold us for a while. When are those sonsabitches gonna bring us some goddam wood, anyway?"

Ma said it should be soon. She said Wayne, who looked after Pa's truck at the Farmers Union, will bring us Uncle Phil's wood. But later Wayne showed up with just a few sticks and threw them onto our porch. "It's all I could find," he said. Eddie came later and sawed it and split it, and we had enough for a few more days.

It snowed again, and fierce winds drove folks inside. We huddled around the kitchen stove and burned trash in the fireplace. We complained and waited for midafternoon and a fire in the furnace. Ma called Uncle Austin again, and he said he should have some wood out pretty soon.

"That's the last time I'm going to call him," she said. "He's no help at all."

"You know, Clarice," Fern bitched. "Austin's crew has got wood out for Rachel and for Ed Higgins and for the store. They ain't gonna bring us any wood. I just know it."

Ma sat helpless and waited while the plow stayed stuck in the Edes Road snowdrift. In a few days, when the village roads were cleared, Aunt Marion and Uncle Lawrence brought us a few sticks of stove wood in the back of Lawrence's bakery wagon, and we burned it in our furnace. And we kept scrounging. Fern tramped back to the old shed, and Ma tried Uncle Phil again, but no luck. Then in February, Wayne took Pa's truck to the Burt Mitchell place again and found a woodpile that belonged to Uncle Austin. Ma had said she would not call him again, but she did.

"Sure," he said. "Take a cord and a half anytime."

"See," Fern said to Ma. "I told you he wa'nt gonna bring you any, and I was right."

Wayne brought us the cord and a half, Eddie sawed and split it, and Fern and I lugged the furnace-size sticks to the cellar. We had wood enough to stay warm for a month. We relaxed. We were rich.

Lack of firewood, more than any other hardship, was the most telling on us that winter. Temple suffered its most severe winter in memory. The snow and the cold paralyzed us. We dawdled in bed mornings. We huddled around the kitchen stove. We had a warm house for only a few hours each day. Pa and his family, Fern said, had failed us.

Thank God for Fern. She buoyed our spirits, sawed and split what little wood she could find, shoveled snow, kept us moving, and bitched about the folks that should be helping Ma. "I hope them sonsabitches are warm. Somebody oughta tell the barstards we got chilled potatoes rottin' in the cellar. Maybe they'd like to help us eat 'em."

Wayne would bring us more wood in March, after we had run out and the fires had gone cold again. By that time, we had run out of money, too.

Pa had left Ma with no cash, just a small savings account in Farmington, a promise of a monthly check from the army, and a prospect of income from the truck. Ma didn't receive the monthly check. One month, two months, and still no check. After the first month, when she learned we hadn't received money, Aunt Marion assumed Ma was helpless and called somebody at the county office to demand our pay. After the second month, Uncle Austin, chairman of the county draft board, said the check should be coming pretty soon. In

March, three months after Pa had left, Ma asked Pa's lawyer to write a letter of inquiry to the army.

We had never had much money, nor had we much opportunity to spend any. Ma had preserved vegetables from our gardens. Pa had raised animals or shot deer for meat. The cows furnished milk and butter, and the chickens supplied eggs and an occasional Sunday roast. Ma had made us a few clothes. Pa had chopped most of our wood, made repairs to the house, and used the auto junkyard to keep the truck and the roadster going. We had spent our cash on taxes, shoes, a few clothes, groceries we couldn't produce ourselves, and gas for the truck. But without the army check, we didn't have cash except for Pa's savings account.

We stopped spending. Bills went unpaid. We acquired, through Uncle Austin's generosity, bread and canned soups and flour and macaroni at the general store on credit. We went without meat. We stopped using kerosene to build the wood fires. We received garage bills for repair work on the truck, and Ma either sent them to the Farmers Union or tossed them in the stove for heat. We were used to living without much cash, but some things we missed. Ma complained to Pa that mostly she wanted just one steak or a can of kerosene or a pint of fresh oysters from Lowell's for a stew. But Pa wrote that he wasn't getting paid either and to send him money from the savings account.

Ma tried to avoid using Pa's saving account for herself, but she used it to pay for Christmas and to see a doctor. Whenever Pa asked, she withdrew money and mailed it to him and implored him to improve his poker game. She bought a pint of his favorite whiskey, carefully packaged it, and dispatched it to him. He asked for more, and she sent it. She borrowed money from Uncle Austin to visit her sick father in Kennebunk and told him she would pay him when her check came.

One day she went to see Uncle Roy Stinchfield, Pa's brother-in-law and manager of the Farmington Farmer's Union. Pa had let out his truck to the Farmer's Union to use in their business and arranged for

Uncle Roy to pay for its use and keep a separate account of the profit. Ma believed the truck would earn money for Pa, as it had before he left.

"Roy," Ma told him. "I need money. I could use some of the profits from the truck, but all I get are bills. Do you have a few dollars?"

Roy, at least a foot taller than Ma and sporting a white shirt and bow tie and nervous tic that made him look like he winked when he spoke, hooked his thumbs under his suspenders and, with a half-wily grin on his face, sputtered, "What do you need money for?"

"Roy. I'm broke. I'm not getting the money the army promised. I don't know why."

He winked his nervous tic, hitched up his pants with the inside of his arms, and coughed, "How much do you need?"

"I've used Elliott's savings account until it's nearly gone. I need to pay some of my bills. Except for Austin, I can't buy anything anywhere. I'd take twenty dollars, if you have it."

"The truck hasn't earned any money, you know."

"But you've used all the gas-ration tickets I had, and you wanted more, and Wayne says he's busier than ever. Where'd the money go?"

He waved a handful of paper at her. "There isn't any money. Only bills to pay."

Ma paused. Roy was being difficult, and it would do her no good to stay longer. "Well, I thought the truck was supposed to make some money for us. That's what Elliott said when he left."

Roy hitched up his trousers again, twitched, and handed her some overdue invoices. "Here. If you need money, maybe you can collect these. I haven't been able to."

Not to be outdone by Roy's brush-off, Ma hunted down the men who owed the Farmers Union money. She presented Roy's invoices, told them how badly she needed the money, and collected a total of thirty dollars from two of them.

Again, Ma had been reminded, as she had told Pa many times, that his family would not help her. They disliked her, she had believed, and would ignore her and take advantage of her. Now, in the middle of a terrible winter, she was trapped in her prophecy. Still, although annoyed and frustrated, she felt it best to pursue harmony rather than hostility. But she was denied at every exchange. I anguished at the sight of her contending with Aunt Marion and Uncle Austin and Uncle Roy and being rebuffed by each of them. I felt sorry for her, but I could not help her. I listened and made no demands. I kept the woodbox filled. I completed my barn chores on time and was attentive to my school work and stayed out of trouble. But it was obvious to me that Eddie and Fern and Wayne and our neighbors were our source of strength. Ma could not rely on Pa's family. Later, I would learn how much they could hurt her.

Chapter Six
FORT BRAGG 1944

You'll be taught foot drill, the handling of a rifle, the use of the gas mask . . . You'll be initiated into the mysteries of the kitchen police . . . You'll drill, and drill, and drill . . . Most of what you are taught will impress you as utterly useless nonsense, but you'll learn it.

—Marion Hargrove, *See Here, Private Hargrove*

P a spent his first night in the barracks shivering and sleepless on an iron-mesh cot, curled under a blanket with his arms wrapped around himself, pondering how far he had come. Startled by the 5:30 A.M. bugle, he was among the first to report to morning formation on the misty parade ground. The calisthenics came easy to him, warmed him, and eased his uncertainty.

For two weeks at Fort Devens, Pa suffered physical and mental exams, inoculations, and military indoctrination. He waited in line naked, his modesty, or what was left of it, abandoned. He was issued uniforms and a duffel bag and taught military courtesy and hierarchy and organization. He boxed his civilian clothes and mailed them home, wrote Ma that he was being transferred, and told her to wait for his new address before writing him again.

A troop train transported him from Boston to Fayetteville, North Carolina. He traveled all day on the Seaboard Coastline Railroad and arrived in darkness, rain, and fog. A bus took him ten miles west to Fort Bragg in the sand hills and rich farmland of piedmont North Carolina. There he moved into wooden barracks that had been thrown together and furnished with iron-mesh cots and footlockers in 1940 to house an instant army.

Assigned to the 3rd platoon, Battery B, 5th Training Battalion, he sent Ma a picture postcard of a 155-mm howitzer and his new address. The postcard arrived in Temple on December 21, 1943, and I knew then what I had suspected—for the first time in my life, Pa would not be home for Christmas.

He had little time to think about his circumstances. He was quickly thrust into a strict regimen of military conduct. He was directed to salute military rank, to obey the orders of his corporal, and to keep his uniform clean, polished, and pressed at all times. He was stripped of his freedom and identity and issued dog tags bearing his name and serial number to be worn around his neck. Basic training was a new way of life for Pa, opposite to the freewheeling habits of an unfettered country boy.

Pa trained in artillery. The first morning, the battery assembled on the parade ground and listened to the drill sergeant's instructions, "Attench . . . Hut! We are going to drill you people in close-order marching. If any of you can't keep up, fall down someplace where you won't be in the way. For-r-rwar-r-rd . . . Har-rup!" They marched for three hours. Over the damp ground and through rain-filled puddles, the drill sergeant ordered flanking movements, columns left and right, and rearward maneuvers until they had marched more than ten miles. The unfit tired and faltered. One dropped out, and the 3rd platoon went on without him. Pa suffered from sore feet and mental paralysis. Marching in a stupor, he unconsciously turned the wrong way. "Your other left, mister. Your other left," the drill sergeant yelled, and Pa had to think his way through lefts and rights. Day after day, he performed close-order drill and calisthenics and ran the obstacle course until they became a way of life.

Pa learned the fine points of KP—kitchen police. He served food, scrubbed the kitchen floor, polished pots and pans, disposed of garbage, all on a regular basis. He washed dishes, made his own bed, cleaned windows, sewed on patches, and mopped the barracks floor. Fern, when she heard of his new skills, exclaimed, "Jeez, Clarice. When El comes home on leave, we can take a vacation."

Pa served on guard duty one day each month. Afraid he would foul up if he were presented a challenge on duty, he wrote down his instructions and kept them in his pocket. He walked his post, talked to no one, and carried a loaded rifle and written commands, "Halt, who goes there?" or "Corporal of the guard! Post number seven!"

After a month, the 3rd platoon set out on a twenty-five-mile march. They marched in combat boots and wore full packs on a cool and rainy winter day. Pa grew tired and nauseous; he suffered from chills and shortness of breath. His feet stopped hurting and went numb. He fell behind, finished after the others, and reported to the camp hospital with a fever. The doctor confined him, and he developed a hacking cough. After three days rest, he had recovered and reported back to training with the 3rd platoon.

Pa trained in the operation of 155-mm and the smaller 105-mm howitzers: how to aim and fire, solve a surveying problem, and break down, repair, and reassemble the guns. He took notes, which he reviewed at night, and practiced with the gun crew day after day until their movements became automatic and precise.

In February 1944, the army reviewed Pa's classification test and interview results and, to take advantage of his skill and experience driving a truck on Temple's unpaved and hilly roads, transferred him to the 1st platoon to train as a truck driver. But then they directed him to forget the skills he had acquired in civilian life and taught him the army way. He learned precise movements, techniques for driving off-road and on pontoon bridges, and driving loaded and unloaded trucks. In the motor pool, he learned the maintenance routine: how to disassemble and replace engine parts and how to keep records. He drove in motorized marches over Fort Bragg's sandy roads and practiced firing .30- and .50-caliber machine guns, which in combat would be mounted on a truck's cab.

At the end of February, I received a postcard. "Hey, listen to this," I said to Ma. "Daddy says when he gets home, we can use the car for a boat. He knows how to float it."

"I'm sure he does," Ma said. "But I'm not going in it with him. You can if you want."

"He also asked me if I'm keeping the woodbox full. Why does he always ask me that?"

"He's probably cold. Write him and tell him we ran out of wood a month ago."

"He won't be there." I told her. "He's going into the field on maneuvers."

Battery B moved into the field in trucks. They towed howitzers and carried ammunition into Fort Bragg's dusty flatlands. The men rode in the back of the trucks on two rows of wooden benches under canvas coverings and stowed their duffle bags on the floor between them. They bivouacked in tents and ate K rations from mess kits—sealed cans of meat and ham and eggs, cheese and crackers, and powdered drinks. The rations were warmed on gas pocket-stoves and proved to be adequate for their purpose.

The battery was out three days firing at fixed targets, moving and setting up the guns at new locations, and firing again. They camouflaged the guns with netting and brush and were taught how to defend their positions with grenades and rifle bayonets. Pa called on his lifetime of experience with firearms and earned a Sharpshooter Badge with the M-1 carbine. He learned how to identify and disarm booby traps and mines, and he practiced driving his truck in a convoy after dark without lights. On the last night out the temperature fell, and he slept curled tightly in his sleeping bag with the drawstring snug over his head. In the morning the battery stood in freezing temperatures and received its evaluation. The sergeant said that 1st platoon had performed well and showed signs of becoming a team, but that there would be more work in the field before the end of basic training. Their performance earned them a weekend pass.

Pa had to pass a footlocker inspection before he could leave the barracks Saturday morning. He cleaned and secured his equipment, refolded his clothes, and carefully placed everything in its proper spot. He polished his combat boots and stood them beside his locker. He cleaned and oiled his carbine, opened the bolt, and laid it across the top. He buffed his shoes to a high gloss, shined his brass belt buckle, and put on a fresh uniform. Last, he pulled the hospital corners of his bunk blanket so tight he could bounce a half-dollar on it, then he waited. When the sergeant came by, Pa stood at attention and said, "Good morning, sir."

"Good morning, soldier. Stay out of trouble tonight."

"Yessir," Pa sighed and headed for the bus station.

He and his pals from 1st platoon boarded the bus for a fifteen-minute ride into Fayetteville, once a bustling port city on the Cape Fear River but since 1940 a military town catering to the soldiers who passed through Fort Bragg on their way to war. On arrival they went on the prowl in search of the bars and public houses they had heard so much about in the barracks. In bar after bar, they drank dime beer, ate pickled eggs and boiled peanuts, and laughed. The air reeked of alcoholic smog, and noisy soldiers muffled the juke box. Pa drank as much and as fast as he could and moved from one beer hall to the next. Late that night, he and his disorderly pals from the 1st platoon were ambushed by the military police and escorted back to camp, a dismal ending to Pa's first brush with Carolina society.

He wrote Ma about his trip to Fayetteville, confessing that he didn't get a chance to see the city. She wrote back that he should do his sightseeing first and the "Bars and Rails" after. She also wrote a disturbing account of untrue rumors circulating in Temple.

She and Fern had been accused of partying and entertaining carousers, Ma wrote, and although she didn't want to alarm or distract him, she couldn't continue to live in Temple and be slandered for no reason. She asked him for permission to move to her parents in Kennebunk. He turned down her plea to leave Temple and ignored her story of rumors and her doings there. He may have outright believed her denial of misconduct, or his silence may have indicated a curiosity. But instead of backing her or offering her understanding, he asked her to send money and a pint of whiskey, if she could. His private's pay of twenty dollars a month was apparently not enough to drink in Fayetteville and gamble in the barracks.

The army had banned crapshooting, but poker was rampant—and Pa needed cash. He told Ma he wasn't getting paid, and she believed him. Broke herself, she sent him money; money from his savings account; money from the Farmers Union if Uncle Roy coughed up any; or money that Uncle Austin would loan her. Her loyalty to Pa, if measured by her attempts to make him happy, was faultless. But, incredibly, he would soon hear more about her behavior.

Following one of his pleas for money, Pa received alarming letters from Aunt Marion and Grandma Luna. They alleged that Ma neglected Nancy, Patty, and me and suggested that he should let them—his sister and his mother—take us in and care for us. He answered their letters, wrote Ma that he had received their allegations, and cautioned her. He then turned to soldiering again.

Pa became proficient with truck driving and maintenance and developed confidence in army life. He didn't admit that he liked it, but unless he was sick or the gnats were chewing on him, he avoided grumbling about training exercises in the field, or living in a tent, or the long hours. He studied and learned. He wore a gas mask, rehearsed bayonet drills, read maps, tossed live grenades, and fired his rifle. He ate well, worked hard, and sweated through calisthenics, close-order drills, and twenty-five-mile marches. In April he wrote me that he was preparing for a big parade.

After seventeen weeks of learning and practicing under hardened sergeants and corporals who had fought a generation ago, Pa finished basic training. He had arrived green and terrified in the cold of winter, but by the warmth of spring he had become a soldier. The battery could drill together and sing cadence two hundred voices strong. When the 5th Training Battalion passed in review in perfect cadence and with eyes right, a band played in the foreground, while in the background a veteran sergeant muttered to himself with pride and headed for the bus stop for the next load of incoming recruits.

Pa and seventy-two other privates, forty-five of them pre-Pearl Harbor fathers, were ordered to report to the 8th Armored Division at Camp Polk, Louisiana, on May 7, 1944. He headed for the train station and home. He needed to see Ma.

Chapter Seven

*The snowplow got Staples Hill plowed out last week so that
the Duleys can now get out with a horse. They've walked all
winter.*

—Aunt Marion, April 1944

Despite the brush-off by Pa's family that snowy and cold winter, Ma's friends did not desert her. One by one, day by day,
they came and sat at the table in the barren surrounds of her colorless
kitchen while Ma ironed or cooked or squeezed wet-washed clothes
through the Easy's hand-cranked wringer. Each day I watched her walk
a mile in that drab kitchen, and between the cookstove and the counter
and the table and the dishpan, she wore pathways in its faded linoleum.
In April and May, she washed windows and curtains, and scrubbed
smoke stains from the pale beige walls and wood cabinets. In early
summer she painted the ceiling or the linoleum or the cabinets and
woodwork or the porch floor. In midsummer she canned peas and
spinach and beet greens over hot fires at dawn, and in late summer,
Swiss chard and green beans and beef stew and blueberries. During fall
she pickled cucumbers and stored potatoes, turnips, carrots, and beets
in dry sand in the cellar. As winter came on, she cleaned soot from the
stove, warmed the kitchen with wood, and received her friends and
neighbors there.

Callers came, it seemed, every day and gave the kitchen life. Ethyl or Rachel usually came in the morning. Anna arrived in late afternoon, Nellie anytime. Lucille dropped in when she was home from the shipyard. Aino on her way to the store, and Hilma came when she was in the village. They came with news or to ask about Pa or to reassure Ma or to exchange gossip. They sat at the kitchen table and sipped coffee or tea and many times left a gift on the oilcloth, a loaf of homemade bread or a jar of applesauce. They came in friendship and to spend time with Ma.

Others came to the kitchen for orders. Eddie listened to Ma tell him how many roosters she wanted killed, plucked, and put in the icebox; where she figured the stovepipe was plugged; or that she needed a tree cut or a leaky pipe repaired. Wayne came to the kitchen and asked where she wanted the wood dropped or the bagged grain stored or if he could bring her anything from town. It was to the kitchen that Grandpa C.F. came on Sundays to sit at the table with Ma. She served him tea, and they exchanged letters from Pa and heartened each other that he was well. He listened to Ma's worries and heightened her spirit, and when he left promised he would come back. Fern came to the

Fern Knowles poses on the front lawn in April 1944

kitchen to take a load off her feet and to listen to Ma wail about Pa's relatives. And Ma listened to Fern try to sort out her life.

Fern's divorce from Elmer dragged. He walked back and forth in the road, hung around the place, and rapped on the door once in a while. Occasionally he came in and, while Ma retreated to another room, he and Fern spoke in low voices. Otherwise, Fern paid him no regard except to complain about his loitering. Although she showed coldness toward Elmer, I was not convinced. She liked men to notice her.

Gus, a local logger who lived alone, came to see her one Saturday, and she invited him to the movies at the State. She returned late, and Ma asked if she had a good time and if anything happened.

"Good time?" Fern howled. "Do you know what he did? He was drunk, an' I wouldn't take him in the theater with me. So guess what? He sits in the car for two hours sipping a pint while I eat popcorn and watch Sonja Henie—I think it was called *Wintertime*—with hardly no clothes on cut figure eights or somethin' in the ice. He musta froze his arse. Pro'bly the pint kept him warm."

"So was he still there when you got back?" Ma wanted to know.

"Yeah, he was there. An' likkered up good too. An' you know what—haw, haw, haw, haw—he tol' me he loved me, for chrissakes. Musta been the likker. He wanted me to come live with him. Said he'd marry me." She laughed again. "And new shoes."

"What about new shoes? Come on. Tell me."

"He said . . ." She paused and her eyes twinkled. "Said if I'd marry him he'd buy me new shoes." And she laughed some more.

Ma smiled. "What did you say then, Fern?"

"Jeez. What would you told him? I told him to shush. He was just talkin' anyway. I took him home. Gawd. I'm a married woman—I think."

"Was that all you did?"

"Hell, yes. I didn't do nothin'. But he wouldn't stop all the way home. When I left him off, he asked me in. I thought about it an' said maybe some other time. Call me when you're sober, I told him."

Fern couldn't restrain herself. I stood there and listened to her crow that a man craved her, laugh that she told him she was a married woman, then plot to dupe him into another meeting. I wondered how I'd ever know whether to trust a woman.

Gus called again and asked Fern out. She dolled up in a blue pleated skirt, a fluffy white blouse, a matching three-button suit coat, and pinned a sparkling silver brooch on the lapel. She rubbed on fake nylon stockings from a bottle and wore stylish black pumps on her little feet. A picture of poise and grace, she beamed at the prospect of Gus's company again and waited in the kitchen, looking again and again at her reflection in the window. "Don't I look nice? Johnny, don't you think I look nice?"

She waited and paced the floor, but Gus didn't show. And he didn't call. I guessed he knew Fern's divorce was not ended. "Where is he?" she fussed. "Is he standin' me up or what?" She blamed Elmer. Said he had probably told Gus there was no divorce yet. "Damn!" she cried. "I had my mind set on them new shoes tonight. I'm all prettied up and, dammit, he's not gonna show. Life's a bitch," she said and looked at me, "Ain't it, Johnny?"

Elmer came to see Fern again. They sat at the kitchen table and whispered. Ma shushed us kids and crept into the dining room and listened, her ear tuned to every sound. She heard nothing until Elmer shut the kitchen door on his way out. Then Fern told her what had happened. "He's afraid I'll discombobulate the hearing," she said. "Doesn't want me in the courtroom."

"What did you tell him?" Ma asked.

"I told him of course I was goin'. I want the folks to see the discarded woman dumped by Elmer because he liked foolin' around better."

"Did he know when the court is?"

"It's tomorrow. But I ain't goin'. He said he wouldn't ask for the hundred and wouldn't be mad at me afterward, so I said I'd stay away."

"How you going to know what happened?"

"He said if I stayed around tomorrow he'd come tell me." Fern had closed a deal, for money and probably some attention from Elmer later. I imagined Elmer thought he, too, had a bargain: He could stay close to Fern and still have his freedom. I wondered how I, a nine-year-old kid, would ever learn what I needed to know to get through life. I supposed I was learning now and should be keeping notes.

The next day, Fern paced back and forth over the linoleum and talked a streak. "I don't know yet what happened. Elmer said he'd come to tell me. I been watchin' out these windows all day now, and I don't see him nowhere. He said last night if I stayed home he'd come tell me. I'm supposed to be a free woman, but I don't know if I'm married or single."

I couldn't see that it made any difference to her. But she ached to know. She couldn't sit down or stand up or do anything but pace from window to window and wait for Elmer. "Here he comes! Elmer! Come in!" Ma shooed us all into the front room, shushed us down, and bent her ear toward the kitchen again. After Elmer had left, Fern sat motionless. "He don't know neither," she said. "He said he couldn't tell. Imagine that, he couldn't tell whether he got a divorce or not. So what am I supposed to do now?"

Later, Elmer walked by the house with a new girlfriend. Then Fern knew what to do. She went to town to have her hair styled. Gus was coming again, and she wanted to be prettied up for him. She would get the new shoes this time, she said.

Until then, I hadn't been concerned about men around the place. Wayne, Eddie, Lester, Ted, and the others came to bring wood, repair the house, milk the cows, and perform other man-jobs Ma and Fern couldn't manage. They came to work, to help Ma take care of the place. But I feared that Fern, after her divorce, would tempt a new breed. Men might come to hobnob with her, to drink a stubby of beer and hang out. I didn't like it. I could picture the hurt to us if men hung out here. Aunt Marion would be livid. The neighbors would shun us. And Pa, when he found out, would rant at Ma.

To keep Fern from entertaining at the house, Ma started to go out more, too. She asked Fern to take us to *So Proudly We Hail* at the State, an account of army nurses on Bataan who wouldn't surrender. Pa had written that he had watched it at Fort Bragg, and Ma felt compelled to go. The air in the roadster was brutally cold. Nancy and I closed the rumble-seat cover and huddled together in the dark, and I pounded my feet together to try to keep them warm. The movie reminded Ma of Pa, and she cried and said she loved it. But I hoped Pa would wait for warmer weather before he went to the movies again. I suffered cold feet, and not until I could stand on the hot-air register at home were they warm again.

Ma would invite Wayne and Ethyl, or Eddie and Nellie, or sometimes Rachel to come on Friday or Saturday nights. They played records on the three-dollar Victrola Ma had given me for my birthday and sang along to "You Are My Sunshine" or "Mairzey Doats" or "She's Too Fat" and drank Krueger ale. Or they listened to *The Gene Autry Show* or *Inner Sanctum* on the Emerson. Sometimes Ma and Fern went to Ethyl's place, or they all went to Hilma's and Lauri's for a Finnish steam bath and talked afterward by the light of a kerosene lamp around Hilma's kitchen table. We usually left early, so Nancy and I wouldn't get overly cold in the roadster. Ma wrote to Pa of these times and invited him to protest her innocent goings-on, but he kept silent.

One night Eddie and Nellie invited Ma and Fern to come to their place. They lived in the shadow of the dance hall and were said to host boisterous parties. Ma hesitated to go, but Fern persisted, "Of course, we're going. We ain't gonna miss a party at Eddie's, not now when I'm a single woman."

Ma had a peculiar way of saying no to a party. She would say she supposed she shouldn't go, and then she would, especially if she could go with friends. Eddie and Nellie were good friends of Ma's, and Eddie was our fix-it man in Pa's absence. He and Nellie, a free-spirited New Sharon woman he had charmed after he came to Temple, lived together in the village center. Ma went there with Fern on a Saturday night and took Nancy and Patty and me with her.

Fern carried two quarts of Krueger ale in a paper bag under her arm, and Ma held onto Patty's hand when they stepped up onto Eddie's porch in the dark and stomped the snow off their boots. At the sound, Nellie opened the door and chattered on about how good it was we could come.

"We wouldn't a missed it," Fern said and stepped inside. "Where can I dump this bag? Gawd, it's hotter than hell in here. Open a window or somethin'."

The inside was given over to the party. A dozen or so people seemed to shimmer there in a vague blue haze. They sipped from a glass or a mug, gnawed on Finnish hardtack bread, and shouted at each other over music that came out of a radio somewhere. Eddie put a log in a black-iron woodstove, and smoke rolled out and mixed with the crowd. Ma's gang was there: Wayne and Ethyl, John and Bernice, Weston and Marguerite, and Rachel. The rest I didn't know. I guessed Eddie had not invited Gus, and Elmer was absent too, leaving Fern free to search the crowd for male companionship. She pried the cap off a quart of Krueger and poured two glasses nearly to the rim. Ma settled Nancy, Patty, and me on a couch in a corner, brought us each a glass of ginger ale out of Eddie's refrigerator, and fished some comics and a book from the Hardy Boys mystery series out of her oversized purse.

"Here, Clarice," Fern said. "Here's a glass I fixed for you."

"Gosh, I can't drink all that."

"It's yours. Take it."

Ma took the glass and sipped, and she and Fern went to the kitchen. A pang of self-consciousness struck me. I felt conspicuous and wondered if we were showing disrespect for Pa. I opened the Hardy Boys book and stared at its pages.

Soon, amid loud stories and laughter, I overheard Eddie plunk the strings of his fiddle. I moved across the room and stood where I could see him. Red-faced and unshaven, his dark hair long off the sides of his head, he sat in a straight-backed chair, the fiddle tucked under his chin. He picked at a string and adjusted a peg. He wiped his leathery hands and fingered the crossbow. Folks went quiet as he slithered the bow across the strings, and as it moved faster, they began to rock to "Pop Goes the Weasel." Eddie stopped and wiped beads of moisture from his brow. Then he played the tune a second time, and the bow seesawed over the strings, and Fern sang and slammed her hand on her knee at the "Pop!" and grinned at Eddie. Eddie played "Turkey in the Straw," and Fern twirled so fast her pleated skirt flew up above her chubby knees. Nellie yodeled and danced alone in the center of the floor, then yodeled again.

Eddie stopped, and he and the others moved the chairs back against the walls, lifted the table to a corner, and rolled the rug aside, leaving the center of the room bare. "Find a partner," he said and tucked the fiddle under his chin again and played some old tunes I hadn't heard before.

Folks took partners and danced to the rhythm of Eddie's fiddle in that little space. Fern lured a short man to her arms and pushed him and pulled him around the floor. Ma and Rachel waltzed, and then Ma danced to a slow tune with a man I didn't know. I went back to the couch and the Hardy Boys. Eddie played a polka, and the floor shook like a shivering dog. He switched to "Lady of the Lake" and the chair backs rattled along the walls. Eddie played one tune after another, and the folks danced round and round on his kitchen floor.

Late into the night, when the beer glasses were empty and the fire had gone dark, Ma woke us and helped us·into our coats and mittens. Then Fern lifted Patty, and we went out into the night air and walked home.

"Eddie sure knows how to do them kitchen breakdowns, don't he?" said Fern.

Ma laughed, unaware then of the price of a little fun in Temple, and told Fern she might go again sometime.

Although Fern's men friends did not hang out at our place, Aunt Marion grew critical of Ma's socializing. She had heard of the goings-on in town and was convinced that Fern's disgraceful presence, as she called it, in our house pointed Ma toward sinful behavior. Henceforth, the family relationships were strained even further. Aunt Marion avoided mixing with Ma; in fact, she didn't talk to her except when she called and quizzed her about Pa's letters. Grandma didn't talk to Ma at all because Ma associated with Fern. Ma talked to Grandpa C.F. because he was gentle and helpful and supportive, but Grandpa C.F. didn't talk to Grandma or Aunt Marion unless forced to—they thought him naïve and accused him of being tipsy most of the time. Ma had stopped talking to Uncle Austin because he didn't listen. Aunt Marion didn't *talk* to anyone; she shouted because she tried to over-power everyone, except Ma, into liking her. I was just a kid, but I knew all this was silly. Pa's family, except for Grandpa C.F., acted like chil-dren.   Grandpa C.F. kept coming to see us on Sundays, but he didn't talk about what went on at his house. He showed concern for us. "How are things going? Are you getting along okay? Is there any-thing I can do for you?"

"Yeah, kid, there is," Fern answered. "You got your boots on? C'mon outside. I got a new camera."

"Me?"

"Yes, you. An' the kids an' Clarice, too. In front of the house by the bay window, where the star is hangin'."

We stood on the snow in our shoes. Grandpa C.F. wore rolled-down and a coat that covered his cardigan. He tipped his fedora back, clenched his pipe in his teeth, and put a hand on Ma's shoulder. She said later that she nearly burst with affection for the old man.

"Smile now," said Fern. "You too, sourpuss," she said to Grandpa C.F.

I pushed my army hat back, stuck my chest out to show off my Fort Bragg

Grandpa C.F. poses with Ma and us at our place in April 1944. Note the star hanging in the window.

sweatshirt, and smiled. My sisters, in pigtails and hair parted in the center, laughed, and Ma, mindful of the dark times she'd suffered, managed a grin. Grandpa C.F. struck his postmaster's pose, and Pa's star showed proudly in the window between him and Ma. She wrote Pa later that, in the midst of her being upset and hurt by his family, Grandpa C.F. placed his hand on her shoulder and brightened her moment. Unfortunately, the moment did not last. She had been upset, worried, stern, and short-tempered for a week or more—about what I didn't know—and she would remain so.

In the coldest of winter, it was not enough that the temperature had plummeted to twenty degrees below zero and that by March snow had piled to enormous depths and outback roads were still shackled by snowdrifts. Other matters troubled Ma. She was edgy and unusually silent and stern. Nancy, too, thought her bothered. Pa's letters stopped coming. For more than a week, she didn't hear from him. This hadn't happened before, and she became anxious and worried. Each day she went to the store twice and waited at the postal window for Grandpa C.F. to sort the mail, waited for letters from Pa. But there were none. I didn't know what had happened, and Ma didn't either until Pa eventually wrote and told her.

Aunt Marion and Grandma Luna had written letters to Pa and complained about Ma's behavior. They had told him that Ma went to parties, stayed out late, and left us alone and unfed. They had told him that Ma and Fern were seen carrying cases of liquor into the house and frequently entertained men there. They had told him that Nancy, Patty, and I roamed unsupervised around town at all hours and that we chummed with seedy characters around the dance hall on Sunday mornings. They had told him he should turn his children over to them to care for while he was away.

Ma was devastated. "Of course, men come to our house. They bring us wood, they thaw the water pipes, they milk the cows and bring us grain."

"They're bringin' wood today," Fern said. "Are we supposed to tell

'em not to bring it. We're out again, for chrissakes. An' it's cold here."
I could hear the logs clunk against each other as Wayne tossed them off
the back of Pa's truck, and I wondered if Aunt Marion was watching.

"Should I go tell them not to come back tomorrow?" Ma asked.
"Who's going to saw it up?"

"Not me," said Fern. "Leave 'em alone. They'll do it. You need 'em
to bring grain, too. You gonna let your cows starve?"

"We could probably get a bag of grain in the rumble seat," Ma offered.

"No ma'am. I ain't liftin' nothin' like a bag of grain. For chrissakes,
they ain't doin' no harm. Eddie killed your chickens and slaughtered a
pig. And he cut a tree hangin' over your house, stuff you asked Austin
to do and he ignored, which he's very good at, by the way. Where the
hell do they get off talkin' about the men who come here?"

Ma was so distraught she couldn't talk.

Fern kept on. "An' bringin' in boxes of likker. That's rich. We can fix
that. Just tell the A & P to stop puttin' groceries in likker boxes so we
won't be seen luggin' 'em into the house. Damn! How long do we have
to put up with that woman spyin' on us?" Fern stopped and shook her
head. "An' I suppose that the friends you an' Elliott had when he was
home—Eddie and Nellie, and Wayne and Ethyl, and all them—they
can't be your friends no more. If she has her way, you won't have any
friends a-tall."

"I know it, Fern. I just wish Elliott would let me leave. Why in heck
won't he release me from this town? I'd be gone in a second."

I knew Fern was right. Aunt Marion watched us, and the more she
watched, the farther her chin jutted out. And Ma, trapped in Pa's resolve
that she stay in Temple, either stayed in the house or paid the
price for being visible. I imagined a clash ahead, and I fretted about it.

Ma withdrew deeper into herself. Her face filled with worry; her
eyes stayed red; her thoughts constantly wandered. She stopped visiting
her friends and spent her days inside. She stopped asking Wayne
and Eddie for help. She and Fern bought grain for the cows and

trucked it home in the rumble seat. To shop, she traveled to Farmington and back with Weston, the mail-stage driver, and they gossiped about Grandma Luna's righteousness. Fern talked in unfinished sentences or in doublespeak about things I didn't understand. Ma hugged us for no reason and said things that worried me. "Don't you worry, kids. Everything is going to be all right." Every time I heard her say that, I thought of Eddie's words to the chicken we had for Christmas dinner.

She wrote Pa and declared that his kids were well cared for and that she would kill herself if they were taken away. She told him that she was a nervous wreck, "… as shaky as I can be," and pleaded with him to keep writing, that she couldn't bear not to hear from him. And she stated again that she hoped to be away from Temple soon.

Thankfully, Pa kept writing letters of support, letters of caution, and letters of concern. He wrote that he trusted her, and not to leave Temple. Ma stayed in Temple, but not before she described the consequences to him. She wrote Pa that "I don't think you know what you're asking. . . . No one is allowed to come to the house, there isn't a neighbor I can call on, and I can't drive to get to town. You won't be home until six months after the war ends, and nobody knows how long that will be. . . . Where will that leave me? . . . I shall go plain crazy. It wouldn't be so bad if we lived near the stores and I could walk to them."

Ma argued that she couldn't stand it there without him and offered to be in Temple whenever he came home. She had actually thought he would permit us to leave. We stayed.

Meanwhile, Aunt Marion, anxious to rescue Pa's kids from wickedness, waited for a letter, but she did not hear from him. She waited longer, then she called Ma. "Have you heard from Elliott lately?"

"No, I haven't," Ma said. "He's missed a few days, but I expect to hear from him anytime." And then she added, "How have you been? If you have a few minutes, perhaps you'd like to come up and read his last letter." Aunt Marion declined.

Fern, when she heard that, came alive. "I can't believe you asked her up here. After the way she's dumped on you? Someone should kick your arse and teach you not to pussyfoot up to the likes of her."

"She's not coming, Fern. She questions what she's done," Ma said, "and won't show herself. I could tell. Maybe she'll be sorry someday. Anyway, I might be gone soon." Ma was still having delusions that we might actually leave. I wondered why we couldn't just stay in Temple and not squabble. I thought something good had to happen soon and hoped for Pa to come home. But despite my fantasies, the backbiting continued until Fern took charge for what turned out to be the last time and, so she believed, freed us from Aunt Marion's hurtful accusations.

But first, Aunt Marion, in her campaign to learn what Pa was doing about her letter, turned to me. She came to the school and asked to see me. In the hallway outside of the classroom, she asked in a low voice, "Johnny, has your mother heard from your father lately? Has she gotten a letter?"

I was surprised to hear the question. Aunt Marion was usually the first to know when a letter arrived from Pa. She had stood in the post office mornings and waited for Grandpa C.F. to sort the mail, then brought Pa's letters to our house. "Yes," I said. "We had a letter yesterday."

"What did he say? Did you read the letter? How is he?"

"I didn't read it, but he talked about being busy training and going to the movies."

"Oh? Is that all?"

"I don't know. That's all Mommy read to us."

"Okay. Well, I have to go. You haven't been to see me lately. Why not? When are you coming down?"

"I've been busy, but I'll come sometime." The truth was that Ma had been trying to get me to go, but I objected. Aunt Marion was too good to me; she was always giving me something, a toy, or money, or a book. But many times she had nothing for my sisters, and I was embarrassed by her doting on me, so I avoided her house when I could.

After her visit to the school, I suspected that Aunt Marion worried whether Pa would answer her letters or had simply tossed them away. By then, she may have doubted that she had acted properly. Perhaps she imagined he was upset or angry with her. In time, she wrote him again. "You have, no doubt, received Mother's and my letters . . . but we are hoping you appreciate the word coming from the family rather than from an outsider, if you hadn't heard already." He would now know she was being helpful, and he would be thankful and not angry, or so she thought. But it made little difference to Ma what Aunt Marion thought. Ma reckoned with a new calamity at home.

Fern, during her time with Ma, had been innocent of any diplomacy. She had spoken clearly and directly in graphic English. Sitting at the sewing machine one day in March, eating peanuts and stitching a pair of slacks for herself, she looked up at Ma and said, "Clarice, I'm gonna leave."

"You what?"

"I'm leaving. I need money. I'm gonna get a job in the shipyard like Lucille. That's what these pants are for."

"But what am I going to do without you?" Ma hadn't noticed that Fern had energized her to look after the place by herself—to stack wood, make clothes, turn the northern spy apples into pies, flour into doughnuts, and have a little fun—and she resisted Fern's desire to leave. But Fern had decided to go, and there was no changing her mind.

"Don't worry, Clarice. You've got your feet under you now. And your money has started to come. There's plenty you can do." And then she paused. "Besides, I don't think I'm going to the shipyard anyway. I ain't been feelin' too good lately, and Dr. Weymouth thinks I'm knocked up. I'll pro'bly just' go home to Phillips. Anyhow, I'll stop bein' a pain in the ass to Marion."

Fern stayed until the snow had melted and Pa was due home on furlough. She may have wanted a job in the shipyard, and she may have been pregnant. But, I thought later, the controversy with Aunt Marion was the difference. Fern's presence in our house, along with her failure to calm Aunt Marion, inflamed the controversy. She knew she wasn't helping Ma as much as she was hurting her. If she stayed, she believed she would attract more trouble.

Fern had been a godsend that winter. She had found firewood under the snow, bucked it up, and lugged it. She had shoveled the walkways, driven Ma shopping, and taken us to the movies at the State. She had cooked, stitched clothing, scrubbed floors, and driven off the drunken Bauer Small. And, of all things, she had cleaned out the privy by shoveling a cardboard box full three times and lugging the stuff to the manure pile behind the barn. When she finished, she washed her hands and said to Ma, "There. That's done. I was some damned sick and tired of that pile bumpin' me in the arse every time I sat down."

Fern had taken charge, and Ma had relaxed and felt secure. Most important, she had brought out Ma's spirit and erased her dreadful loneliness. But despite Fern's rescue—or perhaps because of it—Ma was immersed in an unfortunate falling-out with Pa's family that he would need to resolve himself. The conflict languished, but didn't die. Pa, as far as Ma knew, hadn't answered Aunt Marion's incriminating letters, but she, alone again, continued to moan over Pa's refusal to let her leave Temple and longed for him to come home.

About the time Fern left, Pa wrote me a postcard that he had shined his shoes, polished his belt buckle, pressed his pants, and was ready to parade in front of a general. Basic training was over. "Mommy," I said. "He's coming home! Will I see him in his uniform?"

Chapter Eight

A TURNING POINT AT HOME

For it's hi! hi! hee!
In the field artillery,
Shout out your numbers loud and strong. . . .
—Major Edward L. Gruber,
The Caissons Go Rolling Along

At the end of his basic training, Pa sidestepped Aunt Marion and wired Aunt Christine, his Farmington sister, for money to come home. He likely sought to avoid coming under Aunt Marion's overt persuasion in her attempt to liberate his children from the clutches of Fern and Ma. Or perhaps it was Christine's turn to send him money, or he thought her husband, Roy, would cough up some cash from Pa's truck account. In any event, he couldn't ask Ma. She had sent him cash out of her first government check, but it had disappeared in a barracks poker game when he boldly attempted to parlay it into a train ticket home.

Pa arrived home for a two-week leave on April 24, 1944, Nancy's eighth birthday. The Blue Line bus from Lewiston brought him to Farmington, and Christine drove him to Temple. I heard her Buick pull up in front of the barn and the engine shut down. A car door slammed shut, and Pa came into the kitchen, upright and stiff in army dress khakis and carrying a duffel bag. His face was lean and weather toughened. His hair had been clipped close, like a stubble. Nancy hid behind the kitchen stove. She, who in December had tearfully begged him to write her, didn't know him. He looked different, she said, like a stranger, so long away from home she had forgotten. Ma knew who he was, for sure, and threw her arms around him and kissed him and kissed him. I stared at him, imposing in his uniform, erect and fit and smiling. He hugged Patty, and he hugged me, and Nancy came out from behind the stove. He talked about the train, the late bus, and that he hadn't slept.

This is the first time I have seen him in uniform. He wears a dress khaki coat, buttoned tight against his chest, a necktie tucked neatly between the third and fourth buttons of a tan shirt, creased khaki trousers that barely reach highly burnished shoes. He is adorned with an array of gold buttons and insignia that, it seems, blink like so many stars in the night. He stands straight, like soldiers I've seen in movies or in *Life* magazine, and commands the kitchen.

"Why do you have to tuck the necktie into your shirt?" I ask.

"The army doesn't like things to hang loose," he says. "It's unsafe and messy. 'Secure it,' they say. 'Go by the book.'" He walks into the front room. "The place looks just like I left it," he says.

"We've lived in the kitchen." Ma answers.

He tosses his duffel and his coat and tie onto the bed, changes into slippers, and returns to the kitchen. "You've lived here, in one room?"

"Except when we slept," she says. "We had to—or freeze to death."

He eyes me and grins. "How about it? You filled the woodbox today?"

"Not yet," I say.

He looks out the window and down the road, and then back at us. Ma stands at the stove; Nancy, in back, peeks around Ma's dress. Patty dangles her legs over the edge of a chair, and I perch on the sideboard. Water drips into the pail at the sink. I wait for someone to speak as though, one by one, we will introduce ourselves. Pa paces over the black-and-white linoleum and doesn't notice Ma has painted it. He puts the flame of his Zippo to a cigarette, draws the smoke deep inside, and exhales. Across the room, Ma watches him. He stares into her eyes. It's coming. I know it is.

He hesitates, then speaks. "Marion said she found the kids hungry and dirty, late in the evening, you not home. She took them home and fed them. Where were you?"

Ma is nervous. But at the same time, she is infused with a consciousness of this moment. She has waited for this chance. "Look," she says. "Do they look mistreated to you? Look at them. Clean. Healthy. Well fed. Do they look like abandoned and abused children? I have done nothing wrong. Believe me."

"What did happen then? Tell me." He is solemn and composed.

"It was Fern. After her divorce, she played the party scene to the hilt. I went to Eddie's and Nellie's once with her, but I could see it wasn't for me. But she kept it up, with her boyfriend, Gus, and Eddie."

"Did you run around with her? That's what Marion says."

"It's always Marion, isn't it? Yes, Fern and I went out, and the children, too. We went to the movies. We took a steam bath once in a while. We went to see Wayne and Ethyl. And one Friday night, like I said, we went to Eddie's and Nellie's. But, believe me, I did nothing wrong. Fern's gone now, so it's over. I just stay here in my cave."

Pa persists. "But I still have to deal with Marion. I told her to wait 'til I was home. Why did you bring Fern here, for chrissakes?"

"Why did I bring her here? You certainly must know." Ma rolls on like a flood. "I told you I didn't want to stay here alone. I was hellishly lonesome, even scared. I needed someone around. Good thing Fern was here. She wasn't here two days before your drunken friend Bauer pounds on my door in the middle of the night, put up to it by his playboy buddy, Austin. Fern had the guts to get out of bed and yell through the window for him to get his . . . his *rear end* out of here and never come back."

Pa tosses his cigarette butt in the stove and smiles. "I'd like to have heard that."

"Your damned ungrateful and self-righteous family treated me like cold coffee. They would have nothing to do with me. They ignored me, except when you wrote me a letter, then Marion would run right over here with it and want to read it first." Ma stops, wipes her eyes, blows her nose, and looks up again. "Besides, you forget that you left us in a blizzard with no wood and no money and no way to get anywhere. What were you thinking of? I needed help. You spend four months in the South having your meals served to you on a tray and gambling away your pay and all the money I could send you, then asking for more. And whiskey, too."

Pa shakes his head, as if he shouldn't have brought it up. "Clarice," he says, "I've had it rough, too. I've been damned miserable, worked my ass off every day, sick a lot of the time. You got no idea what I've been through. And now this."

"But I needed Fern. She was the biggest help I could ever have. She split wood, drove the car, did housework, kept me company, and cheered me. She stayed with the kids when Father had his heart attack and I had to go to Mother's. I don't know what I would've done without her. She looked after me. I was so lonesome and desperate here that I would have abandoned the place and gone to my folks, even if you didn't want me to. And she cleaned out our privy, too! Something else you didn't do."

Ma stops, as if waiting for him to say something, but he's quiet, and she starts again. "And now after all that and making it through the winter, I might lose my children. Elliott, I would go crazy. I would kill myself."

Pa takes out another cigarette and lights it, the smoke of the last one still in the air. "I wrote to Marion," he says. "Told her I wanted to talk to you first."

They are silent a moment. Then Ma turns away and gazes out the window toward the pasture. "I agree Fern attracted gossip. She had men friends. She went to parties, especially after the divorce. But God, Elliott, she was such a help. I'd have never made it through the winter. And believe me, I'd never do anything wrong. I just want you home here, and to love me."

"I trusted you, you know."

"Can't we just be happy the few days you're home. God knows when I'll see you again." The handkerchief comes out again. She's scared now, and so am I.

"I'll speak to Marion," he says.

That is all he says—"I'll speak to Marion."—but I can tell it's over.

The next day friends came to the house to greet him. Fern was first. He thanked her for helping Ma, and they drank a stubby together and laughed at the privy project. Aino came down the hill and stopped and told him her son Tarmo was in England. Wayne drove in and they talked about the truck. John Hardy came, and they talked about army life. Later Grandpa C.F. walked up from Aunt Marion's and greeted him. They—Pa in his uniform and Grandpa C.F. in his cardigan, jacket, and fedora, with a briarwood clenched in his teeth—went to the backyard and walked together.

They walked carefully. Spring had scarcely come to Temple. Snow had melted, and water puddled in the low places. The ground was wet, the garden untilled. Trees were barren of leaves and the pasture waited for new grass. Remnants of split firewood lay strewn about, and the

Pa and Grandpa C.F in the backyard during Pa's first furlough in April 1944.

pasture gate hung open. I followed them. Pa jammed his hands into his rear pockets and said to watch out for the mud. Side by side, they meandered, more intent on talking than on walking. Pa showed off his muscles to Grandpa C.F. and said the army knows how to get a man in shape. Smiling, he spoke of his training, the days and nights in the field, and firing the cannons. He described the North Carolina winter, warm compared to Temple, no snow and fair enough to train in the field. Grandpa C.F. asked about the food and if Pa liked army life. Pa said he tried to like it, but the training was demanding and tedious. He would train next in Louisiana, in an artillery battalion, he said, as a truck driver and would likely haul gasoline or ammunition to the big guns at the front.

They wandered to the stream bank and looked down at the swollen and silty rapids. Pa asked Grandpa C.F. if he had caught any fish yet. Too early, Grandpa C.F. said, maybe in two weeks. They walked among the abandoned autos. Grandpa C.F. asked Pa who will plow the garden. Pa didn't know. They walked along the lane in silence, and each likely mused on the other's presence. They had come together for only a few moments. Soon it would be over.

Pa's furlough passed quickly. He called on his family and talked quietly and alone with Aunt Marion. Mothers in Temple brought him news of their sons and wished him well. He avoided the poker game at the West Farmington Fire Company.

He spent his time quietly obliging. He moved the hog to its outdoor sty, repaired the backyard chicken coop, and rebuilt fencing in the cow pasture. He spent evenings at home where we played Go Fish and ate popcorn. He put on his uniform, and he and I walked side by side to the store. He stood beside the woodstove and recounted his experiences, the long marches, the artillery fire, and the bars in Fayetteville.

For several days, with bucksaw and ax, he cut maple, birch, and beech trees along a stone wall on the far side of the pasture. He worked alone and stacked the downed wood to season and dry in the summer sun. Perhaps he felt the guilt of our cold winter. Maybe the exercise kept him fit. Together we lopped grownup bushes and filled mud-ruts in the field road leading to his cuttings. "Wayne can come in with the truck when the road dries up and oad out the wood," he said. "You can come with him." Later, Eddie would saw and split it to fit the cookstove and stack it in the woodshed for me to toss into the woodbox for Ma.

Pa and his bucksaw take time out from cutting firewood behind our place in April 1944. Note the snow on the slope in the rear.

He and Ma enjoyed each other and spent time together, a steam bath, a ride to Farmington in the roadster, a visit to Aino's. The talk had ended any visible tension between them. But he seemed overly quiet, like his talk with Aunt Marion may not have gone well, or that he worried about joining a combat division and going to war, or that he missed his pals. He and Ma played records on my Victrola, drank beer together, and talked late into the nights.

In the second week, he took sick with a cold and left for Camp Polk with congestion and plugged sinuses. He left us alone again, but he left us with hope, with the coming of summer, with wood for the fall, and with the image of his service star hanging in the front window. Two days later, he arrived in Leesburg, Louisiana, and took a bus to Camp Polk. He didn't know it then, but after a summer in Louisiana, the rigors of the European war would seem refreshing.

Chapter Nine
VICTORY GARDENS

*When butter became scarce, they added yellow dye to mar-
garine to make it look like butter. When sugar was cut back,
they added corn syrup and saccharin in cakes and cookies. They
planted Victory Gardens in their backyards. . . .*
—Doris Kearns Goodwin, *No Ordinary Time*

After Pa left for Louisiana, Ma was alone again, yet at the same time, she wasn't. Fern dwelled inside her, and Ma drew on stored inspiration to kindle her energy. She attended to life with confidence: she smiled more, cared more, worried less, and seemed content in the new and quiet bustle of her solitude. She was more in control of herself and less persuaded by doubt. Pa, I was sure, had calmed her and confirmed her faith in herself. She had thoughtfully vented her fears and her feelings to him, and he had understood and appreciated her. She no longer fought against his absence and accepted the reality of seeing it through. Yes, she was alone again but not suffering from it.

Aunt Marion, too, after Pa's quiet talk with her, seemed to change her attitude toward Ma. She telephoned the day after Pa left. Ma stood at the phone, held the receiver to her ear, and tipped her face up to the speaker. "Yes, I'd like to go," she said, "and thank you." Smiling, Ma hung the receiver back on its hook and said, "I think your father has had a talk with your Aunt Marion. She invited me to ride to town with her."

After the abuse Ma had endured over the past months, I was surprised that she could smile in Aunt Marion's presence. It looked as though she had, in a moment's time, upgraded her emotions and accepted Aunt Marion's outreach as sincere. Anger and gloom had been replaced by forgiveness. Ma seemed content when she greeted Aunt Marion in the driveway, and she came home in the same good spirits. Maybe, I thought, Ma will be satisfied with Temple and not want to go to Kennebunk.

Aunt Marion invited Ma to a party at her house for a Temple sailor on leave. Ma had seldom been asked to visit Aunt Marion's and had never gone there on her own. For her to visit uninvited would be to hear Aunt Marion say, "Why, hello, I didn't expect you. I'm very busy, but come in for a minute before I have to go." And then Ma would be stuck with Grandma, who would lecture her on strict and righteous living as if Ma hadn't already learned the puritan life from her own parents and retreated a hundred miles to get away from it. But she smiled again and welcomed the invitation.

The party was followed by another invitation to shop in Farmington and then a summons to Uncle Austin's camp at Varnum Pond to cook hamburgers outdoors and catch sunfish off the dock.

Nancy was puzzled, "What do you think this is all about? Why is Auntie May so friendly all at once?"

"I think Daddy told her to be nice to us."

"You mean she doesn't want anything from us?" Nancy, like me and Patty and Ma, was accustomed to Aunt Marion demanding something in return for her friendship.

"She probably doesn't want Fern to come back. She didn't like Fern," I explained.

"I don't think she likes Mommy either," Nancy said. "Is she trying to help Daddy or what?"

"I think he asked her to be kind to us, to be friendly, so he won't have to worry about Mommy so much."

Aunt Marion persisted in her friendship toward Ma. She walked to our place from the store, sat at the kitchen table, and talked to Ma over a cup of tea. She and Ma shared Pa's letters and gossiped about Uncle Austin joining the navy. She seemed sincere to Ma, and one day she said, "Why don't you come with me for a steam bath at Aino's on Saturday?"

A Finnish steam bath was a luxury that came with living in Temple, and chances had been scarce for Ma since Pa left. "I'd love to," she said.

But on Saturday, Aunt Marion called and apologized that she had to stay at home. "Why don't you go with Viola," she said, "and I'll watch the kiddies."

"Yes, of course I will," Ma said, "and thank you for the offer," and she went to the bathhouse with Pa's sister-in-law Aunt Viola, a pleasant woman who worked at the general store and never said a crabby word to anyone.

For some Temple folks, a Saturday night visit to a Finnish home for the weekly wash down was the social event of the week. Families and friends gathered there, and groups bathed in turn. Some people brought beer, and others even made reservations. Most lingered over conversation in the kitchen afterward.

Constructed by the Finns when they immigrated to Temple, steam bathhouses consisted of two rooms: an anteroom that served as a changing area and a bathroom with a barrel of superheated rocks perched over a wood fire surrounded by tiered benches. Bathers splashed water into the barrel of rocks and sat naked in the steam, and a week's accumulation of dirt sweated out of their pores. They sponged off the grime, splashed more water into the rocks, and endured the topmost bench their skin could tolerate. Lusty he-man bathers cooled down with a frolic in the snow outside the cabin door; the more genteel splashed cool water on themselves and retreated to the anteroom to dry off. Some snow bathers fortified themselves first with a stubby of beer or by being whipped on the backside with birch branches. In later years, I came to believe that the objective was not to rid the body of dirt in the pores but of sin in the soul. Cleanliness, for some, was a by-product of godliness.

Before Pa left for the army, we had enjoyed Finnish steam baths as a family. The bathhouse of choice for us, among the several in town, was Hilma and Lauri's. In the woods behind their house, they had built a small, low-roofed log bathhouse that looked like an old-fashioned ski chalet. We tramped there through snow, shivered in the barren anteroom, and hung our clothes on spikes driven into wooden timbers. In the privacy of these woods, we bathed in the dim glow of a kerosene lantern, the five of us naked as peeled popple, smothered by oppressive heat that seared our lungs and—for Nancy, Patty, and me—turned our tender skin carmine.

In the hot room, we each regulated our own degree of discomfort. Pa, naturally, sat on the top tier of the three-level bench. He hacked away at his cigarette cough, splashed water onto the scorching rocks, and sweated out a week's worth of grime and sin. Ma chose a midlevel perch and held a pan of lukewarm water to splash on herself and soothe her overheated skin. Nancy, Patty, and I sprawled in the dampness of cool water I had splattered onto the hot floor and searched for a breath of lukewarm air. Ma handed me soap and a washcloth, then held out a pan of cool water that I dashed over my head to rinse off the sludge. Pa, after he had suppressed his cough and cast off his grunge, went outside and fluttered in the snowpack. I followed to the anteroom and rejoiced in the cool air. I toweled myself to a sticky dampness and groped for my clothes in the dark. Nancy vowed never to get dirty again. Years later, Patty would refer to these nights as good, clean family fun.

Although it seemed unnatural to me for men and women to bathe together, I needed an occasional bath someplace. In summer I could swim in the stream. But the winter alternative to a steam bath was two inches of lukewarm water in a galvanized wash tub in a cold kitchen. I preferred my character-building in the overheated shed of a steam bath, whether with mixed sexes or not.

Thus, in the spring of 1944, Aunt Marion used the Finnish steam bath to express friendship to Ma. And when Aunt Marion couldn't go with her, she provided Aunt Viola as a substitute, while Patty, Nancy, and I played Go Fish with Aunt Marion. Ma looked to me then like a full-fledged member of Pa's family, as though they had finally discovered her and wanted to include her in their doings.

Meanwhile, the earth warmed, and Raymond Knowles and his two-horse team and plow cantered about the village into side yards and backyards and front yards and turned over garden plots everywhere in town. President Roosevelt, in a call to Americans, had urged the planting of sustenance gardens, Victory Gardens he called them, to offset labor shortages on the nation's farms. "Work the soil and raise food," he had said.

Soon, the smell of newly turned soil and manure seeped through the village. Folks cultivated their garden plots, then smoothed them and formed seed rows in the fresh earth. But Ma, wearied by the winter behind her, was not facing up to what seemed to her a formidable undertaking.

"Mother, are we going to have a garden?" I asked her.

She thought a moment. "I don't know if I can handle one," she said.

"But we'll help. The president says we should plant a Victory Garden."

"I don't know," she said. "I would have to spade it up myself, and . . ."

Ours was more than just a kitchen garden to be nibbled at. Two garden plots adorned our backyard: one outside the kitchen window on the high ground by the lane, bordered on the back by two McIntosh apple trees; the other, the lower garden, next to the stream bank behind the barn. A manure pile stood outside the cow-stall window and supplied both gardens—perhaps a tenth of an acre in all—with state-of-the-art dressing.

In past years, Ma and Pa had grown vegetables in quantities to last all year and preserved and stored them in the cellar. They put away peas and pickles and Swiss chard and spinach; string beans and shell beans and beet greens and beets; turnips and potatoes and carrots and corn; and pumpkins and squash. They put up enough greens and reds and yellows for our winter, enough to last into the following spring when the gardens would take life again.

But time to plant has come, and the gardens need plowing and mixing. Ma is not inclined to take on the burden without Pa. So she does nothing and waits, for what I don't know. Then Mrs. Mosher, our neighbor across the road, notices the fallow backyard and calls Ma on the hand-cranked telephone. Do you need the gardens plowed, she asks, and says someone will be over with the tractor, and there will be no charge. Ma is surprised and pleased. She says thank you and to tell Mr. Mosher to help himself to our manure pile. After the plow leaves, Ma beams at the freshly turned earth, and we start work on our gardens.

We call our plots Victory Gardens to make President Roosevelt happy. Ma concedes Patty, Nancy, and I each a bit of space on the end of the upper garden, and we hoe furrows and toss the winter's buildup of rocks into a pile at the edge. Ma is not a creative gardener, but she shows us how to plant as she has seen Pa do it.

"Here," she says, "sprinkle some fertilizer into the rows and mix it with the soil, then cast a few seeds and carefully cover them with a little dirt. Use the hoe to drag more dirt over the tops and tamp it down firmly."

Following her example, I plant the furrows with radishes, lettuce, and beet greens and stick the empty packages over a stake at the furrow's end to tell me what is growing in each row. Finally, I sprinkle water over the rows so the seeds will sprout. But that's not enough; it hasn't rained since the snow left, so I shower my furrows every day, and soon the radishes are up.

For the remainder of the upper garden, Ma works alone, crouched beside each open row, her hands stained and her dress soiled by the garden dirt. She casts peas and places bean seeds and sprinkles beet, carrot, spinach, and Swiss chard seeds into the open rows, covers them lightly, then tamps soil over the tops. She dribbles water over the seeds and puts empty packages on stakes at the ends of the rows as if she can't tell spinach from Swiss chard. "I am not the gardening connoisseur your Aunt Marion is," she says.

Aunt Marion tends one of the finest gardens in town and produces profuse quantities of plump, sweet-tasting vegetables. Her success comes from treating her vegetables like she teaches school. In the classroom, she instructs her students and expects them to learn. If they don't attend to her teaching or don't catch on to the subject matter, she simply applies more of the same—more reading, spelling, flash cards, and recitation—until they learn. There can be no failure in her classroom, and she expects the same in her garden. Plants that lag are gardened, but not coddled, until they grow. She doesn't talk *to* her garden; she talks *about* it. "Of course it's going to grow," she says. "It's not likely I won't have peas by the Fourth."

Soon Aunt Marion wants to see our garden. Ma is nervous, but Aunt Marion admires our work and says what a fine job we've done and helps plant the lower garden. She shows Ma how to side dress the rows with composted cow manure from our pile and says to keep both gardens watered until it rains again. And she comes back the next day—to see how it looks, she says.

Grandpa C.F., who tends a garden of his own, tells Ma the plants need more water and shows her how to work the soil with the big-wheel cultivator. "There," he says, "that looks good, don't it?" You woulda had all weeds growing here pretty soon."

"Marion said you were growing watermelons this year. That so?" Ma asks.

He leans the big-wheel against the shed and says, "That word's getting around, is it? Yeah, that's so. I planted some watermelon seeds in an old sawdust pile by the woodshed. Gotta do something to stay ahead of the crowd."

But when Grandpa C.F. returns to his watermelons and cucumbers, and Aunt Marion to instructing her peas to grow faster, Ma is left with two gardens to care for. She works alone, except when Nancy or I pretend to pull a few weeds. She often wears a dress in the garden. She says she wants to look nice if company comes, but she drips sweat, pops blisters, wrecks her hair, and is soon stained with dirt and mud. When someone comes to visit, she is embarrassed and has to change into clean clothes. She complains that she can't lift her arms to clear the supper table or wipe the dishes. And her garden lags.

Gardeners in Temple competed with each other. Each wanted to be first: the first to plant, the first to harvest, the first to grow the newest variety. At the general store, folks were careful what they said about their gardens. They checked out the competition before they described the situation in their backyards. A gardener already knew about his own garden. He needed to pick up tips from his neighbors and find out where he stood. Even Old Carr next door, silent on his own garden, sometimes probed Ma for progress, "Yer corn spindled, I see." Grandpa C.F. grew the only watermelons in town that year and only then announced to no one in particular, "I 'spect I'm the first."

The last week in June, Aunt Marion brought Ma peas from her garden, "The earliest I've ever had," she said. "They're the first in town."

"Congratulations!" Ma said. "I saw it in the paper." Ma didn't say a word about her own peas, which had barely bloomed. But in spite of Ma's inexperience and her self-acclaimed inferiority, her gardens provided generously.

Aunt Marion kept calling on Ma. She brought fresh vegetables and letters from Pa, and she offered to take Ma shopping or on errands. One day she telephoned, "Christine and I are going to Waterville tomorrow. Is there anything you need?"

Ma thought a moment. "Well, the roadster has a broken spring—the main leaf—and Eddie says there isn't one in the junkyard. Could you go into Montgomery Wards and see if they have one? Thank you, Marion. I appreciate it." She hangs up and looks at me.

"She asked me if she could help. I figured I might as well try."

Aunt Marion arrived the next day with a new main leaf for the roadster in her trunk, new summer shorts for me, and new flowered sunsuits for Nancy and Patty. I think Ma believed then that Aunt Marion was for real, that she actually wanted to help and didn't have a secret reason for being friendly. It occurred to me, too, that Aunt Marion took pleasure in being helpful but would sooner or later expect Ma to settle up. I hoped she would be up to it. Meanwhile, I put the thought out of my mind, stopped anticipating another clash, and looked forward to the rest of the summer.

When school closed, I did not receive a report card. Ma, who had taught at the Village School for Mrs. Stolt the last month of the school year, carried it home herself, unseen by me. Nancy's too. Fourth grade had been hard, and I worried that I hadn't been promoted. I knew Nancy had likely passed, but Ma didn't say anything about me, so I eventually asked, "Ma, will I be in fifth grade in the fall?" She smiled and nodded, and I smiled, too, relieved that I would not suffer the embarrassment of having my fourth-grade classmates sit in a higher row or of having my younger sister catch up with me.

Ma dressed us up properly to go to graduation at the dance hall. We each stood on the podium and, in front of a crowd of parents and friends, blurted out memorized pieces. Robert Suomi, the only graduate, received a diploma, and we listened carefully to his calm valedictory piece, "Sail On, Sail On." Aunt Marion compared our performances with her own classes at the Red Schoolhouse in West Farmington and praised Nancy and me for the fine job we did.

Later I wrote Pa about my summer doings. I told him that I had been swimming in the stream, in the deepest pool on the intervale, where the current curled tight against a steep bank before meandering to the millpond behind our place. Nancy, whose swimming ability was ahead of mine, had showed me the dog-paddle stroke, and on hot summer afternoons we paddled across the pool to where the low flow had exposed a sandy beach, then stroked back again. I had eaten radishes from my Victory Garden, I reported, and caught three sunfish at the pond, and that Uncle Austin had plopped them into a pail of pond water for me to take home. I had picked blueberries, I wrote, and Ma had made blueberry pies and showed me how to make a blueberry turnover. I wrote that I was sure glad to hear from him, and I thanked him for the T-shirt he had sent from Camp Polk, and I said that, yes, the woodbox was full. I announced that I had a job, which actually turned out to be more than one.

That summer, for the first time, I worked for money. I had worked plenty in the past, but Ma and Pa hadn't paid cash for a full woodbox, a well-fed calf, a stacked woodpile, a weed-free garden, or a clipped lawn. By 1944, I was old enough and strong enough to be of service to folks in town. The money I earned was mine to spend at the general store for penny candy and ice cream, at the State for a Saturday matinee, or at Newberry's Five and Dime in Farmington for a toy. Ma no longer needed to finance my indulgences. She could send the extra cash to Pa.

First, I sold *Grit*, a weekly newspaper of good news, remarkable people, and curious places. The papers were delivered to the general store by the mail stage, and one afternoon each week I filled my paperboy's bag with folded newspapers, slung it over my shoulder like a real paperboy in a real city, and delivered *Grit* to folks in the village. I crossed lawns, short-cut through backyards, sidestepped cow dung, and kicked stones in the dusty Temple roads. I left *Grit* on porches, between doors, and inside sheds. I handed them to folks who paid me on the spot, and I returned later to collect from those who were not at home. I charged seven cents per paper and could keep three of it, plus tips. Each week I deposited forty-five cents into a large brown envelope that I kept in my bedroom.

I mowed two lawns for pay. Mrs. Mosher had looked at the mowing job on my side of the road, thought it good enough for her, and asked me if I would clip her lawn. Thanks to Pa, I knew what a bad job looked like and applied his lessons to her grass. Each week, I mowed, trimmed, clipped, and removed until I thought Pa would be satisfied. Mrs. Mosher gladly paid the price we had agreed on, money that also went into the envelope.

Aunt Marion paid me a generous amount to clip her grass, a lawn half the size of Mrs. Mosher's. And she graciously complimented me and tipped me with homemade oatmeal cookies and lemonade, reminding me to come again the next week.

I labored in Great Uncle Shay's haying crew. In 1944, haying crews in Temple had been ransacked by the war and were made up mostly of older men, kids, and women. I worked with Aunt Marion, her cousin Bertie Hodgkins, my cousin Marilyn Stinchfield, and Eddie Fontaine. For two hot and sunny days, in the shadow of a wide-brimmed straw hat, I raked hay scatterings with a long-toothed bull rake and pitched them onto a wagon. I tread on the hayrack's top-heavy load and lugged water for the crew and for the oxen. I didn't know I was working for money until two days later, when Uncle Shay sent me a dollar and asked me to come again.

I didn't know the value of labor in those days. Fortunately, most folks didn't ask me how much for the job; they simply paid me something. I suppose it was too little in some cases and too much in others. But in every case, I was satisfied, even when Ma asked me to clean the barn. She said she'd pay me what I wanted if I would pick up the clutter, store the tools we'd left lying around, toss out the trash, and sweep the floor. I told her I'd do it for a dime, and she quickly agreed. "Is that all you want?" she asked.

"Yeah, that's enough." I didn't want her money at all—I knew she needed it worse than I did. And I knew the dime would get me into a Saturday matinee at the State. "Just find me a ride to the movies on Saturday," I said.

My career as a paperboy, which turned out to be over at the end of

Uncle Shay's 1944 makeshift haying crew. Left to right: John Hodgkins, Marilyn Stinchfield, Bertie Hodgkins, and Eddie Fontaine. Aunt Marion took the picture. (Temple Historical Society)

that summer, convinced me I did not want to be a businessman. Each week when I finished work, I couldn't see that I had accomplished anything except that I had added forty-five cents to the brown envelope. For me to buy a paper and sell it at a higher price without adding any usefulness or value to it seemed a worthless endeavor. I had only walked around town, which I did most of the time anyway. On the other hand, when I clipped grass, raked hay, watered oxen, or cleaned the barn, I saw a constructive result and took considerable satisfaction in that. If I completed the job fast and in good order or did more than was asked, my employers were happier and hired me again and sometimes, if they could, paid me more. I was happier, and my brown envelope swelled.

Work in those days differed from before the war. The young and the strong—one-tenth of our town—had gone soldiering. Women worked in factories and tended stores, women and children worked in the fields, and old men worked in the woods. Families helped each other hay, cut and stack firewood, tend and butcher animals. My friends, and Nancy's too, worked in the summer. At home and for our neighbors, we painted sheds, lugged and stacked firewood, and levered dump rakes in haying crews. There was little play, but when we could, we spent our hot afternoons at the swimming hole in the loop of the stream. Every day, women and kids and older men met the challenge of filling in for absent soldiers.

Ma did the same. Although she had relied on Eddie and Wayne and Lester to help with Pa's work, amid the recent controversy over goings-on at our place, she resisted calling them, afraid they would set off another fracas and more gossip. For the first time, she thought that if she worked harder herself and relied on Pa's family to encourage and back her, she could manage the place alone. The challenge would prove too great.

Chapter Ten
CAMP POLK

Eighth Armored Division training for overseas combat received a thoroughgoing inspection last week by officers of XXI Corps. . . . Inspection officers saw units in quick march, on the machine gun range, and in the classroom.
—*Armoreader,* Camp Polk 1944

O n May 1944, the Allied invasion force was poised on the English coast, set to strike across the English Channel in a massive attempt to establish a bridgehead on the European continent and push the Germans out of France and into their own country, where they could be surrounded and defeated. United States, British, and Canadian assault troops had rehearsed landings on England's beaches, airborne soldiers had jumped again and again into England's farmland, and armor and artillery battalions had trained in tactics on England's hillsides. But success of the assault was not assured. The Germans, under Field Marshall Erwin Rommel, had constructed a coastal barricade of formidable defenses and positioned their armies along two hundred miles of the French coast from Pas de Calais to Brittany in anticipation of the eventual invasion. By May, General Eisenhower, Supreme Commander of the Allied forces, knew when and where the invasion would strike and played a psychic chess game with Rommel in an attempt to confuse him. Rommel, across the Channel, read flawed and deceptive intelligence reports from his staff, watched the sea, and waited for the strike.

Also in May 1944, the U.S. 8th Armored Division moved into barracks at Camp Polk, Louisiana, and waited for replacements to fill out the division's ranks. Formed at Fort Knox, Kentucky in 1942 to train armored-division cadre, the 8th had transferred to Camp Polk in 1943 to prepare for combat. The division comprised three tank battalions, three infantry battalions, three artillery battalions, and ordnance, engineering, maintenance, and medical support units. For a year, it had prepared for deployment to the European war, the past five months bivouacked in tents at Camp Polk. In April, the maneuvers had ended, and the division's privates and privates first class had been transferred to replacement depots in the war zones.

Pa reported to the division at Polk's South Camp on May 7 and was assigned to Service Battery 405th Armored Field Artillery Battalion. A replacement private, a truck driver, he would train to haul ammunition to the three firing batteries of the 405th. That first night, he crawled into an upper bunk in the barracks and lay in the dark and the heat among strangers with whom he shared nothing of the past. They shared only the present—the barracks, the mess hall, the toilets, the training—eventually they would share the war. Pa felt neither sleepy nor awake. He thought of the war. He thought of home. He thought of himself. He wished he had a drink.

The next day, the division assembled at Camp Polk's amphitheater, the Bowl. Pa sat stiffly on a wooden bench and, as stifling Louisiana heat swelled up around him, listened to the Bowl's loudspeakers blare out the voice of his commanding officer, General William Grimes. In the next few months, Grimes said, the division would be turned into ". . . trained and disciplined soldiers . . . an effective combat unit . . . proud to be fit and ready for battle." Pa sniffled and coughed; sweat trickled down his back and soaked his shirt. He listened to Grimes carry on about evaluations and how hard work and discipline will keep them alive and only the best will make it and how they may be the ones to deliver the knockout blow to the Germans. After thirty minutes, Grimes announced that two hundred fifty girls would be imported from Leesville, Crowley, Mansfield, and Beaumont to a welcome dance for the division at the Field House Saturday night. He then dismissed the eleven thousand soldiers.

Pa pushed himself in the smothering heat of the Louisiana flatland to catch up with soldiers who had trained with the battery for a year. He learned and practiced small-unit tactics; received instructions in map reading and radio operations; ran through the infiltration course in daylight and again in darkness; fired the M-1 carbine and .30- and .50-caliber machine guns; tossed grenades; received instructions on controlling artillery fire and truck convoying; retrieved communications wire and laid it out again; and maintained his truck and his weapon. Twenty-five-mile marches kept him fit, and he played first base on the battery's softball team. But after a few weeks, when thermometers began to register in the nineties, Louisiana turned into what he termed "Lousyana."

On June 9, the division set out on field maneuvers. They started before daylight: a convoy of tanks, half-track personnel carriers, self-propelled 105-mm howitzers, loaded trucks, and officers riding in jeeps. They moved along Camp Polk's dusty roads into the rolling prairie of southwestern Louisiana. Pa's battalion bivouacked near a grove of loblolly pine, pitched pup tents, and dug latrines in the soft sand. They set up 105-mm howitzer firing stations, filled sandbags, and built breastworks. They erected camouflage netting over the guns and sprinkled it with loblolly branches. Pa, at the wheel of a two-and-a-half-ton six-by-six truck hauled ammunition from Camp Polk's ammunition dump to the firing batteries. Division headquarters furnished target coordinates, while soldiers at the firing stations simulated combat conditions, fired live ammunition at unseen targets, and were evaluated on their performance. At night, they ate hot meals from a field kitchen set up in the shady pine grove and crawled exhausted into tents and bivy sacks. On weekends, they hiked to South Camp.

They were in the field four disagreeable weeks. Pa, unaccustomed to the relentless heat, dehydrated. He wrote Ma and complained of sickness. Fine bayou sand blew under his eyelids, lodged in his combat boots, and stuck to his sweaty skin. Wild pigs invaded his pup tent and stole his food. Chiggers gnawed on him; blood-sucking larval mites that hopped on his body, slipped under his socks, nuzzled in his armpits and crotch, and left him with a ceaseless itch. He fought back: he drank water, taped his clothes shut, scratched his crotch, and singed the chiggers with lighted cigarettes. But suffering prevailed. Thermometers registered more than one hundred degrees. Soldiers fried eggs on the hood of a jeep. The Camp Polk ammunition dump exploded.

On a weekend break in the midst of maneuvers, Pa met Frank Pierce. Frank appeared beside him in South Camp's post exchange, or PX, as Pa paid for cigarettes and chewing gum. Frank spoke first. "Are you sure you have enough money for that chewing gum?" he asked. "I saw you playing poker last night."

Pa answered him. "Don't you play?"

"I played some in the back rooms of Philadelphia pool halls, but not much in the army. It was tough enough for me in Philly."

"Driving a truck and playing poker has been my life," Pa said. "Comes in one hand and goes out the other. I'm used to it."

Frank laughed. "The army must seem to you like you haven't left home."

"That's what my pals at home say, but they don't know about the chiggers. I lived all my life with blackflies and mosquitoes, but they're nothin' like these goddam chiggers. You have chiggers in Philly?" Pa asked.

"No. No chiggers in Philly. Whadda you do for 'em? They're buggin' the hell outta me, too."

"You and everybody else," Pa said, "I don't know what you do for 'em. I mostly scratch, but my ole lady says to put nail polish on 'em."

"Does it work?"

"I imagine it would, but I can't find any nail polish in this hellhole. You got any?"

Frank laughed again. "You're lucky you're married. Good advice like that is hard to come by. Maybe I should get married."

"Then you could be like me," Pa told him. "I just scratch and put up with the chiggers like everybody else. We'll be gone from here soon anyway."

"And the Germans will be shootin' at us, too," Frank answered.

Pa looked at Frank, scratched under his arm, and said, "I think even that'll be better than these goddam chiggers, believe you me."

Frank, two years older than my father, had joined the army a few months before Pa and was at Camp Polk when he arrived. Two of the oldest soldiers in the battery, they would remain friends throughout the war and longer.

After four weeks in the field, the division returned to South Camp barracks. Pa listened to veteran sergeants lecture on devious German soldiers, innocent-looking booby traps, seductive German women, and syphilis. He wrote Ma and complained of sore feet and nausea and chigger bites and the worsening heat. He was broke, he confessed, and hoped he would be promoted but it didn't look likely. The youngsters, as he called them, were getting the stripes. And among his grumbling, he wrote that he was preparing to go overseas, then asked Ma to send him money and whiskey.

Although Ma didn't know he might have preferred battling the Germans to the chiggers, she did her best to keep up his morale. She asked him to not think about going overseas. "Just learn how to stay alive," she told him. She urged him to soak his feet in soda and water and sent him nail polish for the chiggers. Against the wishes of Aunt Marion, who had discovered his gambling affliction in a letter to Ma, she sent him money and whiskey. I suppose she felt he had earned his transgressions.

In August, the division went back into the field. They practiced large-scale tactics, passing an armored division through an infantry division to exploit a bridgehead, and refined the use of their equipment. General Patton had shown in France that tank advance had become the most effective technique to penetrate an enemy's front. Pa's battalion practiced support of tank advance with mobile artillery and direct fire. At the end of August, the division returned to South Camp fit for deployment.

Pa cheered the end of his joyless summer. In the field, he had worked in miserable conditions. He wondered why they sent him to the hot, flat, steamy bayou to learn to fight in northern Europe. There had been no explanation. During periods in camp, he had seen an occasional movie and played softball for the battery, but he had shown no enthusiasm for either. He was in the field during South Camp's July Fourth competitions—machine-gun carry, grenade throw, litter-bearer race, and the wall scale—and was glad of it.

No orders came down from General Grimes. Rumors circulated they were getting a new commander, that Grimes was not going with them. They organized their gear and waited. Furloughs were issued, and Pa wrote that he was coming home, this time for three weeks. He longed to get away from Camp Polk.

Meanwhile, Brigadier General John Devine took command of the 8th Armored Division. Devine had landed at Utah Beach on D-Day as commander of the 90th Infantry Division's artillery and had battled across France, his long-range howitzers playing havoc with German tanks, armored vehicles, and soldiers. In consideration of his battlefield performance, General Eisenhower ordered Devine to Camp Polk to take charge of the 8th armored. A combat-tested general would lead the division into the European war.

Chapter Eleven
EDDIE

I get so blue sometimes.
—Ma, July 1944

n inspection of a map of Temple in 1944 would have revealed, as it would today, five ponds—Drury, Mud, Staples, Jesse, and Grants—within its boundaries, and one pond, Varnum, that Temple shared with Wilton and Farmington. Of the six, only Varnum Pond lured summer folks and vacationers. Although nearly the entire body of water sat in Wilton, the summer cottages scattered along the northerly shore were in Temple. Jacob Wirth, the famous Boston restaurateur, and Isabel Israelson, a not-so-famous New Yorker whose notoriety resulted from being nabbed skinny-dipping in the pond—Farmington's water supply—both owned cottages there.

Mark Mosher, of Cowturd Lane, Temple, owned two cottages where his family reclined on lounges on sunny afternoons and plied motorboats trailing salmon lures at twilight. Farmington's Dr. Pratt owned a cottage perched on a bluff overlooking a small cove. Albert Lowell, proprietor of West Farmington's general store and meat market, spent weekends at a cottage on the northerly shore, but the owners of the cottage at Pine Point, the most idyllic site on the pond, rarely revealed themselves at all.

Uncle Austin moved into his cottage on Varnum Pond as soon as summer heat pressed upon the village. He traveled back and forth to his store, except on Sundays when he would cast a salmon lure into the center of the pond, set his pole next to his boathouse, and sleep on the cottage porch. It was at Uncle Austin's that I first caught sunfish, experienced a motorboat ride, and ate a hamburger cooked over an outside fire.

It was here, during the good times when the Hodgkins family were disposed to being pleasant to each other, that we celebrated summer holidays. It was here that Aunt Marion invited Ma and my sisters and me to celebrate Independence Day, 1944. That day Uncle Austin flew the American flag, and Sam Johnson, one of his drinking pals, came and lit firecrackers—one-inchers, cherry bombs, and torpedoes—and launched tin cans into the air on the nose of Roman candles. Nancy, Patty, and I waved sparklers and toasted marshmallows and ate second servings of watermelon. Ma lounged on the porch, talked to Aunt Viola and Elspet Johnson, and welcomed the break in her lonely routine.

After Independence Day, Ma's summer settled into a sweatshop regimen. Each day, she toiled in the garden, weeding and cultivating and harvesting, her once-blistered hands toughened to the hoe handle and the cultivator. At dawn, she heated boiling-water baths and canned vegetables in Ball jars. She kept the house, washed and ironed clothes, scrubbed woodwork, and washed windows. She churned butter and bottled milk and sold the surplus. Ted Campbell continued to milk and care for the cows, but Ma avoided asking Lester, Wayne, or other men for help. When she needed firewood cut for canning, she bucked it herself. But the weight of two gardens, hungry livestock, a constant search for wood, and a never-ending need for house repairs kept her chronically fatigued. When the weight became too heavy, she called Eddie Fontaine.

Born in Quebec, Eddie had left there as a teenager and migrated to Maine by way of Vermont and New Hampshire. He worked as a carpenter, lumber-camp cook, and handyman. At forty-something, he was Temple's most common answer to the question, who am I gonna get to fix my whatever? In his five years in town, Eddie had repaired stone foundations, lined wells, cleaned and pointed brick chimneys, grafted apple trees, tended cows, slaughtered animals, and carved ax handles for the loggers. Rich in French heritage, he was an accomplished fiddler and country dancer. An uncommonly versatile man, he was quick to help anyone who treated him justly.

Unmarried, Eddie bartered a small apartment in Brackley Hall from Uncle Austin and lived there with his girlfriend Nellie. Thickset and strong from years of muscle-work, he tended Uncle Austin's barn animals, pitched hay in his fields, fixed everything at the general store, and occasionally pulled a crosscut saw in his logging crew.

Nellie, high-spirited and unpredictable and thought by some to be either a little wild or daft or both, adored Eddie. But she possessed a roving disposition, and occasionally, when she thought Eddie was spending too much time fixing the broken lives of women in town, she stomped off in a huff to her mother's in New Sharon. When life with her mother or her want for Eddie became intolerable, she would reappear, singing, yodeling, and dancing her way to the general store, and Eddie would take her in and comfort her. Eddie and Nellie were a team. They buoyed each other, cared for each other, danced with each other, needed each other, and were respectful and forgiving of each other.

One heat-filled day that July, as the dust lies flat and motionless on our road, and the buttercups droop in Mrs. Mosher's field, I stretch out in the shade of the front-lawn maple and search for a cool breath. The air is trapped in this valley and takes on the sun's heat like air in an oven. It lies on the skin and strengthens. Those who have not deepened their pain by fanning themselves with a folded newspaper in search of comfort have not known a Maine summer day. The cows in the pasture stand motionless. Horseflies seek shade. I turn my eyes toward the village, and sweat breaks out on my face.

The village is still. Occasionally I glimpse a person on a brief mission into the sultry afternoon. He, or she, walks quickly between two houses, dumps wash water out the back door, or steps outside and cuts a handful of beet greens. There is no sound. Like a silent movie, the character moves purposefully into view for only a moment, then exits from the picture, and the village is still again.

Then, in the center of the stillness, I see Nellie turn onto Cowturd Lane and stride toward me. As she moves closer, I see she wears gum-rubber boots, a wide-brimmed hat, and that she twirls a rope. I can hear her hollering and singing. I like Nellie. I had never thought she was daft or boneheaded, but I don't like what I see now. I call to Ma. "Mommy, where's Eddie today? Isn't he coming for the cows? Nellie's out here."

Ma doesn't answer, but obviously Eddie is not coming. Today Nellie is here after Uncle Austin's milk cows, and I watch her for fear that she, a stranger to the cows, will make a mess of it and perhaps stir up Uncle Austin's fierce and horny Durham bull that shares the pasture with the cows and wails all night, unsettling Mrs. Mosher.

Nellie turns into the lane, lets herself through the pasture gate, and moves toward the cows. "Here, boss," she says. Shy, they back away. She stumbles on prickly pasture thistle and mutters, "Damn," then, louder, "Here, boss. Here, boss-boss-boss." She grabs one by the collar, ties the rope to the metal ring, and goes for the other. She whistles and shouts, "Here, boss-boss-boss," and twice flusters the milk cow off. Then reasoning that she should approach quietly, she whispers "Nice bossy, nice bossy," and the cow calms. Nellie ties her onto the rope in the same manner as the first, breaks into song again, and leads them both toward the gate.

The Durham bull, a spectator until now, follows her. Nellie opens the gate, and I, uneasy, get onto my feet ready to run. But she lets herself through and into the lane and quickly closes the gate behind her. She sets off for the road, cows in hand. Relaxed now, she pushes the cowboy hat onto the back of her head and starts to yodel. The

Durham is barred at the gate and, frustrated, gallops back and forth in the animal path next to the fence. Ohmygawd, I think, the bull is aroused by Nellie's yodeling. He grunts and snorts along the fence, then turns and rears and snorts again. Nellie, Eddie's cowgirl, yodels and hollers and sings her way down Cowturd Lane until the bull can no longer bear it. In one bound, he clears the pasture fence and charges across our front lawn in the direction of Nellie and the cows. I knew it, I think to myself, and I dash for the barn. "Mommy! Mommy! Come quick!"

The bull pays no attention to Ma and me and thunders in a beeline for Nellie and the milk cows. Nellie shrieks and runs for Uncle Austin's barn. Her gum-rubber boots thump in the road, and her big breasts bounce up and down under her shirt. She yanks the Jerseys along behind her and yells, "Oh, my Lord!" But the wood fence between us and Old Carr's garden is in the Durham's line, and he tears through it, splintering rails and scattering palings, and comes to a halt in curmudgeon Carr's pea patch tangled in wire and down on his front knees. I nearly melt. Old Carr tolerates no disruption of his orderly life and is given to outbursts of temper whenever a harmless pebble launched from our front yard lands on his metal roof. He will be furious.

The Durham struggles to his feet, snorts and shakes his head, then drags the wire fence into Old Carr's strawberries. By this time, Carr is there yielding no ground to the bull, wielding his cane, roaring an assortment of profanity, and driving the Durham back across his garden through the hole in the fence. Ma, who has retrieved a hoe, helps him usher it into our barn. I drag the barn door shut, and Ma goes inside and calls Uncle Austin.

"You better get someone over here to take care of the Durham," she shouts into the phone. "It's in our barn. Carr is raving mad, and I've just about had a fit. I need my fence fixed, too. And you can tell Nellie to stay the heck away from your cows from now on."

I'm proud of Ma. She shows uncommon courage here, challenging that vicious bull and speaking up to Uncle Austin, too. And now she has to deal with Old Carr.

Next morning, Old Carr is out repairing his garden. Pa called him Old Carr and never got along with him very well. He was cantankerous, ornery, walked with a cane, and I suppose seemed older than Job to Pa. I never really knew him, but I took butter to him and Mrs. Carr once in a while. I was timid and careful when I was over there, but Old Carr didn't uphold his reputation in my presence. Maybe Mrs. Carr muffled him.

Ma goes over to see him. He looks at her, "How do you like chasin' cows around all day, Ma'am? Don't you think it's about time Austin and Eddie got their goddam cow business straightened around so we won't have to put up with this abuse anymore?"

Ma says softly, "Yes, Albert, I do."

He raises his voice, almost yells, "Waal, first thar's cowshit all over the road that nobody cleans up. Then thar's bellarin' all night by that damned lovesick Durham, and Marie has to call Austin at five o'clock in the mornin'. An' now lookit this." He stops and stares at his pea patch and strawberries, now a tangle of torn and uprooted plants and strewn fencing. "I'm goddam sick of it. I've loaded my .30-30, and I'm gonna use it the next time one of them four-legged bastards as much as looks my way." He's so mad he stops and looks up at the sky and lets the rage pass. "I told Austin that last night, too, and he goddam well better been listenin'."

"Well, I'm sorry, Albert."

"I know you are, Ma'am."

"I wish it hadn't happened. And I told Austin a thing or two myself."

I didn't think Uncle Austin was very helpful. He seemed to be agreeable and full of assurances but of little substance. He sent Nellie and Alex Goldsmith, an elderly part-time laborer and woodchopper, to put the Durham back in the pasture, and he came later to see that it was done and tell Ma that he would repair the fence—but he didn't fix it. Uncle Austin liked to call himself a farmer, but he wasn't one; I never knew him to milk a cow, clean a barn, or take heifers to pasture. To me, he played the role of supervisor of some farm work, and not a very able one at that. Ma, on her half acre, was as much a farmer as Uncle Austin.

Nellie was neither a farmer nor a supervisor. Her strength was being present. Big hearted, she would agree with whatever was happening but begged clear directions. I saw her as Eddie's partner, the life of his parties, but incapable of controlling circumstances by herself. I didn't blame Nellie for the ruckus, but when I saw her coming up the road with the rope I knew the peaceful scene along Cowturd Lane would be upset.

Eddie was of a different ilk. Ma, like most folks in town, turned to Eddie when she needed help. He was strong, stable, and dependable, a problem solver who showed up on time and knew what to do. I thought Eddie was genuine and truly sought to help Ma. He knew we needed him. He had experienced differences himself over money with Uncle Austin, knew firsthand the conflict with Pa's family, and stepped in to help Ma when she asked.

When Fern left and Ma faced taking care of the place herself, Eddie was her one departure from the self-imposed rule of "no men around the house." He fixed a broken window, cleaned the smoky stovepipe, and set out tomato plants and side-dressed them with manure. I helped him find the well hidden in the bushes beyond the pasture, and he pumped water through the plugged pipe to force out the rust. He brought whiskey for Ma to send to Pa, and Ma asked him to furnish the firewood supply for the coming winter. He agreed, and she paid him with the fattened pig and told him she would borrow Pa's truck for him to use and furnish a crew to help saw and stack the wood inside. Ma relied on Eddie considerably in those solitary days.

He harbored no animosity or grudge against anyone who treated him justly. Ma kept his friendship, used his help, repaid him when she could, and was not self-conscious about it, except that she was aware of the explosive nature of Pa's family and the potential for her to be black-listed again. So she was careful but not limiting, although Nellie, when she accompanied Eddie, made Ma nervous. Nellie interrupted the tranquility, and Ma worried when she hollered or danced or yodeled that Aunt Marion would be displeased again.

Eddie showed Ma how to drive the roadster, but she resisted driving alone. He and Nellie took us to *See Here, Private Hargrove* at the State, a movie they said showed what Pa had done at Fort Bragg. They took us swimming in Chesterville at a muddy beach on Crowell's Pond, where Ma said two-headed leeches that sucked blood with both heads lived in the muddy bottom. None of us spent more than eight seconds in the water: Patty spent her eight seconds shrieking at the thought that she shared the pond with slimy, two-headed bloodsuckers; I spent mine fearful that I would grow weak from loss of blood; Nancy, quiet and suave, grinned at our antics and stayed out of the pond.

In midsummer, Eddie suffered, as he had before, a setback in his re-lationship with Nellie. Unpredictable and impulsive, she suddenly looked at Eddie and said, "I'm goin'. I can't take it anymore, and I'm goin' to Mother's." And she was gone.

Eddie, outwardly as tough as a wagon-driver's ass and never one to fret or allow himself to be tormented, muttered okay and I'll be here when you want to come back. Ma was the fretful one. Although she fussed when Nellie sang and hollered and disturbed the neighbors, she didn't want her to run away. But Nellie flew, like a parakeet with no compass, to only God knew where, and Ma feared Eddie would go, too. But Eddie went on as though he didn't care—he knew Nellie would be back.

Ma fell into melancholy that summer. Her spirits foundered; the blues took over. She was overcome by the enormity of her chores. Pa's expectations weighed heavily on her frail faith, and she suffered despair. She looked into the backyard and saw no horizon. The gardens sported beet greens, Swiss chard, peas, spinach, string beans, and more, all to be canned over a hot stove in the hottest summer in one hundred years. She needed to buck the backyard alder and the slabwood strewn there for the early morning fire. And the winter woodpile, three cords of four-foot sticks, sat there, too, to be fitted and stacked inside.

She looked to the front and saw the hole in the fence that stared back at her like a menacing one-eyed Cyclops and the threatening elm tree that hung over the kitchen roof and needed to be cut and stacked in the cellar. She looked at Patty, Nancy, and me, and saw her helpless brood to care for and knew her care would be evaluated by Aunt Marion and Grandma Luna. She looked in the barn and saw it was full of animals to be tended. She looked at the calendar, saw another winter coming, and shivered. She looked in the mirror, and she stood there alone. She needed to talk to Pa, to speak some words that haunted her; she needed to unload her exhaustion. She reached for a pencil and a sheet of paper and, in words now faded by the years, cleansed herself of the bottled-up feelings she could no longer hold back.

The words went straight to the heart—her heart. It was classic Ma. She wanted him to love her, support her, believe in her, and open his heart to her. She needed his love worse than he knew, but she feared that speaking her suppressed feelings would risk what little affection he held for her. So first, Ma validated him: "Please don't feel as though you can't ask for money. I have kicked myself around because I even told you what they said. The money is yours, darling. You have always taken good care of me. . . . And please never again thank me for money I send to you. . . . It hurts too much. The money is yours. . . . Skip us, darling, and think of yourself."

Aunt Marion had criticized Pa for gambling away money when his family had little or none for themselves, and the criticism had touched his conscience. Ma calmed him and promised to send more. She was in Temple for him, she wrote, to care for all he had left behind, just as he had always cared for her. She overlooked that he had left her in Temple against her will, alone in winter with no wood, no money, and a troublesome flock of grating relatives. Instead, she endorsed his inexcusable behavior. For in her heart, Ma doubted that he loved her.

"I seem to have got started on the letter I have wanted to send for a long time," she wrote. "You know, when you were home you didn't act as though you wanted me. And I have thought that you never loved me as much as I did you, but that was something that you couldn't help, perhaps. . . ."

The time had come to tell him that she deserved more of his love. She accused him of indifference toward her, that he had not shared his feelings with her, and that, in fact, he didn't love her. But not to risk losing the little attention he did extend to her, she exonerated him. If he chose not to love her, she reasoned, he probably couldn't help it; she accepted him nonetheless. She chose to be the villain. The gentle and prim woman had revealed her deepest needs and feelings to him, but before he could absorb them and ponder on them, she had pardoned him—but not his family.

Aunt Marion and Grandma Luna, Ma wrote, had in the past imposed unnecessarily harsh judgments on her. Ma felt that she still walked on thin ice, and she suspected they were waiting for the ice to break. So she was careful, she went on, not to provoke his relatives into writing more hurtful and deceitful letters to him. But still they demanded to read the letters he wrote to her, and she implored him to write *one* letter to her alone, one that she could keep next to her heart.

"I have often thought I would like to receive one letter from you," Ma wrote, "that I could keep to myself, but the family has to see them all."

His letters to Ma, picked up in the post office and brought to her by Aunt Marion, had been so impersonal they could have been read aloud around the woodstove in the general store without embarrassing either him or her. But she begged for words of love, longing, and personal feelings.

In the end, Ma accepted the blame for her feelings. She lacked confidence and felt that whichever way she turned, someone would be disgruntled, and she would be the worse for it. She sought to do a good job for him in Temple, but the difficulties of carrying on alone were more than she could handle, and she admitted she had failed him at times. She told him, however, to never mind her troubles: "Dr. Lovejoy said yesterday it was a pity and crime that you went. He said you could have stayed home if you had wanted to. But it's done, darling, and I'm proud of you, if that means anything at all. Forgive the letter. I get so blue sometimes. I've held it in so long I couldn't help it."

Her long overdue outpouring of irritation, insecurity, and intimacy was, unfortunately, likely to fall on deaf ears. Pa was not given to sentimentalism and did not customarily speak or write of such personal matters as love, absence, yearning, and dreams. I suspect Ma convinced him, as she did herself, that her sagging emotions were her fault.

Meanwhile, Nellie, in self-imposed exile with her mother in New Sharon, comes back to town for a Finnish steam bath with her friends. I see her in the road singing a cowboy song on the way to the general store. Eddie, no dumbbell when it comes to women, ignores her, but she stops him on the road and begs him to let her come back to him. She misses him. Eddie tells her to wait. He has to think about it.

But Eddie doesn't need to think about it for long. He comes to see Ma and tells her Nellie has been gone so long the apartment is a hellish mess—dirty dishes, muddy floors, stuff scattered all over. He asks Ma if she'll wash the dishes and sweep the floors so Nellie can come home to a clean house. Ma agrees that she will and writes to Pa that Eddie does so much for her she can't refuse to help him. Pa doesn't say anything about it, but Ma knows it's the right thing to do. But I think she is taking a chance walking to Eddie's house, past Old Carr's and Bertha's and Uncle Austin's.

After three hours pass, she stomps back into the kitchen, her slender face contorted and fire-red. She looks at me with furious eyes, ex tends her arm straight out, and points a blanched-out finger down the road. "Dammit. I've done it again," she says. "Leave it to me. I'll hear about it, I'm sure."

"What happened, Mommy?"

"What happened? Nothing. And that's the trouble. I was done. I'd washed the last dish and was ready to leave. And then John and Bernice came to talk to Eddie."

I ask again. "So what happened?" Ma is taking too long to tell the story. I want to know the ending. "Tell me what happened."

"Just wait. I'll get to it." She swallows a sip of water. "I was all done. John and Bernice asked me to wait while they spoke to Eddie and then they'd walk home with me. So I waited. And then, wouldn't you know it, Austin came to talk to Eddie, too. And there I was sitting at the kitchen table, the house half full of people. Thank God I wasn't drinking a glass of beer." She stops and stares at the floor; her face softens slightly. "At least I told your father I was going down there to clean, because now he'll sure as . . . as *heck* know I was there, and there's no telling what they'll tell him." She shrugs, puts a half smile on her face, and looks out the window at the weeds in the garden. "Oh well, I always seem to be in the wrong place at the wrong time."

Later, she heard from Pa, who wrote that she needed to explain her actions to him. She recounted the story. She was there, she told him again, to clean Eddie's house before Nellie came back. Unfortunately, she was in the wrong place at the wrong time, as always, but she was innocent of wrongdoing.

The old anxieties flooded back over me. The hassle had erupted again. I became painfully aware that Aunt Marion's so-called friendship was low on trust and truth and high on suspicion and indictment. Ma could trust Aunt Marion to come around and insist on reading Pa's letters, then tattle to him when Ma went to a movie or helped a friend, but she couldn't trust her to know the truth or have any respect for Ma's life. Ma was still kept outside the family fence. It didn't matter what she did; she couldn't change Aunt Marion's mind-set.

Near the end of August, before the heat of summer faded, Eddie came to saw the wood he had trucked and dumped in the backyard. Preparing firewood, a crucial and continuous chore among Temple folks, required the patience of Job and careful attention to several sequential events. Firewood keeps its own calendar: there are seasons for cutting, for splitting and stacking, and for drying and seasoning. The calendar for wood to be ready to comfortably heat a Temple house is longer than a year; often the loggers cut the next year's supply in the same season the current year's wood is dried. But the wood Eddie had brought to us had been cut a year late and was green with sap and moisture. Nevertheless, we had no choice. For the coming winter, we would burn before drying and seasoning took place.

Eddie is a quarter mile away when I first hear his contraption, an assortment of barking engine noises and rattling parts, coming up the road. Nellie is perched beside him, smug in her open-air seat, looking every bit a missionary to someone in distress. Eddie parks his menacing-looking rig by the wood pile. "Nellie's the only crew I got t'day, ma'am," he says to Ma. "An' my sawin' rig needs three people."

Eddie has stripped the body and rear seat from an old Plymouth sedan and placed a second engine sideways on the frame just behind the front seat. A steel shaft joined to a large, circular, saw blade has been set up crossways on the rear of the frame and connected to the driveshaft of the sideways engine by a belt twisted once to drive the saw blade clockwise. A platform has been positioned on a slider beside the saw to form a carriage wide enough to steady a four-foot stick of wood. When the carriage and stick are pushed forward into the spinning saw blade, the stick is lopped into stove length pieces.

"I can help, and so will the kids," Ma says. "I'll put on some slacks and boots."

"Gloves too, ma'am," Eddie says.

Eddie is the master of his Rube Goldberg contraption. He sets the sideways engine's hand throttle on high, shifts into first gear, and eases the clutch to start the belt. The sputtering engine barks, then roars; the belt shrieks through the twist; and the saw howls and calls for a stick, a pit orchestra's prelude to the wood-sawer's ballet.

The crew—Eddie, Nellie, and Ma—works silently in the din of Eddie's contraption. Eddie points at Nellie and motions to the three cords of wood stacked behind her. She slides a log off the pile and places it on the carriage, then Eddie nods to Ma and pushes the carriage. The saw whines a moment, and Ma catches the cut piece and tosses it behind her to start a pile. Eddie spots the log, pushes, and the saw whines again. Ma catches the second piece, and Nellie works another log off the pile. This pantomime—lift and place, push and cut, take and toss—goes on for an hour, graceful and precise, before Eddie shuts down the rig and takes a break.

Ma collapses on the nearest log. "Whew! I'm tuckered," she whispers.

Eddie, sweating the clean sweat of a laboring man, goes to the kitchen and dips water from the enameled pail. Nellie and Ma drink, then drink again. Nancy, Patty, and I toss the sticks down the open bulkhead into the cellar.

No one talks. In ten minutes, Eddie stands up and wipes his forehead. "Well, let's get this job done. I've got ten cords at Duley's t'saw t'day, too, soon's I can." Those are the last words for another long hour. He pushes the starter button, and again the crew acts out the wood-sawer's choreography until Nellie's pile of logs disappears. Eddie shuts down the saw and goes to fill the dipper. Returning, he hands it to Ma. "Well, ma'am, that should hold ya awhile."

"Gawd, I hope so. My arms are shaking so now I don't think I can hold this dipper."

Eddie and Nellie climb into the seat of his remnant of a touring car and head for Duley's. Ma goes inside to write Pa before the evening mail. Without complaint, Nancy, Patty, and I lift and carry and toss wood until the sun is low. Working with firewood is important to us.

Without it, we will face another cold and embarrassing winter asking for help or searching for wood. I prefer work. So do Ma and my sisters.

Pa had written that he was coming home, and Ma, unsure what mood he would be wearing when he came through the door, made herself anxious anticipating his homecoming. Since she expected criticism from her cleanup caper at Eddie's, she wanted to avoid any allegation of neglect at her own house, so, once the wood was in, she set about cleaning. In the days before Pa's arrival she cleaned windows, washed and ironed curtains, scrubbed and waxed floors, asked Eddie to repair the front step, and directed me to mow the lawn. She hoped so much for a pleasant reunion.

Chapter Twelve
ACROSS

*Paying high tribute to the 8th Armored Division . . . Brig.
Gen. John M. Devine said Saturday, "I don't think I've seen a
better looking group of soldiers who were better trained than
this division."*

—*Armoreader,* Camp Polk 1944

O n the strength of one hundred dollars Ma had wired him, Pa
boarded the train in Leesburg August 30 and arrived in West
Farmington on September 1. Uncle Austin met him at the station.

Ma had dressed up the house for his homecoming. To make the
place attractive, she had toiled long hours and stocked the cupboards
with custard pie, homemade biscuits, and fresh oysters for Sunday stew.
Yet, she was unsure he would appreciate, or even notice, her setting the
place in order.

She waited in a dither for Uncle Austin's Chrysler to cross the
bridge and turn onto our road. What would be Pa's mood—would he
be excited to be home, or would he be cool and unmoved, warm and
pleasant and pleased to see her or tired and irritable? Although I was
eager to see him and admire his soldiery look and listen to his stories
about the big guns, I feared for Ma.

Pa arrived midafternoon in the lingering heat. He wore a summer uniform, and sweat had stained his back and under his arms. His skin had darkened from the long days in Louisiana, and his muscles showed firm and taut. Ma smiled at him. "Welcome home, honey. You look wonderful," she said and hugged him tightly and kissed him. "You must be feeling better."

He greeted her warmly. "It's cooler here, and I could sleep on the train."

He dug into his duffel and pulled out a gift for each of us. It was unusual for Pa to bring gifts, unless they were useful, like shirts or books. He didn't buy playthings: I had just two childhood toys: a large, metal dump truck that one of his friends had brought to our house for me, and a windup bulldozer with rubber treads that Pa had given me one Christmas. He handed Ma an embroidered pillow top. I don't recall what he had for Nancy and Patty, perhaps a souvenir handkerchief or an army doll. For me, he brought a wood sculpture, a carving of four soldiers in a jeep emerging from Louisiana's piney woods. They wore field jackets, combat boots, and steel helmets. It was not a toy but an ornament, a souvenir, a keepsake. I set it on a shelf in my room and inspected it at bedtime and the following morning for a detail I might have missed. I cherished it. For the first time in memory, Pa had given me something I didn't need. It wasn't to wear or to work with or for school, nor was it something of his own that he was letting me keep for a while. It was for me from Pa. I didn't know how to say thank you.

The next day, he took Ma in the roadster to the Saturday dance at Chesterville. They met friends there and drank Krueger ale from quart bottles, danced the polka and the waltz to the music of Herschel Paul's orchestra and returned home late, laughing. Friends came on Sunday, and Ma made oyster stew, and they drank more ale.

Pa relaxed during his leave and was cheerfully lazy and noticeably pleased to be home and with Ma. He paid no attention to Ma's relationship with Aunt Marion. He showed no interest in the wood or the garden or the animals. He let Ma manage the place as she had in his absence. He and Ma spent his leave time together enjoying each other: they bathed together in Lauri and Hilma's Finnish steam bath; they drank quarts of Krueger ale and sipped at flasks of Southern Comfort; they gathered apples at the Merrill farm; and they drove to Phillips to see Fern and stayed up late and laughed. They felt themselves at the height of life. Time had stopped.

Pa called on his friends at Blackie's barbershop and the poker table at the West Farmington Fire Company.

Pa poses on the front lawn during his September 1944 furlough.

He laid down bets on the trotters at the Farmington Fair. His friends came to the house, and there was more Krueger ale and laughter. He wore his uniform and posed for pictures. He showed off his fitness and talked of training and the big guns. Pa was happy—he felt valued and respected, valiant, and seemed thrilled to be a soldier. I was refreshed by his cheerfulness, and I was proud of him.

When September was half over, Ma said to us, "We're going to a party."

"Where?" I asked.

"At Uncle Austin's camp at Varnum Pond," she said. "It's a party for your father. Take your fishing pole. Show him how you can catch a fish."

Pa drove us there in the roadster. On the way, he detoured to the old

Dean place to look for deer dung and half-eaten apples in the unkempt orchard. "There are deer here," he told us. "But I'll be gone when the season comes."

He drove up a long hill overlooking Varnum Pond and stopped again. The land there lay dormant. The camp road descended through a grown-up hayfield showing aster and goldenrod and black-eyed Susan and disappeared into a layer of thicket against the shore of the pond. Across the pond, the hardwoods were tinged with rising reds and yellows, and the spruce and fir shined emerald green. The pond was deep blue and slightly rippled by a fresh and clean northwesterly breeze sliding over Mount Blue. The passage of a Temple summer was being foretold on its hills. We turned in, then walked up through high grass into another orchard.

Pa looked at the apple trees, old and tangled and bent. "We'll need hard cider this time next year when I get back," he told Ma. "Perhaps Eddie can pick up some apples here and take them up to Howard's and fill up our barrel."

Ma smiled at what she characterized as nonsensical. "If you think it's necessary, I'll ask him," she said.

Uncle Austin's camp had been tidied up for the occasion. An American flag flew from a pole in the front yard. Someone had printed a sign that read "Good Luck Elliott" and tacked it to the porch rail. Aunt Viola had clipped the grass. Aunt Marion had set up card tables and folding chairs under the pines and hemlocks. A motorboat and a skiff sat ready at the dock.

Pa pulled up between two pine trees and shut down the roadster. The yard was strewn with cars: Chevrolets, Chryslers, Buicks, a Ford station wagon with wooden sides, and a small truck. Folks had arrived and grouped in clusters or beehives or sets. The largest cluster stood around a table on the porch where an assortment of bottles, pitchers, and glasses sat for the drinkers to enjoy. Food preparers, talkers, fishermen, and three little-girl cousins made up the other sets. Pa greeted the drinking set, poured himself a half-glass of whiskey, then circulated to the fishermen.

Pa didn't bring his fishing gear; he didn't fish on the pond. In other years, he fished on the stream and frequently filled his creel with trout. He endured the tales of the pond fishermen and was curious to watch their antics, but pond fishing bored him.

He stood near the shore with Grandpa C.F. and Sam Johnson and watched Uncle Austin climb into the motorboat with a fishing rod in his hand and motor to the center of the pond.

"Watch him," Pa said. "He's putting out a line. He doesn't fish like the rest of us."

Uncle Austin fished like he farmed and logged, which meant that he didn't actually fish at all. Near the pond's center, he cast his line and lure into the water, then laid the line back to the dock. He stuck his rod in the bushes by the boathouse and spoke to Pa, "Keep an eye on that line for me, will ya?"

"How long you going to be gone?"

"I'm goin' up to the porch and take a nap. If the line shakes, come get me."

No one had ever seen Sam Johnson—a drinking pal of Uncle Austin's—fish either, but every time he had an audience, he told fish stories. "So I'm fishin' with Phil," he said, "up on the Carrabassett. Well, I'm not really fishin'. I just went along to do the drinkin' while Phil fished." He told the story like Pa's brother Phil worked for him.

Pa stood there with his glass and listened.

"Phil's doin' a fine job pullin' in trout," Sam continued. "At least he is 'til a car comes along and out steps this hulk of a man in a blue coat and leather-top boots and a patch on his coat that looks like a star. Looks just like a Texas Ranger. He steps down and asks what we're doin'. Waal, he can see what we're doin'. Phil's fishin' an' I'm drinkin'— lucky for me he's a game warden and not the liquor inspector. He wants to see Phil's license, which he looks at, and then wants to see the fly

Phil's usin'. He takes one look and says, 'Waal now, Mr. Hodgkins, that fly of yours can't fly too good hangin' onto that worm. Did you know that?' And he writes him a ticket right there."

"How much did them trout cost him, Sam?"

Sam reached down behind a pine tree and pulled up a whiskey bottle, refilled his glass, and placed the bottle back behind the tree. "I dunno, but I bet he coulda had three or four pretty good meals at Stewart's Diner."

Grandpa C.F., the only other fisherman in the set except for me, straightened his necktie and turned toward the pond. "Jeez cripes, Sam. Any fish you catch should be embarrassed. I'm goin' fishin' now. Watch how it's done." Grandpa C.F. seemed more conscious of the fisherman's heritage. He rowed the skiff far enough into the pond for it to be quiet and sat there, a small flask of whiskey in one hand and a pole in the other, and sipped and tried to coax a fish up to his hook.

Hungry, I meandered to the food-preparers cluster. Aunt Marion laid out a raspberry jellied salad on a serving table and followed that with carrot salad, fruit salad, whipped-cream salad, pineapple salad, candied salad, cranberry salad, tossed vegetable salad, bean salad, and potato salad. Earlier, she had put out plastic drinking cups, utensils, paper plates, and paper bibs for the kids. From the Chevy's trunk, she fetched hot dogs, hamburgers, egg-salad sandwiches, rolls jammed with tuna fish and mayonnaise, potato chips, coleslaw, peanuts, oatmeal cookies, and two wooden Coca-Cola cases filled with various soft drinks. Ma, Aunt Viola, and Elspet Johnson stepped up to fill out the beehive of food preparers and help Aunt Marion assemble the tables and chairs and display the food, and to ooh and aah over such beautiful salads. But Aunt Marion refused any help. "I'm just fine," she said. "I'll take care of setting up."

"Let me do that."

"No. You go enjoy yourself. I'll do it."

"But I want to help."

"No. I know how this should go. And I want to do it." And she banished them to find a beehive someplace else.

They joined Aunt Christine and Grandma Luna and created a talking beehive. Uncle Roy, to avoid being trapped in what he referred to as a hen party, looked for a different cluster. He spied Harvey Smith, who owned a gas station in Farmington, and Sam Johnson at the bar and joined them in a drink to prop himself up for the afternoon and to find out if Harvey's business was slow, as he alleged his own to be. Pa, not interested in Roy's poor-man stories of low sales and high expenses at the Farmers Union, refilled his glass from Sam's bottle behind the tree and looked for another cluster.

Uncle Lawrence and Ken Brooks, a regular at the West Farmington Fire Company card games, gathered up some paper and twigs and formed a fireplace cluster around the flat-stone barbecue grill. Lawrence, Aunt Marion's husband and a house-to-house bakery goods salesman in faraway Augusta, was usually a refreshing relief from the pressures of Pa's siblings. He organized baseball games, beano fests, and Saturday night dances in Temple, but he didn't take a position on how other people should live. Nor, unlike Aunt Marion, did he carry around an agenda of righteous and proper achievements for himself and others to carry out. In his bakery truck—what Ma called a cookie wagon— he called on farmers and rural folks each day and spent four nights a week at a rooming house in Augusta with little reward except for Sundays and holidays off. He had been elected to Temple's Board of Selectmen for several terms and was, I thought, one of the few totally honest people in town.

Pa drifted to the fireplace, the least likely cluster, he thought, for a contrary discussion, and asked Uncle Lawrence, "How are your Red Sox doin'?"

Lawrence, a Red Sox zealot, kept a portable radio by his side and rooted for his idols to accomplish the impossible, overtake the St. Louis Browns and win the American League pennant. "Those bums are the same as always," he answered. "They start out the year damned good, but look at 'em now when the games count. They can't hit nothin'." He will spend the afternoon in predestined misery listening to Jim Britt's languid account of his Boston heroes fulfilling their destiny. "Hear that? Struck him out. I knew it."

Pa fired his Zippo and lit the paper under the twigs Ken and Lawrence had laid in the fireplace. Then Lawrence added two larger sticks, blew into the fire, and sent sparks floating up through the hemlock canopy before turning to Pa. "Johnny's been with me on the route once or twice this summer."

"Did he like it?"

"Seemed to."

I could have told Pa there wasn't much for me to dislike. Uncle Lawrence and Leo, a schoolmate who was enough older than I to work for pay, saw to the customers, while I sat and read a Big Little Book and ate jelly doughnuts and raspberry turnovers. I was like a pig in mud.

Pa smiled and said, "He wrote me about flat tires and getting lost on the route."

"He got a kick out of that," Lawrence said, "after it was over. But I think he was a little worried at the time. He's growing up. He'll be okay."

Traveling on the bakery truck, sometimes for overnight trips, had taken me to places far beyond the bridge in West Farmington to sights I hadn't seen before: an airport, a city street, a dairy farm and a silo, men working in factories and office buildings, a rooming house, folks eating meals in restaurants, kids buying sundaes at ice-cream stands, and sandlot baseball games beside the road. After each trip, I had told Ma my stories and written a letter to Pa.

In the stone fireplace, the fire burned to a bed of red coals and Lawrence and Ken flipped hot dogs and hamburgers onto an iron grill and watched them sizzle. Pa sipped from a glass and told them how big the chiggers grew in Louisiana and said that he hoped he'd never see another one.

Suddenly, Aunt Marion interrupted the hives and clusters. "C'mon! The food's ready," she yelled. "Where is everybody? Someone wake up Austin. Here, Clarice, grab a plate. Hot dogs on the fire. C'mon! C'mon! Food needs to be eaten. My gosh, where are those appetites?" She gave every laid-back guest her personal attention and refused to think that someone might not eat two helpings. "Hurry up. Hurry up," she kept saying.

The beehives buzzed and stirred, and the drinkers filled their glasses from the nearest bottle. Uncle Austin woke up and strode down to the shore to see if a fish had been dumb enough to get tangled in his line. "Anyone watching this pole? Do I have a fish on yet?" he asked no one in particular.

I wasn't hungry. I wanted to listen to Pa talk about Louisiana.

"C'mon, Elliott," Aunt Marion told Pa. "You look like you need some poundage. Lawrence, put that plate of hot dogs on this table. Johnny, you want two, don't you?" Uncle Lawrence dished up the main course of hot dogs and hamburgers to the serving tables, which Aunt Marion had adorned with a rainbow of salads, soda pop, potato chips, homemade rolls, cookies, and a cake.

I filled a paper plate with a hot dog, sweet-tasting jelly salad, and two oatmeal cookies. Folks were strewn here and there, on the porch, in lawn chairs, on a bench next to the water, and on the dock. I sat on a rock and balanced a paper plate on my lap and ate jelly salad with a plastic fork and a hot dog with my fingers.

"There's more to eat. You have to finish it up," Aunt Marion announced, but no takers went forward. Ma and Aunt Viola whittled out sticks for the little-girl set to toast marshmallows, and I asked Pa if I could fish. He said maybe later and joined Sam Johnson's storytelling beehive. I knew I shouldn't bother him. It was his party. They wanted his time. They all knew what he had not yet said—that next for him would be the war. He would go across and not be back until it was done. They wanted to be with him and talk. I did, too. I stood with him and Uncle Phil, Uncle Lawrence, Uncle Roy, Sam Johnson, Ken Brooks, and one or two others and listened to Sam tell another story.

"So I'm drivin' my '42 Chevy—got it from Del before they stopped making 'em—up to Rangeley to do some fishin' in . . ."

"Fishing!" Uncle Phil interrupted. "Chrissakes, you can't fish. Don't you remember? You was goin' up there to do some drinkin'."

"I did all my drinkin' before I left," Sam said, "and that's why I got in so much trouble. I got pulled over in Phillips, and the man in the blue suit says to me, 'You been drinkin'?' I said I hadn't had a drink for a week—couldn't get it nowhere, rationing and all. So he forgets about the drinkin' and asks me where I'm goin' on a Sunday. I says nowhere, maybe Rangeley, and he asks me if I gotta permit. Permit! I say. What for? Then he tells me I can't drive anyplace unless I'm on my way to work. Work? I say. Chrissakes, I don't even have a job, so he writes me a ticket. Jeez, did you know there's a goddam ban on just drivin' around? Believe it or not, I got pinched for drivin' around sober. Now whadda ya' think of that?"

"So how do you get around to pick up groceries and stuff if you're too drunk to walk and too sober to drive?" Ken asked.

Uncle Roy twitched, yanked on his suspenders, and tugged at his trousers with his elbows. "Guess he'd hafta ride a bike," he said.

I hated for the afternoon to end. The pond was a gentle place. Folks had come together here and taken pleasure in each other. Ma and Pa had joined in the good-natured talk and banter. Folks had respected them, included them, and joked with them. Pa sipped and talked in the man-cluster and guffawed at Sam Johnson's stories. Ma's talking bee-hive turned into a cleanup hive, and they burned the paper plates, washed and stored the plastic forks for next year, and helped Aunt Marion put away the tables and chairs. Grandpa C.F. took off his tie, hung it on a peg by the fireplace, and went to sleep on the couch. Uncle Austin snored on the porch while his fishing line waggled in the bushes by the dock. The little-girl set hiked to Pine Point, and I fished. The man-cluster talked, gossiped, reminisced, laughed, and discussed the war. Pa told them he'd be going across next, and each man shook Pa's hand, patted him on the back, wished him well, and said give 'em hell. But it wasn't easy for Pa to go.

Back home, when the time for Pa to leave descended upon us, Ma said to him, "I don't like this. I can't let you go, not this time. It's a war you're going to."

Pa did not want to go back to Louisiana. He recalled the oppressive heat, the chiggers, the dehydration, and the sickness he had suffered. Perhaps he could manage being at war, he thought, but he knew Louisiana in the heat would still be hell. "Maybe I can stay home another week," he told her.

Ma stood by the phone while he called Camp Polk.

He hunched down and spoke into the mouthpiece. "My wife is sick. I need to wait here for her to get well enough to take care of the kids. Should only be another week." He waited for an answer. When he finished, he turned to Ma. "I can stay a few more days."

Ma smiled and slid her arm around his waist. "Thank God." And then she turned serious. "Do you think anyone was listening in on your call?"

"Probably," he said.

Ma didn't appear sick to me. Pa had fast-talked the army into his staying home. My soldiery image of him was shaken. I wished he hadn't made the call.

At the end of the week, he hugged Ma. "I have to go," he said.

"I know," she answered. "Please be careful."

Pa arrived at Camp Polk on October 2, in time for the change in commanders. Brigadier General John Devine, a veteran of the Normandy landings who had fought with the 90th Infantry and 7th Armored Divisions in France and had earned the Bronze and Silver Stars, was taking command of the 8th Armored Division. General Devine praised the readiness of the division and committed himself to instilling a fighting spirit in the soldiers. He immediately ordered the division to prepare to move overseas.

Pa welcomed the news. He wrote Aunt Marion that, especially after being home, Camp Polk was a hellhole. He would have been willing, I suspect, to give Louisiana to the Germans right then and call it even.

For two weeks, Pa's battalion inspected and inventoried 105-mm howitzers, two-and-one-half-ton trucks, and fighting equipment and, except for what they condemned as unfit for combat, marked it for shipment. They processed purchase orders and invoices for shipment of new equipment to the embarkation point. They greased and crated rifles and machine guns. Each man packed a duffel bag.

Word came on October 26, and the battalion boarded troop trains for the staging area at Camp Kilmer, New Jersey. For four days, Pa lounged in his bunk, stood in chow lines, waited in toilet lines, played poker and craps, and traded stories with his pals. Through Mississippi and Alabama, they passed bare cotton fields, empty sharecroppers' shacks, and skimpy-looking piney woods. At Atlanta, they turned northeast and passed through Columbia, Raleigh, and Richmond. The train moved slowly and frequently stopped on small-town sidings and waited for scheduled trains to pass.

As time went on, Frank Pierce—Pa's friend from Camp Polk—grew uncomfortable and complained to Pa of the noise, the chow lines, and the crowded compartments. "But I guess," Frank said, "if it looks like a boxcar, sounds like a boxcar, and rides like a boxcar, it must be a Pullman."

"We're headed north," Pa answered, "and there's no chiggers up there."

North of Washington, the grass had turned brown, and the trees were bare. At Camp Kilmer, a drab countryside greeted the troops. Pa arrived on October 29 and moved into a two-story, barn-like, wooden barracks. He practiced dry-land boat drills thirty miles from the dock, learned that from then on his mail would be censored, and received an opportunity to write a will. He mailed me a postcard picture of the

George Washington Bridge and wrote that the weather was much cooler and that he had been to a show. It was the first censored piece of mail we received from him. The censor's stamp was, I suspected, Pa's way of telling me that he couldn't say much, but the picture and the cool temperature told me he was moving. Pa didn't try to cheat the censors, but he tried to tell us, subtly, about his doings. Later, in Europe, he wrote Ma that he couldn't tell her where he was, but they had a daughter by the same name. In five minutes with a sixth-grade geography book, she located Nancy, France.

Pa wrote to me more often as the time approached to ship overseas. In the beginning, he had written to Nancy, Patty, and me only when Ma pressed him, but in the days leading up to his shipping across, he wrote freely and frequently. He wrote, as he had before, to ask me to be good, do my schoolwork, and keep the woodbox filled; but he also described what he was doing, that he had been in the field, was in a new place, or had seen a movie.

I think the reality of shipping across brought a change in his attitude toward his family. He needed to bond with us and longed to reveal to us and have us recognize the danger he was exposed to. But he, a quiet man in whom reticence was a primary virtue, didn't reveal this directly. Instead, he wrote often and told me whatever the censor allowed. He expected me to understand and accept the unsaid that he might not return. Ma said he longed to be closer to me and was writing to me willingly, not because she had persuaded him. I prized and saved his mail and wrote him often and described my days at home.

Ma, suffering in the dreamy, dazed afterglow of his extended and romantic holiday, said he left New York Harbor feeling lonesome for us, but I didn't believe so. I thought he was focused on the war and wanted us to be proud and support him, which we had, except when he fibbed to the army and shattered my feelings. I needed time then to come to grips with my letdown, but I was over it as he faced the voyage across.

Late on November 6, 1944, Pa, his duffel perched on his shoulder like a stick of pulpwood, hurried up the gangplank of the troopship *George W. Goethals*. The next morning, the *Goethals* and three other ships, with the 8th Armored Division packed tightly into their compartments, steamed out of New York Harbor, past the Statue of Liberty and Fort Hamilton, and through The Narrows into the swells of the North Atlantic. Outside the harbor, the crew uncovered an antiaircraft gun aft and test-fired it. They rendezvoused with a convoy, and destroyers sporting antiaircraft guns and antisubmarine depth charges took up stations on their perimeter.

They steamed a circuitous zigzag route. To confuse German U-boats, the convoy zigged southeast toward Africa, then zagged northeast toward Iceland. From the deck of the *Goethals*, Pa looked over the rail at what seemed like a hundred ships bobbing in twenty-foot ocean swells. Out of his view beyond the transports, a screen of U.S. Navy destroyers searched for U-boats. Frank came on deck. "How many ships are out there?" Pa asked him.

"I don't know, but as near as I can tell, they take up the entire ocean."

"I counted over thirty-five," Pa told him, "but I doubt if I can see half of what's out there."

"Well," Frank said, "if they're like the guys down below, that would mean about fifty thousand soldiers are puking their guts out. Gawd, I've never seen so many guys sick. If they were all up here puking over the same rail, they'd tip this thing over."

"You been sick?"

"No. You?"

"No. Must be our age."

"One guy down below said he puked eight times in an hour and a half. Said it was like going up and down in an elevator all day."

"Means we can get seconds on steak," Pa told Frank. "And the guys playing poker aren't that sharp either."

"So your money will last a little longer, will it?"

The *Goethals* rolled and pitched in the swells for eleven days. Each day, the troops participated in a lifeboat drill, a session of calisthenics, and an hour's instruction in French and German. Impromptu amateur talent shows, movies, poker, boxing matches, chowtime, and stories of life at home killed the remainder of each day.

On the twelfth day at sea, the *Goethals* approached Plymouth Harbor in southern England. The *Mayflower*, full of Pilgrims, had left Plymouth in 1620 and turned back twice before sailing alone for sixty-five days to reach what would become Plymouth, Massachusetts. In 1632, William Hodgkins I and his son William II left Plymouth, England, in a ship whose name remains unknown and arrived in Plymouth, Massachusetts, seventy days later. Pa was a tenth-generation descendent of William I and the first of that line known to have been back to the homeland.

As the *Goethals* entered Plymouth Harbor, Pa saw piers and docks crowded with troop transports and merchant ships set against the cut stone and marble construction of the Royal Citadel. Behind the Citadel, stone buildings, hotels, shops, and church steeples, some showing damage from German air raids, formed a sightly backdrop; it was as pretty a place, he wrote Ma, as he had ever seen. The battalion boarded a troop train that night and traveled to Tidworth, England, arriving after daylight on November 19. In a cold rain, they moved into tents on Windmill Hill, a sloping, muddy, clay field. The trip from Louisiana had taken twenty-four days.

Chapter Thirteen
THE VILLAGE SCHOOL

Dear Daddy,
. . . We are making a blanket down to school and have it over
half done. . . .

—John Hodgkins, September 1944

B| ack in time when the population of Temple grew and spread and developed the town, ten school districts were created for educating the young. In his *History of Temple: Its Rise and Decline*, Dr. Richard Pierce referred to Temple's schoolhouses, at the height of the town's rise in the mid-1800s, as "citadels of ugliness." He wrote that they were poorly constructed and lacked the rudimentary necessaries—light, heat, and teaching supplies—for schooling to be effective. Teachers were ill-paid, and their competency was defined by their ability to maintain order, which was considered paramount. In some districts, classes were held in homes; in others, schools were closed during the winter term. Students often left school to work on the family farm; for many others, the district system was, in Pierce's words, a "bad institution."

During the later decline, according to Dr. Pierce, the town abandoned and closed district schoolhouses for lack of students or qualified teachers, and districts were combined. Ironically, as the town eliminated school districts, primary education in Temple strengthened: the town improved the remaining schoolhouses, hired trained teachers and paid them adequately, purchased uniform textbooks, and regulated the school year. But as the town's decline continued into the twentieth century, the consolidation of school districts also continued until, in September 1944, one schoolhouse remained active in Temple—the Village School, where Nancy, Patty, and I went for our education.

Each day, we walked a quarter mile to the schoolhouse, and on most days we walked home for lunch. On the way, we scuffed at the dirt or rustled colored leaves or flailed at fresh snow or sloshed in the mud or stepped carefully around fresh cow turds. We passed three village homes, each with an attached barn and a sunny spot for a garden. The only noises we heard were our boots striking the road, the stream rumbling under the bridge, or a car whining its way through the village. Sometimes Miriam came down the hill or Leo rushed out his door to join us, and we chatted or gossiped about romances at the school.

Artist's depiction of the Village School in the early 1940s. (Leslie Swank)

The white-clapboarded schoolhouse, prominent in its plainness, stood well back from the road. Raised entrances left and right under its gabled front led to the interior. A flagpole affixed to the front projected above the ridgeline. Two large sugar maples—one was first base, the other third—defined the playground, except that baseball games required outfielders be positioned across the road, in front of Aunt Marion's windows. Our recess and lunch-hour games of hopscotch, tag, kickball, and baseball had worn away any evidence of grass, and we played on a hard and sometimes dusty surface. In spring, we bypassed the rock-solid playground and played marbles in the soft roadway, where we could mold a small hole to entrap the agate and the tiger's eye. Mornings and at the end of recess, we waited on the playground for Mrs. Stolt, schoolmarm and guardian of the grounds, to ring a bell. We then queued up at the entrance, marched inside, hung our coats on hooks in the hallway, and went directly to our seats.

Inside the schoolroom we sat in nine rows of seats and desks, from kindergarten on our right to eighth grade on our left. In September 1944, I sat in the fifth-grade row, alphabetically with four other classmates. In my row, as in the others, Mrs. Stolt reserved the front seat for recitation and as a place where any one of us would sit and refocus on her lessons if she thought it necessary. In front of the empty seat sat Mrs. Stolt's imposing wooden desk, cluttered with her schooling necessaries: pencils, pens, chalk, paper, textbooks, homework papers and workbooks, and a school bell. Behind the cluttered desk, across the top of a wall of slate blackboards, she had constructed the loopy and curvy Palmer Method alphabet, cursive letters of ascenders and loops and descenders and free-flowing tongues and tails, which, if we learned to form them correctly, would conceal our personalities from handwriting analysts forever. The cluttered desk and the wall of blackboards behind it made up Mrs. Stolt's instructional center where her teaching took form and shape.

In the rear of the schoolhouse, two doors led to the his-and-her privies. To my left was the entry hall from the playground where coats hung on metal hooks and a pail of water and a tin dipper sat on a bench. To my right, a woodstove—its firebox served by beech and maple stacked next to it—warmed the room. Natural light flooded over us through three large windows on each side, and the pale glow of two overhead light bulbs illuminated the room.

Learning had no distractions here. The bare room was softened only by a clock with Roman numbers on its face and a bulletin board to display our work. Except for the occasional one- or two-fingered request for a trip to a privy, which required Mrs. Stolt's approval, we sat quietly. We read, wrote, solved math problems, prepared for recitation, struggled with workbook exercises, or listened to Mrs. Stolt teach an upper-grade lesson while we waited for her to attend to our row.

She taught from her left to her right, from the lower grades to the upper, one row at a time; first reading, then language, then arithmetic. Each class lasted about ten minutes and was a review of the previous day's assignment and a rudimentary presentation of a new lesson. In the afternoons she brought history, geography, and science to our rows.

A pleasant but exacting woman, Mrs. Stolt had come to the Village School two years earlier. A dogged teacher who did not tolerate nonsense, she expected students to be prepared and attentive to lessons. She did not tolerate indifference or indolence. When necessary, she tended to us individually, and when trouble appeared on our report card, we didn't fault her for our failures. I liked her and credited her with improving my grades, although some—Ma and Pa and Aunt Marion—would give the credit to me. We were a team: she taught, and I learned.

After Mrs. Stolt came to the schoolroom, Ma continued to substitute now and then. Whenever she stood in front of the rows and taught us, Patty thought the schoolroom was blessed by divine intervention. To her, school with Ma as the teacher was like staying at home, only more fun. Her friends were seated next to her, the room was warm with lots of paper and crayons, and Ma was there, too. But Nancy didn't like to have Ma teach. Ma made her repeat lessons over and over until any thought of getting favored treatment from her mother had been banished from the schoolroom. I thought Ma a first-class teacher, but I could see she didn't take pleasure from filling in for Mrs. Stolt. She came to the school on short notice, un-prepared, and would fumble around Mrs. Stolt's desk to find the lesson plan for the day. Failing to discover Mrs. Stolt's intentions, she would teach something else we had already learned or make up some other way to get through the day, and I'd be

Ma, schoolteacher at the Village School, poses on the village bridge in February 1932.

embarrassed at her dillydallying. But when, as in the case of Miss Pinkham's exit, Ma taught a long time, she planned ahead and organ-ized herself, and I was proud to watch her deliver the lessons.

But now Ma is home, and Mrs. Stolt, who seldom misses a school day attracts my attention. I am sitting at my fifth-grade desk. Two rows away, Mrs. Stolt stands in front of the seventh grade. She holds a text-book in her wiry hands, fingers chalk, and looks out over her reading glasses. Four students, Alice and Albert and Keith and Leo, look up and acknowledge her silent presence at the head of their row. Today's lesson, she tells them, is the area of a circle. She retreats to the black-board and draws a perfectly round circle, labels its diameter twelve inches, and asks, "Alice, how do you determine the area of a circle? The formula was in your workbook lesson."

Alice doesn't know, nor does Albert. Keith flips the pages of his workbook in search of the answer. Mrs. Stolt points to Leo, but he won't know how to figure the circle's area either.

Leo is a would-be playmate. He and his mother live in the village with his grandparents. His father lives elsewhere. At an early age, Leo learned to work hard from his grandfather, who keeps animals and works a team of horses. Leo is big and strong and self-conscious and hides his sensitivities in a blunt, crude, and offensive personality. He is brainy, but because he thinks intellect will degrade his domineering character, he hides his mental strength. I call him my would-be friend—if he wasn't a bully, he would be a friend. He leads the conflicts on the playground; he is arrogant and sarcastic; he creates disagreements, then tries to settle them by swinging his fists. But I spend time with him and have absorbed more than one pounding in my attempts to be his playmate.

One day, we are in my backyard after school, and he demands that I help him with his barn chores. I refuse. He sneers and threatens to call the sheriff as though that were an option, and I refuse again. He swings a fist at me and knocks me on my backside. I am up quickly and flail my fists at his muscular body, a body nearly twice the size of mine and as hard as a bag of old fertilizer.

He knocks me down again, and I know I'm outmatched. I grab a ski pole and swing at him. The pole ricochets off his shoulder into his face.

"Hey there, sonny boy," he says. "Take it easy. You could hurt somebody."

Another time, it is winter, and I am in the snowy road with my sled, sliding on the hill by my house. Leo and Myron, an eighth grader who feigns a pleasing nature but is actually a devious instigator of trouble and many times Leo's accomplice, are there, too, and they attack and pummel me so ruthlessly that Mrs. Mosher comes out of her house across the street to my rescue.

On another day, I am in the kitchen, my face bruised and red, and Ma thinks I should go to the doctor. I tell her that I don't like to fight, that I want to have friends and play games, run in the lanes and explore the stream bank with them. But Leo is a bully. He ridicules my failures on the school playground and shoves me around in his barnyard. I put up with it all. Ma despises his belligerence and says she is not going to put up with his bullying, but she does nothing about it.

Now Leo is in front of Mrs. Stolt's pointed finger.

"Leo, tell me how to find the area of this circle."

"I can't, ma'am. I don't know." He is indifferent to his failure. After all, Alice and Albert didn't know either.

Upper-grade arithmetic is the highlight of my day, and I sit erect, alert to Mrs. Stolt's lesson. Because the seventh graders have told her they don't know the answer, I have raised my hand. In the past, Mrs. Stolt has called on me now and then. Today, she prefers that the seventh graders learn their lessons from her, but I leave my hand up anyway.

Mrs. Stolt reviews yesterday's lesson and uses wheels, silos, telephone poles, and the pail of water in the hallway to illuminate the lesson. I put my hand down and look for something else to do.

My learning at the Village School did not all come from textbooks and classroom work. In September 1944, twenty-three kids made up Mrs. Stolt's nine-row audience, and I learned from knowing them. Though we all came from the same small-town culture, some were vastly different from others, and different still from me.

The rows included shy kids, like me, who worked barn chores, tended gardens, and played simple games of hide-and-seek or tag. But there were also exuberant kids who batted baseballs on the playground, worked dump rakes, or drove tractors. There were kids whose fathers worked away, didn't work at all, farmed unsparingly, or drank unrelentingly. There were kids whose parents had little money and others whose parents furnished new clothes whenever the seasons changed.

Each person in that schoolroom had a unique quality, and from them I learned confidence and conversation and common sense. And I discovered tolerance, learned acceptance, and gained friendships.

We also tended to America in that schoolroom. We pledged allegiance to our flag each morning and learned the forty-eight states and their capitals. We celebrated the patriotic holidays with remembrance ceremonies and fitting lessons. We practiced good citizenship.

We worked to help win the war. Mrs. Stolt asked us to collect milkweed pods with their tufts of silky hairs and floss that were used in making buoyant life jackets for the navy. After school and on Saturdays, in the fall when the pods had matured but not burst, we searched the roadsides, the fields, the lanes, and the abandoned farmsteads; we filled paper shopping bags with milkweed pods. We were good soldiers.

One day in late 1944, Mrs. Stolt carries a large cardboard box into the schoolroom. It waits beside her desk unopened, as if to tempt our curiosity, while she traverses the room from left to right with reading, language, and arithmetic lessons. After lunch, instead of reading to us from *Peck's Bad Boy and His Pa*, she opens the box, and I see knitting needles and scads of colored yarn.

"We're going to knit," she says and holds up a handful of needles. "The soldiers need blankets and afghans in field hospitals at the front, and we are going to make one. If you don't know how to knit, I'll teach you."

Mrs. Stolt crisscrosses the room casting stitches on needles until every kid has enough to knit a nine-inch-wide piece. She demonstrates the plain knitting stitch, delivers individual attention to the less skillful, and tells us to knit until the piece is square. Some kids knitted at home, and it is second nature to them. I have seen how easily Ma, Aunt Marion, and Grandma knit, and I have worn the mittens and hats they have made for me, but I am slow to learn the beginner's stitch. Mrs. Stolt must correct my slip-ups, and Nancy shows me again after supper how to knit the plain stitch, and I finally pick up the routine.

Knitting wasn't mandatory in the Village School, but every kid above second grade volunteered to knit the nine-inch squares. We knitted at school during recesses, during lunch break, during reading period, and whenever we had time away from schoolwork. We knitted at home and on weekends. Some knit more than others, as if it were a competition, while others completed just one square. "Knitting's for girls—or sissies," said Leo.

Women, then, knitted as part of their homemaking duties, but I had never seen a man knit. However, Mrs. Stolt wanted the school to produce an afghan, and she expected boys to knit, too. I knew Leo would knit, and after a comment or two to puff up his masculinity, he did. Fighting a war, I thought, is for everybody. We conquered our self-consciousness and knitted until that box of yarn—and another one—was gone. We filled two boxes with colorful nine-inch squares and turned them into an afghan, and our afghan went, I imagined, to the snowy fields of France where soldiers huddled in foxholes, shivered on stretchers, or lay in hospital beds.

At the end of the first ranking period, Mrs. Stolt wrote Ma that I was doing good fifth-grade work, a subtle suggestion, Ma told me, that I should stick to fifth-grade subjects and not interfere in her upper-grade lessons. She also wrote Ma that I had improved in my history and geography lessons, likely helped by reading war news in *The Franklin Journal* and *Lewiston Evening Journal* and watching *Movietone News* at the State, and that I should continue to work to improve. Although I stopped interfering in upper-grade classes, I continued to watch and listen and learn from them.

At the end of the year, my fifth-grade report card showed steady improvement in all my subjects in a yearlong effort to convince Mrs. Stolt I was worthy of the sixth grade. I succeeded, but I may not have shown her the child prodigy Pa believed me to be.

The work at the Village School was not all lessons and homework. It was also a stack of firewood beside the woodstove each morning, a full water pail in the hallway, and the recess bell rung on time. We dusted erasers, shined blackboards, and swept the floor clean at the end of the day. We dug up maple seedlings to plant on Arbor Day and cut a balsam fir for Christmas. We picked wildflowers for Mrs. Stolt's springtime desk. Learning had no limits in our schoolroom.

We recognized God in our schoolroom as well. We prayed each morning to start the day, learned The Golden Rule, and practiced it on our schoolmates. We learned the Ten Commandments. We celebrated Christmas—we hung wreaths and swags, decorated a balsam fir with candy canes, and invited our parents to a Christmas program in the schoolroom. In front of our parents and relatives, we spoke memorized pieces, sang Christmas carols, and acted out part of the Christmas Story from the Book of Luke. At one celebration, just as our program ended, Santa Claus burst through the door, wished all a Merry Christmas, and distributed gifts, candy canes, and popcorn balls. We all sang "Silent Night," and I thought God was happy with us in the Village School for inviting Him to be part of our learning.

I took pleasure in the challenge of the Village School. Mrs. Stolt gave time to each student, and the older kids helped the younger ones with workbooks. I made good friends there and I learned to help others. I learned to be on time and reliable in my duties. I suffered no opportunity, however, as Ma wished, to study art or music or sculpture. Consequently, I acquired no sense of style or lyric, poise or beauty— except when Miss Pinkham stood in front of my kindergarten row. Though Ma's expectations for my learning the gentle graces came up deficient, the lessons I learned at the Village School served me well.

Chapter Fourteen
WINDMILL HILL

It's going to be impossible for me to
send any gifts this year, but . . .
—Pa, December 1944

P a had left New York for England before snow came to Temple. Two weeks had passed when he cabled Ma that he had arrived in England safely, and in that two weeks, the fields in Temple turned from autumn brown to speckled white. A few days later, Aunt Marion brought Ma's mail from the post office and sat at the kitchen table while Ma read a letter from Pa, his first since leaving New York. In it, he recounted his trip to England and reported his living conditions on Windmill Hill. Aunt Marion, excited that he was fighting a war for his country an ocean away and single-minded to wear the mantle of custody, copied his letter and took it home for her scrapbook of his experiences.

Now, at the Village School, I fidget on the edge of my seat, restless for Mrs. Stolt to jingle the final bell. Possibly—hopefully—a letter will come for me today. Pa wrote me before he left New York that he would write again as soon as he could. Perhaps he has written, or perhaps he is busy preparing to cross the Channel or at the docks or on a ship or has left for the front already. I worry that he has forgotten. At dismissal, I race across the playground and run the shortcut home. Behind the buildings that line Temple's roads are fields and pastures and orchards and gardens, open-space shortcuts that every boy knows about and uses. I run across Aunt Marion's lawn and behind Leo's barn and over Mr. Mosher's sugary-white field. The path is smooth and frozen dry under my boots, faster than the roundabout dirt road. I have come this way many times; I know it is the quickest way home.

The door slams shut behind me. Ma is waiting and points to the kitchen table where yesterday's newspaper rests and where mail is read. "You have a letter," she says.

An envelope from Pa lies there, addressed to me, unopened.

"It was in the noon mail," Ma says. "Your Aunt Marion brought it. She wanted to read it. She asked me to open it, but I told her I couldn't. It's for you."

I smile and sigh at the sight of the envelope. I usually receive a picture postcard on which he asks me questions: Have you been swimming in the stream? Are you being good? Are you helping Ma? Have you filled the woodbox? But this time I have five pages of his handwriting to read.

"Read it," Ma asks, "And tell us what it says."

I sit at the wooden table and hold the letter to the oilcloth with both hands and, in the fading light, study the words. Pa recounts his doings and hardships and confesses his sadness at not being part of our Christmas. He describes the English lifestyle and sets down the events and experiences he wants to share with me.

"He's in England," I tell Ma. "He doesn't say where, just England. He's camped in a tent on a hillside where it rains all the time. It's cold, and he keeps warm burning coal in the tent."

I imagine I can hear his voice as he patiently describes to me his life in England. He boasts that he invented a lamp to see by, a little kerosene in the bottom of an oilcan and a piece of rope for a wick. Candles don't exist in England, he tells me. Everything is rationed, even coal. He says that he goes to the toilet in what the English call a honey bucket, and a truck comes by each day to collect it, and wouldn't that be an awful job. He writes that the English live altogether differently than we do because they don't have many of the things we have at home. If this is so, I think, the English must be really bad off. He pokes fun at them. Their cars look strange to him, and driving on the left side of the road like they do is unhandy. Well, I reason, since Pa drives the roadster in the middle of the road in Temple, he shouldn't notice much of a change in England.

He explains the complicated English monetary system. I try to explain it to Ma and Nancy and Patty. "He says the English have half-penny coins and quarterpennies, too. And they have threepence and sixpence and shillings, and florins, and half crowns and crowns. Gosh, they have more coins than we do."

Ma remembers when Grandma and Grampa Watson—who were British—used English money. "I know they do," she says.

I read more of the letter. "And they call paper money notes," I say, "like a ten-shilling note, or a one-pound note, or a five-pound note. And he promises to send me some English money when he gets a chance."

Ma chuckled. "I hope he sends it to you before the next poker game."

He asks me if we have snow and if I'm keeping the driveway shoveled. He writes that in England it is nine o'clock by his watch and that it should be four by the clock in our kitchen and the woodbox should be full. How about it, he asks. It's not full yet, I admit, but it will be soon.

He tells me that he will eat Thanksgiving dinner one day late—their turkeys didn't thaw in time—and he has that day off, but the day will otherwise be like the rest. For Christmas, he can send only his best wishes and a promise that he will make it up to me someday—now, he must attend to his present circumstances.

The letter held hope that after he returned home we could be closer.

He had learned from Ma's letters how proud I was of him, and I hoped he would approve of me, appreciate me, instruct me in the ways of growing up, and want to tell me his stories. He would know that I had helped fight the war, too, that I had collected milkweed pods and knitted squares in the Village School for an afghan, and I hoped he would praise me for that. But I must be patient, I thought, for he struggled with duty now and faced danger. And I knew he was determined to see it through.

On Windmill Hill, Pa shared a tent with six other soldiers. Every day, the rain slanted through the tent flaps and puddled on the ground under their cots. They framed a floor to stay above the mud and fashioned a watertight door. They slipped and slogged in the oily clay and shivered in the misty wind that slid over the English countryside. They wore trench coats over their field jackets and scrubbed mud from their combat boots at night. They burned thirty-five pounds of coal in the tent each day and, to contend with seventeen hours of darkness, fashioned crude lanterns out of tin cans, kerosene, and rope. They turned into bed early, wrapped themselves tightly in sleeping bags, and slept curled up on cots. They waited for orders.

By December 1, their trucks, tanks, artillery pieces, and half-track personnel carriers began arriving in British ports, and the division's drivers shuttled the equipment to Tidworth. Pa rode the train to Liverpool. then drove a six-by-six supply truck in night convoy back to camp. He passed through darkened Birmingham and followed southern England's winding and narrow roads, driving on the left side and clockwise through multispoked roundabouts. He drove through dark villages of stone buildings, by shadowy farmhouses behind gated entrances and fallow fields lined with hedgerows of overgrown privet back to the murky fields of Windmill Hill.

In camp, the days went by quickly, and his time for war came closer. His battalion convoyed to the artillery range at Tilshead and fired their new self-propelled 105-mm howitzers. Tank battalions moved to

Salisbury Plain and tested their new M4 Shermans, and infantry worked out battle tactics and fired their M-1 rifles. Medical units dispatched to local hospitals to gain knowledge of battlefield wounds. Battalion commanders flew to France for briefings and orientation.

For battlefield operations, General Devine organized 8th Armored Division into three combat commands—A, B, and R—each consisting of a tank, infantry, and artillery battalion supported by engineering, medical, ordnance, and maintenance units. Devine planned to use each combat command independently; two on the line and one in reserve.

Combat Command R comprised the 58th Armored Infantry Battalion, the 80th Tank Battalion, and Pa's outfit, the 405th Armored Field Artillery Battalion. Pa was part of a fighting unit. He read in *Yank, The Army Weekly* that U.S. forces were moving through minefields in Belgium and pushing up against the German Westwall. Perhaps the war would take him to Germany—possibly Berlin, he thought—before it ended.

A month passed at Windmill Hill before Pa received the mail that had followed him from Louisiana. He read the latest from Ma and a letter from me that I was knitting an afghan at school. In *The Franklin Journal,* he read war news and news of Temple: that Raymond Knowles had moved across town and Mellie Jenkins was back from a trip to Gray. A fruitcake arrived from Aunt Marion, and he put it aside for Christmas.

On Christmas Day, Frank came to see him, and they ate turkey and potatoes from their mess kits and shared Aunt Marion's fruitcake with the men in Pa's tent. "Damned good fruitcake, El," Frank said. "Wish I had a wife who could cook like this."

"It's from my sister, Frank."

"Oh, your *sister?*" He took another bite. "Your sister married yet?"

"Yes, Frank. She's married."

"El, you must know what's going on. You hang around headquarters. When are we gettin' our orders?"

"I don't know any more than you do, Frank. I went to a lecture on what to do if I get captured, so I figure we're going to where the Germans are."

"I heard they counterattacked. Are we going into the line?"

"I don't know, but the brass do. They have meetings every day. So we better be ready. Keep your sleeping bag dry and handy."

On New Year's Day, the orders came down to move at once across the Channel to Rheims, France, for combat assignment. At dawn, the 405th loaded and left in convoy with Combat Command R for Southampton. They went without Pa, who received orders to stay and help load Combat Command B. On January 5, CCB finished loading in a cold rain and convoyed from Tidworth to Southampton in fog and darkness, three days behind the 405th, which had sailed for France the day before. Pa slept fitfully that night, curled in his sleeping bag in a wet tent.

He was among strangers. His pals in the 405th, buddies with whom he had trained and lived and shared the past year, were ahead of him. He was curious to see the residue of war—the destruction and the remnants of prior battles—but he was worried. What was the extent of the danger he faced, and would he measure up when he encountered the battlefield? He thought of us at home and was concerned that his doings were unknown to us. He had told Ma to expect another cable soon, but he hadn't wired it and wouldn't until the move was over. He lay awake a long time.

In Temple, Ma sleeps in the front bedroom, a chamber pot under her bed—no more winter trips to the privy in the dark for her. Nancy and Patty sleep in the room next to mine. Under the blankets, I hear the fierce winter wind whistle through the pasture fence and shake the tin roof over my head and tattoo the snow against my window. I coil into nearly a circle. I am not fearful, but I am lonesome.

Sleep doesn't come. I think about Pa. I don't know where he is. He told us we would get a cable, but it hasn't come. I worry about him, or, perhaps, I worry about me or Ma. We face another winter alone, this time without Fern's help, and Ma says Pa might not come home again at all.

Chapter Fifteen

CHRISTMAS 1944

There is little doubt that I now recall those days with more fondness than they deserve.

—Jimmy Carter, *An Hour Before Dawn*

As the second winter in Temple without Pa approached, Ma showed no interest in preparing for the snow and cold or for the Christmas holiday, nor did she show any sentiment toward being with people. Eddie and Nellie took her to Farmington for early Christmas shopping, but the Christmas spirit did not inspire her. She didn't visit anyone, and only her closest Finnish friends called on her and sat at the kitchen table and talked.

Temple folks directed their energies toward support for the war. Full larders, jammed food-storage bins, and packed shelves of preserves in Temple's root cellars underscored the success of the president's campaign to plant Victory Gardens and grow more food. *The Franklin Journal* reported that the 6th War Loan drive had been a success and that Temple had met its quota of seventeen hundred dollars, about eight dollars for every person in town, a considerable sacrifice—for the sixth time—by economically beleaguered townsfolk.

Aunt Marion, chairman of Temple's fund drive, had solicited bond and stamp sales at every home and had come to the Village School and appealed to the students to contribute. At Christmastime, she launched a campaign to write to soldiers. Outside Grandpa's post office window, she pinned a poster of photos and addresses of the men who were at war and urged townsfolk to send a card and a gift. Mothers, sisters, and caring neighbors sent fruitcakes, cookies, candy, chewing gum, cigarettes, and cards of encouragement to soldiers and sailors in faraway places. The urge to support the war was irresistible, and as Christmas approached, Temple folks gave first to their soldiers and sailors away from home.

At the same time that Temple was so crowded with unselfish and stouthearted citizens, I became dispirited and envious. At other houses, fathers cut a Christmas tree, made gifts for their kids, and took their families on Christmas outings and to family gatherings. At our house, Ma had sent me to the far edge of the pasture for a Christmas tree, but it sat barren and forgotten in the parlor. At the Village School, kids bubbled with excitement and recounted tales of Christmas preparations, but I had nothing exciting to relate. Christmas movies came to the State in Farmington, but Ma had no motivation to take us there. She seemed to take little notice of the coming of Christmas.

Plagued by Ma's indifference, gloom descends upon me and I mope about the house without Christmas in my future. But then, in a seemingly thoughtful attempt to insert some joy into our holidays, Aunt Marion calls and invites Nancy, Patty, and me to visit her. "Come down and see my Christmas tree. It's all decorated," she announces.

Nancy and Patty refuse, and I don't count on the visit to erase my melancholy, but I go to Aunt Marion's to see her Christmas tree. I walk alone between cold snowbanks and smelly cow barns and yapping dogs to her house. It's only a quarter mile by the road, but years by the calendar. Aunt Marion is the first in town to have life's newest conveniences: new car, coal-burning central heater, electric refrigerator and freezer, and hot-water tap. Her house is warm—everywhere—and she keeps an especially hot wood fire in the kitchen cookstove. And I know she will show off her latest Christmas trimmings.

I reach for the storm-door latch. The tension spring squeaks, and when I step onto the porch, the door bangs shut behind me. She knows I'm here, but I knock anyway, stamp my snowy boots on the welcome mat, and wait. I hear her footsteps, then, "Don't wait out there. My gracious, you'll freeze to death." She opens the door. "Come right in."

I reach down to brush snow from my boots.

"Land sakes! Never mind that snow. Come in, so I can close the door."

I see her comings and goings reflected in the mirror-like surfaces of her kitchen stove and refrigerator and sink and tabletop; it's a kitchen that could be used as a Frigidaire ad in *The Saturday Evening Post*. She opens the oven door and pulls out a sheet of hot cookies, and the sugary-sweet aroma tempts my stomach. She wipes her hands on her apron and holds out a flowered plate. "Have a fresh cookie," she says. "Where are Nancy and Patty? Didn't they come?"

"They didn't come. Too busy, I guess." Actually, they have more courage than I do. I didn't want to come either, but I am here because I didn't dare stay home. Aunt Marion's generosity demands compliance, and to explain to her why I didn't come would be impossible. I unbutton my coat.

"Here. Have a cookie. I just made them," she says.

"I'll have one in a minute," I say. But to be polite—I'm sure she has made the cookies for me—I take one in my fingers and drag it up through the sleeve of my coat, and crumbs fall out onto the floor. I'm embarrassed and self-conscious. I wish Ma had made Nancy and Patty come, but they don't take to Aunt Marion's generosity toward me and begged to stay home.

"Goodness gracious. Take another cookie, and never mind the crumbs," Aunt Marion insists. "And come into the parlor."

Grandma is in the parlor seated in a stuffed chair with high arms that, like sideboards, constrain the muddle of books, magazines, newspapers, and writing paper strewed in her lap. "Why, hello Johnny. How are you?"

"Good, Grammy."

"Did you come alone? Where are your sisters?"

"It's just me. They're home." I know she will ask me more questions. She puts me on edge with questions every time I come.

"What are they doing?"

"Playing."

"Is your mother at home?"

Here it comes, quizzing me about Ma's doings. "Yes," I answer.

"Where's Grandpa?"

"He's at the store. Did you hear from your father today?"

"I don't know."

"I hope he's all right. I read in the paper that the Germans had attacked us in Belgium. Is he still in England?"

I'm uncomfortable here. There's a sweet smell of Christmas balsam in the air, but I imagine something else going on, something unknown to me. I wish Nancy and Patty were with me. "He was the last I knew," I say.

Aunt Marion interrupts Grandma before the next question. "Come and see my Christmas tree. Tell me if you like it."

Beyond Grandma, upright in the parlor window, stands the tree. Aunt Marion flicks on its colored lights. "There, what do you think?"

I am unprepared to describe what I see. Branches stretch upward to the ceiling, topped by a doll angel dressed in what looks like a satin wedding dress. Bubbly electrified candles, patterned hanging balls, elongated glass globes, and silvery affectation flaunt the tree's branches. Swoopy, sparkly garlands confine and embroider the tree, as if a kid has outlined its whorls with a glittery Crayola. Christmas presents, wrapped in paper with Santa Clauses and carolers and cozy, snow-covered houses in Camelot, lie at its base. I tiptoe around it over the rag-knit parlor rug while the angel keeps a watchful eye on my whereabouts.

"It's not quite finished," Aunt Marion says. "But I thought you'd like to see it."

Stunned, I say simply, "It's nice." But I initially think it perfect. She straightens a piece of garland. "Oh, do you *like* it?"

But her tree is *not* perfect, and in a moment another word comes to mind—gaudy. She has made the tree too gaudy. My mind spins, and I recall nearly a year ago when she tried to take the three of us away from Ma—for our own good she said then—and how Ma was hurt, how Nancy and Patty and I were frightened, and how Pa spent his furlough trying to reconcile the squabble. I wanted the hurt to be over, but now she stands here, like an idling locomotive with its latent power rumbling inside, dangling her dazzling Christmas tree and, I fear, plotting again to take us away from Ma. I'm frightened by her possessions and her intentions, and an earthly discomfort cloaks me like a cold blanket. I totter on the edge of sickness. I disguise my feelings, but I must get away. I tell Aunt Marion her tree is beautiful, but I have to go. I hurry past Grandma and the shiny white bathroom where, in the past, an ominous flush toilet—no privy here—has frightened me into rushing home rather than confront the surging water. I pass the oatmeal cookies and, coat in hand, scurry out the door.

I walk home slowly and absorb the fresh air; my fright disperses, and my resentment at Aunt Marion's possessions dissolves. I had never minded not having stuff at our house, possessions and accouterments and trappings and the like. Aunt Marion's Christmas tree looked elegant, I thought, and could be featured in *Good Housekeeping*, but it lacked personality. There was no evidence of caring human hands. Where were the homemade trinkets and the popcorn strings and the angel made of plain paper? It was too perfect. A thought came to me: Christmas is not about things, but about people; it's about people who express the joy of Christmas by finding the spirit. I needed to find the spirit, and then Christmas would come to our house, too. Pa wouldn't be there, but his star hung in the window, and he had promised he would make it up to us someday. That was good enough for me. I could hold my head up and forget my sorrow, but I would need Ma's help, and my sisters', too.

At home, Ma was still in the doldrums and roamed around the house in a daze. She bumped into furniture, forgot where she left things, stared out the window, and didn't hear us when we asked for milk or a sandwich or if we could go outside. She had no inspiration to decorate the house, tell Christmas stories, or sing carols. She didn't think we should celebrate, out of respect for Pa's absence I suppose. But I knew in my heart he wanted a happy Christmas for us, and I soon forgot my discontent.

I had put up a Christmas tree, but the spindly fir stood forlorn in the bay window absent any presents, its few ornaments, like unfertilized garden plants, sparse and dull. We had no wreath for the door or swags for the mantle or candles for the windows. Pa wouldn't like that, I thought, and Nancy, Patty, and I strung popcorn onto some of Pa's old fish line and draped it on the tree. We colored plain paper with red, green, and yellow crayons and glued together paper chains for garlands; we cut out paper snowflakes and hung them on the branches; we sliced foil wrappers for tinsel; we fastened cutout letters into a Merry Christmas banner and mounted it on the wall over the fireplace; we cut red-berried juniper in the pasture and tied it to a homemade wreath and hung the wreath on the front door; we tied pine cones to small fir boughs and placed them on the mantle. Eddie took Ma shopping for a Christmas ham, and soon Ma placed presents under the Christmas tree, and the spirit was at our house, too.

Christmas Day in 1944, unlike many other Christmases, is not blurred in my memory. Christmas in Temple, then, was a private matter celebrated by families alone. There were no cocktail or caroling parties, no community Christmas tree, no competition for the biggest toy.

Families shared the day privately and did not boast or exploit their doings. I suspect most folks exchanged gifts of necessity—knitted mittens and caps and sweaters—and perhaps a homemade wooden toy and, like us, spent their day inside, ate their Christmas dinners together, and waited for it to be over.

Ma, as she usually did, shooed us upstairs early on Christmas Eve. "Get to bed now. As soon as you go to sleep, morning will be here," she coaxed us.

Christmas morning we were up early, slept out and full of the gifting spirit, but for no reward. We needed to wait—a timeless truth—for Ma to be ready. She slept late, and midmorning came before she appeared at the bay window in the parlor. Grandpa C.F. came at about the same time, unusual for him who customarily visited us in the afternoon. After the presents were opened, he stayed for the ham dinner.

At dinner, in answer to a question from Ma, Grandpa said that Aunt Marion was not coming.

Surprise showed on Ma's face. "Oh?" she said.

"No," he went on, "she's not coming, and I don't like it either. Said she had presents for the kids and they should come down to see her and open them there."

A hurt look came on Ma's face, and she stammered, "But . . . but I . . ."

Grandpa's words go soft. "Probably they should come back down with me for a few minutes and humor her. I'll come back here with 'em. We'll pop some corn or play Go Fish."

Later, Aunt Marion greeted us at her door. "Why, Merry Christmas. Let me help you take off your coats."

We stepped into the parlor where the tree glittered in the front window and Grandma sat in a stuffed chair. I wished her Merry Christmas. Then Grandpa C.F. spoke through the pipe he held tight in his teeth. "They can only stay a few minutes. Their mother's home alone."

Aunt Marion threw him a look that would frighten a rock, and the tension in the room became tighter than if someone had farted. But she was not to be put off. She had wrapped gifts for Nancy, Patty, and me and set them under her garish tree for us to open.

"Here," she said and picked them up. "These are for you."

I don't recall now what was in the packages—I may not have remembered even for the time it took to walk home—nor do I recall ever revisiting those presents. Aunt Marion's Christmas gifts to us that year were conditional; they must be left at her house, and we must come there to play with them. We were too destructive for her niceties. No one would care for them at our house, she said, and they would be broken.

"I want you to have them for a long time," she wheedled us. "I'll take care of them for you."

I suspect we eyed and fingered them, perhaps even played with them for a few minutes before Grandpa C.F., to our grateful relief, said it was time to go. We offered Aunt Marion our thank-you's, as Ma had told us to do, and with Grandpa C.F. in tow, left empty-handed for home where Ma waited alone.

After Christmas, the doldrums stayed with Ma. Darkness, cold, and long days and nights wore her down. Letters from Pa, the person she loved most in the world, came infrequently. She didn't know where he was, except that he was moving toward war. She didn't know what to expect, except the worst. She often talked of never seeing him again. Understandably, her pessimism turned to fear. She listened to radio broadcaster Gabriel Heater and read the daily newspaper for war news. The *Lewiston Evening Journal* reported the Germans had launched a counterattack and threatened a breakthrough into Belgium and France, but Ma didn't know whether Pa was there. In his last letter, he had warned us that he could not say what he would be doing next but to expect a cable from him anytime. The days following extended into a week, and then another, without word.

I was the next to hear from him by way of a small package mailed in England. Inside were two embroidered handkerchiefs, a few English coins, and a postcard. The coins were a birthday gift for me sent six weeks early, he wrote on the postcard, in case he didn't get a chance later. And he reminded me that ten shillings equaled two dollars. He also asked me to take an embroidered handkerchief to Grandma and one to Aunt Marion. Ma thought he seemed worried.

"He must have been called to the front," she groaned. "Why else would he send you a birthday gift now? Your birthday is still two months away. Or an Easter gift for your grandmother?"

I agreed with Ma. Pa earned about thirty dollars a month in the European war zone paid in the currency of his locale. Since he had been paid on the last day of December, probably in French currency, he had no use now for pounds and shillings, and he had sent them to me.

The cable came a few days later and said that he had arrived in France safely. That's all. The cable didn't tell us whether his division was involved in the fight against the German counterattack. It didn't tell us whether his battalion would be firing their guns or whether he would be shot at or whether he would even be at the front. It was silent, except that he was in France. The cable didn't help Ma's worry.

Chapter Sixteen

WE ATTACK THE BASTARDS

More than once in interviewing veterans of the January fighting, when I asked them to describe the cold, men involuntarily shivered.

—Stephen Ambrose, *Citizen Soldiers*

W hile Pa dozed in the foggy and wet Southampton bivouac, LST #1001 floated empty at Royal Pier, its shadowy hull a threatening spectre. Since 1942, LSTs—jumbo-sized variations of Higgins landing craft—had delivered troops, tanks, artillery, vehicles, and combat paraphernalia to the shores of Africa, Italy, and France. LST #1001, built in the Boston Navy Yard and commissioned in June 1944, would carry Pa and Combat Command B across the English Channel to France.

He woke at first light in a misty soup that lay over Southampton Harbor. Word came to load the ship. All that day, January 6, 1945, Pa and the soldiers of Combat Command B transferred tanks, trucks, half-tracks, and 105-mm howitzers over slippery ramps into the tunnel-like hold of LST #1001. They worked fast, shouted instructions through the fog, and packed over two thousand tons of war armament onto the ship. Pa boarded at 10:00 P.M. in darkness and stored his gear.

He found a poker game and gambled recklessly. He quickly lost over two thousand francs, then looked for a place to sleep.

At dawn Sunday, LST #1001 was still tied to Royal Pier and cloaked in zero-visibility fog. Later, the ship steamed slowly into the outer harbor, dropped anchor, and waited for the fog to clear. Pa went to onboard church services and listened to a chaplain proffer hope and faith and ask God to bless their mission. Pa was unaccustomed to reverence. I had not known him to attend church, nor had I known him to believe he needed to. Perhaps he felt compelled by his circumstances to seek strength and courage and comfort for the dangerous times ahead. But I suspect that in the end, he and the others asked no more from heaven than to be fed and sheltered, to do their duty honorably, and to be alive for the voyage home.

At midday, the fog blew out and revealed more threatening weather. Nevertheless, the crew weighed anchor, and the LST steamed close by the Isle of Wight in the rain and entered the English Channel. It rolled deep into storm-driven sea-swells, white water deflected off the flat-ended bow, and sea spray flew onto the deck like snow. Coffee cups and food trays slid off mess-room tables. The troops stood up to fend off seasickness, staggered against bulkheads and stairways, puked into wastebaskets and toilet bowls, and collapsed on their bunks. Pa lay awake and listened to the worsening seas pound against the hull. They ploughed forward toward the coast of France and, as darkness enveloped them, watched the rain turn to sleet, then to snow.

The next morning they passed the harbor at LeHavre, the city invisible in the snowfall, and continued up the curvy Seine River into the fangs of a furious blizzard. The storm worsened, and wind and heavy snow lashed the deck and tore vehicles loose from their fastenings. Visibility fell to near zero, and one hundred kilometers upriver, they hove to and anchored in the Seine for Pa's third night on board.

Pa's first sign of the war's destruction came at gothic Rouen. American soldiers had driven the Germans from the city the previous

August, and its cobblestone streets and twelfth-century Norman buildings had suffered great damage. St. Vincent's Church had been reduced
to rubble, and Joan of Arc Square destroyed. The Cathedral of Notre
Dame, its immense towers barely visible in the swirling snow, showed
the pockmarks left by American B-17 bombing missions. From the rebuilt provisional docks at the city's waterfront, where the troops and armament of LST #1001 disembarked, Pa looked for the first time on the
sobering aftermath of the war.

At Rouen, they formed a convoy of tanks, trucks, artillery pieces,
and half-tracks and the next day moved overland to Rheims. The
weather turned sharply colder and snow fell hard. High winds, low visibility, and icy roads delayed the convoy's progress. They passed
through Gournay and Beauvais and Clermont and Compiègne, their
stone buildings and cobble streets broken and lined with rubble and, as
Pa wrote later, stove all to hell. They crossed long stretches of agricul-
tural land where snow flayed the convoy and forced frequent stops.
They arrived at Rheims in darkness and found shelter in open barns
nearby the city. Pa burrowed his sleeping bag into a pile of straw and
slept restlessly.

The next day, he drove sixty kilometers back to Soissons in the
storm for a truckload of gasoline, and on his return to Rheims took
shelter in the same barn. He wrote to Ma for the first time since leaving England.

On one side of one piece of paper, he told her what he could of his
whereabouts, that he was in France, and that he was in good health. He
wrote that he was comfortable in the subzero cold, had seen terrible
sights, and was ready to give Field Marshall von Rundstedt a dose of
his own medicine, recompense for the massive winter offensive in the
Ardennes. Finally, he noted that his mail had not reached him since he
left England. When he had finished his brief letter, he took shelter in
his sleeping bag and covered himself again with straw.

In Temple, whenever Ma received a letter, even though it lacked details, she perked up a bit and broadened her smile for a few days. But eventually the loneliness and dispirited thoughts returned, and she would dream of some disaster or believe something had happened to him and spread gloom about the house until another letter arrived—a letter that would reassure her once again that he was healthy and strong in spirit. Now, having heard from him directly from France, her spirits would soon grow.

In the cold barn, Pa huddled in his sleeping bag for an hour or two. At midnight, the column assembled and convoyed out of Rheims to the east toward Pont-à-Mousson. In darkness and blowing snow, the convoy moved slowly over unplowed and icy roads. The temperature reached fourteen degrees below zero. In the difficult driving, a self-propelled 105-mm howitzer slid off the icy surface, and the men worked in cold and snow to winch it back onto the roadway. Low on fuel, they bivouacked twenty-five kilometers from the front in shelled-out buildings occupied by the Germans the month before, while Pa drove another fifteen kilometers to Metz for a truckload of gasoline.

At Pont-à-Mousson, Pa left Combat Command B and went on to nearby Port sur Seille where Frank Pierce and the rest of his outfit, Service Battery 405th Armored Field Artillery, were billeted in open, wind-laced stone barns waiting for orders. Pa wasn't troubled by the cold and snowy weather. In Temple, in deeper snow and colder temperatures than those in Port sur Seille, he had learned to dress warmly and to keep dry. Now, in a French farmer's cow barn, he buried his sleeping bag in straw and waited for war.

Orders came, and the 8th Armored Division was attached to General Patton's U.S. Third Army and ordered to reinforce the front. Rumors were that a German attack on Strasbourg to the east would likely broaden into a large-scale counterattack. The news undoubtedly pleased Pa. At home, General Patton was deemed an American war hero, and now Pa was one of his soldiers.

In Port sur Seille, Pa's battery went on alert. To disguise their presence, they removed their uniform insignia, tore off stripes, and avoided saluting officers outdoors. They stored artillery shells in a World War I ammunition magazine and converted the Café de Seille to a field hospital. Pa received a new supply truck, a Studebaker two-and-one-half-ton truck with a roll-up canvas body cover, known in those years as the "deuce and a half," the most famous truck in America and Europe. He readied it for the battlefield: he removed markings that identified it as U.S. Army, whitewashed it, built sand-bagged walls inside the canvas cover, and mounted a .30-caliber machine gun on top of the cab.

Pa drove to Thiacourt for the battalion's mail, weeks old and full of Christmas greetings. He received twenty-three pieces—letters from Ma, Aunt Marion, Grandpa C.F., and hometown friends, a letter from me, a package from Ma, and several issues of *The Franklin Journal*. He nestled into his sleeping bag and slowly read the treasured letters. From Ma and Aunt Marion he got the news in Temple; from me a request for a new picture—one from the battlefield—and from Grandpa C.F., he read that the new heifer was doing fine at our place. Grandma wrote, too, and she had to keep filling her pen with ink to include all the family news. He read a typewritten note from Uncle Austin with news of Pa's cronies. In *The Franklin Journal*, he read war news of the battles on the German front. The Journal reported that Field Marshall von Rundstedt's winter offensive had reached its high-water mark in Celles, Belgium, and that the Germans were being attacked by General Patton's U.S. Third Army. He read thoroughly and looked for mention of the 8th Armored Division.

Pa, like every U.S. soldier in the war, had an important job to do, but he and the others were isolated from the war's grand scale. Orders came to capture a road junction at a spot on a map, fire the big guns at some map coordinates, deliver a load of ammunition to a firing battery, or drive a colonel to an observation post. They carried out their orders but couldn't see beyond their horizon. They didn't know the big picture; sometimes they didn't even know where they were. They listened to rumors and read the *Stars and Stripes* and *Yank, The Army Weekly* and tried to figure out what was happening.

Now, Frank walks into the barn's hay mow, and Pa looks up from the newspaper. "Hey Frank," he asks, "aren't we in the Third Army?"

"Yeah, El. That's what they told us."

"And aren't we in France?"

"As far as I know. What's up?"

"Well, listen. It says here in *The Franklin Journal* that the Third Army is in Belgium. It broke the German siege at Bastogne and saved the arses of the 101st Airborne Division and is battling now to trap von Rundstedt's army."

"Jeezus, El. That says we're in Belgium? Let me see that."

"Here, take a look," Pa says. "But I doubt if we're in Belgium. The guy in the café can't speak anything but French, and neither can his kid."

Frank reads a moment. "Hell," he exclaims, "this says Patton turned part of his Third Army around and attacked von Rundstedt. That must be why we got the hurry-up call. He wants us to hold the line here in case there's a counterattack."

"So what if it doesn't come?" Pa asks. "What do we do then?"

"We attack the bastards. Hold them right here. Or else they'll go help von Rundstedt."

"Keerist, Frank, how do you know all that?"

"I'm older than you, El. And wiser, too." Frank grins. "And one of the cooks told me General Patton had turned a couple of veteran divisions north to fight von Rundstedt in Belgium and we'd been sent over to take their place."

"Well, I'll be damned. You tell that cook he's right. It says so right here in *The Franklin Journal*."

In the next days, Pa drove his truck northerly thirty kilometers to Metz for gasoline and westerly to Pont-à-Mousson for rations. He then pushed farther west to Verdun, crossing the Moselle at Pont-à-Mousson, and brought back more gasoline. He drove to the ammunition supply dump at Pont-à-Mousson for artillery shells and southerly to Nancy for rations. He drove with confidence in truck convoys over the snowpacked, icy, wind-blown, hilly roads of Alsace-Lorraine. He called on the experience of having hauled heavy loads over the wintery roads of Temple. He felt secure in an insecure world. In Port sur Seille, he walked guard, cleared snow, and wrote home. And he waited.

He wrote to Grandpa C.F. that he was in France and had seen much devastation—bombed-out bridges, destroyed buildings, wrecked equipment and that the French people were in tough circumstances. He wrote of the harsh weather and that he was sleeping in an open barn. He did not complain that he was cold or that his living conditions were rough but instead expressed appreciation for mail and wrote that nothing was more welcome than mail from home. Had he been allowed to, he would have written that he was in General Patton's U.S. Third Army, the army Grandpa C.F. was reading about in *The Franklin Journal*. He would have given Grandpa C.F. the details: that 8th Armored Division had taken up position on the Siegfried Line—Germany's fortified West Wall—that they expected a German counterattack, and that he was on alert to go to the front with gasoline or ammunition. He would have made it clear to Grandpa C.F. that, for Pa, the war was about to happen.

On January 18, as expected, the elite German 11th Panzer Division mounted a strong tank-and-infantry counterattack against the 94th Infantry Division and recaptured Butzdorf and Nennig on the Siegfried Switch, an arm of the West Wall extending into the hills west of Orscholz, Germany. The 94th Division, strengthened by the addition of 8th Armored Division's Combat Command A, regained the two towns on January 24 and, led by CCA's tanks, mounted a drive to break through the Switch Line and capture the high ground at Sinz.

For five days of fighting in subzero temperatures and a winter storm, Pa drove his truck to the front. He drove to Nennig with winter clothing for the 94th Infantry, who were fighting ill-clad in frigid conditions, and he took battle-weary troops off the line to Pont-à-Mousson for hot showers.

When CCA's tank battalion had regained Nennig and Butzdorf and launched an attack against the revetments and through the minefields of the Siegfried Switch, Pa loaded his truck with gasoline, stored his bedroll behind the seat, and drove in a truck convoy through Butzdorf toward Sinz to the battle with the German panzers for the high ground. Snow fell hard, winds gusted, and temperatures stayed bitter cold. In Nennig and Butzdorf, snow built up in the roadway, and the trucks packed an icy-hard path to follow. Beyond Butzdorf, in the fields and orchards of the Siegfried Switch, snow blew across the roadway, gathered on the sides of the trucks, and froze. As the tanks battled for Sinz, Pa returned to Port sur Seille, reloaded, and climbed again past Butzdorf to the tank positions.

As Pa drove, he likely focused on the truck's gauges, as he had once told me a good driver must do. As the truck crawled over the curvy, snowpacked road, he likely recalled the days he trucked pulpwood off Derby Mountain and Wilder Hill in Temple. Surely, he called on all his past experiences in Temple's hills to cope with that severe winter storm.

On the fifth day of the battle, as snow continued to fall and build up in the roadway, gasoline and ammunition trucks could not reach the front. Combat Command A's M4 Shermans battled tank-to-tank with panzers to the outskirts of Sinz but were stopped there by heavy casualties and a lack of gasoline and ammunition. Pa loaded his truck and waited in Port sur Seille for the fierce weather to abate, but after midnight, dangerously low on gasoline and ammunition, CCA withdrew from the battlefield.

Although they failed to hold the high ground at Sinz, the 8th Armored Division had blunted the German counterattack toward Metz and kept the 11th Panzer Division from bolstering the forces at the Battle of the Bulge. But they were bloodied. Twenty-three men had been killed, and two hundred sixty-eight wounded. Six tanks had been destroyed, and four others disabled. They withdrew to Port sur Seille and Pont-à-Mousson where they found coal-heated rooms and passed the hours lying about and waiting for orders.

After the tank battle, in the shadowy light of a sealed-beam lamp, Pa wrote Ma that the weather had been stormy and quite a bit of snow had accumulated. He told her that for the first time in France he had slept the night before in an enclosed room, warmed by a coal fireplace. And he wrote that it was too good to last; he probably would be on the move again soon.

Orders came to move north, and Pa packed his duffel. German resistance at the Battle of the Bulge had disintegrated, and U.S. forces had advanced to previously held positions along the Siegfried Line. General Omar Bradley had reassigned the 8th Armored Division to the U.S. Ninth Army under the command of General William Simpson in Holland. Pa loaded his truck and waited.

He wrote to me on February 2, before he left Port sur Seille. The bitter cold and stormy weather had broken, and it had turned warmer. The snow had settled and melted on the south-facing hillsides, and roads were bare. The war looked good on all fronts, he wrote, and he predicted it might end in a few months. He felt buoyed by his service with General Patton's Third Army, and he was ready for more action. He included a sample of French money for my collection and sent his love to all of us. I, who from the beginning had wanted him to go and make me proud, felt validated. Pa was making history. As he predicted, the end of the war would come and perhaps soon, but not before the 8th Armored Division paid an even higher price in battle casualties.

They left on February 3 for Mheer in Holland. The convoy traveled in a warm rain and passed over tree-lined roadways that meandered through farm country and small French towns where villagers in faded frocks smiled and waved to them. Once-icy roads had turned soft and rutted. The rain had taken most of the snow, but dirty banks of it still lined the roadsides.

At Arlon in Belgium, they entered the oak and beech forests of the Ardennes where the Germans had attacked in the foggy December of 1944. At Bastogne, the scene of fierce Third Army fighting in the bitter January cold, they turned west over the fiercely contested ground of von Rundstedt's bulge to Marche-en-Famenne, then out of the forest again and north to the ruins of Leige where they stopped to rest. Pa and Frank eased their suffering on K rations and apples and pears and wondered what would be next. Pa supposed they were headed for the front, but what would happen there? Would the Germans mount another counterattack? Would Eisenhower order an invasion of Germany soon? How ferociously would the Nazis defend their homeland? Or would the German army, beaten back to its borders, surrender now to save its country from further destruction? The answers would come in time, they knew. But still they wondered.

Later, when they arrived in Mheer, the rain was still coming down. The drivers parked their trucks in an apple orchard, and the troops bivouacked in the shelter of nearby barns. Pa curled in his sleeping bag on a pile of straw and fell asleep, the first time in two days.

Chapter Seventeen
TEMPLE 1945

*I am certainly fortunate in having Marion and Lawrence and
C.F. to keep store for me.*

—Uncle Austin, February 1945

W e spent the cold, snowy winter of 1945 in near isolation.
February, the coldest month
in Temple in ten years, plagued us
with snow; fierce winds threw it
against the house, plugged the road,
and discouraged folks from trekking
into the village to visit.

Fern had gone north to Phillips,
and the people she had attracted
when she lived with us followed her
there. Eddie and Nellie, in a surprise
trip to West Farmington in the fall,
had married and no longer entertained in their kitchen or socialized
with their friends as they had before.
Lucille was still in South Portland,
and Anna, although at home on the

*The author and his two sisters,
Nancy and Patty, stand in a
snow-plugged Temple road in
January 1945*

intervale, wrestled with the difficulties of a crumbling marriage. Marguerite replaced Weston, who had left to serve in the Coast Guard, on the mail stage, and she failed to set aside time in her busy days for socializing. Ethyl and Wayne saw little entertainment in coming to visit us and stayed away. And so did Rachel. Wayne was seldom seen bringing wood or grain to our place in Pa's truck, and Wayne's helpers—Lester and John—wouldn't come without him. Eddie, true as always, came when we needed him. But on most days, except for Aino, Hilma, and Naimi, Ma's loyal Finnish friends, I saw no one chatting with Ma at the kitchen table, and no friends called to invite her to a Finnish steam bath or to the Saturday-night dance in Chesterville.

Pa's kin, except for Grandpa C.F., had taken haughty disinterest in Ma again. They could not avoid it, and Ma, now accustomed to their indifference, was resigned to live without their company. Since she believed they brought only trouble anyway, we passed our time alone and avoided agitating them. I spent my days at school with Nancy and Patty, and Ma spent hers at home by the fire. Evenings, we listened to *Blondie* and *Fibber McGee and Molly* and *Amos and Andy* on the Emerson. Ma tuned in to Gabriel Heater and wrote frequent letters to Pa.

One day, word trickled up Cowturd Lane that Uncle Austin, who had held off wearing a uniform, had lost out in his longtime mind game with the county draft board. Ma's eyes brightened, and a smile came on her face. She did not wish Uncle Austin trouble, she said, but like most folks in town, she felt that the burdens of war should be shared. Except for serving on the county draft board, Uncle Austin had not contributed much, certainly not an equitable share, given Pa's circumstances.

Uncle Austin received his call to the army in February 1945, the last man drafted from Temple. Aunt Viola groaned at the news and shed tears. I saw her at the store wiping her welled-up eyes, and I didn't know what to say. I knew I should feel sad and express some sympathy toward her, but I couldn't. I hadn't felt sad when Pa left; I thought it an honor to hang the blue star in the parlor window. Yet Aunt Viola, like Ma had been, was understandably alarmed that Austin was headed for danger and distressed at being left alone with considerable undertakings to look after. She and Uncle Austin were parents of four-year-old Diane, and another baby was due in the summer. Since their marriage, Uncle Austin had kept animals, managed woodlots, hired workers, and run the general store, duties that required his constant attention. In his absence, the care of his enterprises would fall to Aunt Viola, a burden she perhaps did not embrace but one she could have predicted had earlier town gossip come within earshot.

Until he received his draft notice, Uncle Austin had not contemplated that he would ever be a foot soldier. Folks in town had talked in their kitchens of the prospects of him being drafted, but word circulated that he had other more lofty goals. When Pa left in 1943, as Fern told it, Aunt Marion had declared that Austin would not be drafted at all but would be commissioned an officer. God forbid, Fern had smirked, that he would have to wallow around in the mud with other soldiers. But Ma credited the comment to Aunt Marion's puffed-up perception of Uncle Austin, not to any desire by Austin to wear an officer's hat.

The talk continued, however, and soon Aunt Marion broadcast that Uncle Austin had enlisted in the navy. But in February 1944, Fern brought news from the general store that he had been deferred from military duty. In March, the word was that doctors had detected pus on Uncle Austin's lungs, and he had flunked an army physical. In May, Ma heard that he had passed a navy physical in Portland, and, excited by the news, she quickly wrote to Pa that, at last, Austin was in and would leave in August. But he wasn't in at all. The navy, which had lowered the maximum age for enlistees, disqualified him and placed him back in the draft pool, and folks in Temple stopped speculating on the prospect of Austin ever leaving.

But the county draft board was not finished. In February 1945, fif-

teen months after Aunt Marion had awarded him an officer's commis-
sion and just when folks in town, including Aunt Viola, had reconciled
themselves to his staying in Temple, Uncle Austin's draft number came
up. He endured an army physical in Portland and, absent any sign of
pus on his lungs this time, was immediately put aboard a Boston and
Maine passenger train for the induction center at Fort Devens,
Massachusetts. Four days later, he received a forty-hour pass and traveled home in his freshly pressed army uniform to say good-bye to his
family.

The family reacted straight away and mobilized to keep his dealings
going while he served. Aunt Marion and Uncle Lawrence shared clerk-
ing at the store. Postmaster Grandpa C.F. helped out, too, which
pleased me to no end because he served in good measure over the candy
counter. Uncle Phil, Austin's out-of-town older brother, looked after

the logging and haying crews, and
Aunt Marion, town treasurer, covered for his duties in the town office.
Helping one another came easy to
them, and when Aunt Viola cut
down her workload in the weeks before the baby was born, they picked
up their pace. Though Ma was
miffed at the quick response by
family forces, she admitted they
should be helpful, but accused them
of being unaware of her hurt. She
spilled out her irritation in a letter to
Pa and reasoned that it would obviously be best for her to just ignore
them. I could see, however, that she
had attained a measure of satisfaction in knowing Uncle Austin was

*Uncle Austin stands in
his driveway in his new army
uniform in February 1945*

finally wearing an army uniform—at Fort Bragg, no less.

Pa wrote Ma and expressed surprise that he was training at Fort Bragg and not at a navy station. He wrote that Austin would surely dislike army life but held out hope that he would recall Pa's earlier advice—some like the army and some don't; it's better to like it—and resolve to see it through. But as expected, Uncle Austin found Pa's advice hard to accept and confessed he'd rather be running the store. He wrote Pa that he was not enamored with army life and, unlike Pa, he couldn't take any satisfaction from soldiering. He longed to be in Temple where he said they needed him. More likely, he needed Temple.

Uncle Austin's absence affected many folks in town, and much of the conversation around the woodstove in the days following his exit centered on whether the board should have drafted such a critical figure. He had been generous with goods on credit and had personally overcome the beer shortage in town by trucking Krueger, Harvard, Pabst, and Genesee directly from Auburn in his own truck. Now folks doubted whether beer would be regularly available and whether the store would continue to offer goods on credit.

Loggers, especially, feared Uncle Austin's absence. When deep snow kept them out of the woods, they usually spent their afternoons nursing a quart of Krueger and, without work, needed a credit slip at the store to eat supper. The Finns, too, feared his absence. He had helped them in many ways: to find work, to fill out their annual alien registration forms, and to write letters. They would need to look elsewhere—to town officials, postmaster Grandpa C.F., or Grandma, who had taught them English years before—for assistance.

Uncle Austin's absence also touched town government. He held a public office—excise tax collector—and the annual report of revenues was due. More so, town meeting was coming up, and selectmen had usually taken advantage of his accounting skills to balance the town books. They now found it necessary to call on Aunt Marion, town treasurer, to finish Uncle Austin's work on time and save them from the embarrassment of publishing an incomplete and incomprehensible year-end report at town meeting.

Town meeting was held in March, during mud season, when farmers and loggers were idled by lingering snow and rutted logging roads and had time to contemplate the affairs of Temple. On the town calendar, the year ended in February and at the soon-to-follow meeting, folks could review the past year and not be overly late in making changes for the year ahead.

Town meeting, unlike the social camaraderie of a softball game or a box social, was thought by many to be the paramount act of rural independence, an act of community self-expression usually reserved for the individual. It was a daylong affair, and time was suspended for folks to assemble and fulfill their public duty. A town official lit a woodstove the night before to warm the meeting room. Men finished their morning chores early, and women brought casseroles and breads to serve for lunch. The general store closed for the day. At the Village School, Mrs. Stolt issued instructions for grades five through eight to go to the meeting, sit in the back row, and not make any noise. And she directed us to keep notes of what happened and bring a report to school the next day.

On town-meeting day, in company with eight schoolmates, I walked across town to the Grange Hall. Temple didn't have a town hall: we used the Grange Hall—where dusty images of former masters of the Temple Grange hung on the walls—for town meetings, potlucks, box socials, and entertainment. Years earlier, when I was barely old enough to be in the audience, Ken MacKenzie and his troupe of cowboy singers from radio station WCSH in Portland had come there. They had arrived late, and when MacKenzie took the stage with his guitar, he apologized and told the crowd he had driven ninety miles an hour over rough country roads—twenty miles an hour horizontally and seventy miles an hour up and down—to try to get to Temple on time. The audience guffawed at MacKenzie, and I suspect some folks in town now would say town meeting was entertainment, too. But to me, it took on the appearance of serious business. Sober-faced men and women gathered to conduct the town's affairs and to approve a budget for the next year. They came ready to discuss matters of business, matters of controversy, and matters important to them and their town. I took my school notebook to keep track of the doings for Mrs. Stolt.

I sat in the back row. Folks streamed into the crowded room, greeted their neighbors, and picked out seats. They sat in rows of wooden chairs and faced a head table of town officers—selectmen, treasurer, clerk—and a discussion leader. A knot of town-meeting veterans sat around the woodstove and leaned back in their chairs. Small groups of men stood in the aisle and talked, and women chatted with each other over the backs of their seats. They streamed in until the room was full and every chair was taken.

The townsfolk conducted their business in categories: roads, schools, and elections of town officials. For roads, they chose to spend more money than the selectmen recommended, an unlikely occurrence, I thought, in our cash-strapped town but one that was deemed necessary. Folks had grown tired of dusty and washboardy travel, and they wanted to tar some village roads and part of the busy intervale road and voted to do so. And they voted to pay laborers local men available for part-time work—fifty cents an hour to cut roadside bushes, to spread sand onto freshly sprayed tar, and to shovel snowdrifts out of snow-plugged outback roads.

They were, however, more reticent with school spending and voted to spend less than the year before. Attendance at the Intervale School had dropped to seven students, and the school committee, when asked by the state Department of Education, had agreed to close it and consolidate the classes in the Village School. Townspeople had argued whether it should be kept open. Some had wanted it open for their convenience and because the Intervale School was the oldest school in town and a local landmark. Others agreed that closing it made sense and saved money. At town meeting, the voters took note that the new budget was two hundred dollars less than the previous year and quickly approved it. I made a note for Mrs. Stolt. She would want to know whether she could buy chalk and arithmetic paper for next year, and I would be able to report that the recommended spending had been approved, but not to expect any more.

Folks deliberated longer over the election of town officers. First Selectman Hanson Bailey had announced some weeks before that he would not be a candidate for reelection. Several men—Elmer Knowles, Rueben Campbell, and perhaps Joe Bergeron—were rumored to be interested in being elected. Some were nominated. In addition, John Palmer, a West Farmington real estate salesman who barely lived in Temple and seldom came to the village, was nominated for election to the town's highest office. In the discussion preceding the vote, one person questioned how long John Palmer had lived in town and if he understood Temple well enough to be a selectman. Someone else stated he would make a fine selectman; others spoke on behalf of their own candidates. Voters wrote their choice on slips of paper and slid them folded into the ballot box. A few voters had written their choice before the meeting, or another person had written it for them, and they simply retrieved it from their pocket and put it in the box. John Palmer was elected.

Uncle Lawrence, who had served as selectman for several years, was nominated for reelection to the board without any controversy. It was said he had done a good job, was fair, and always answered the complaints of townsfolk promptly. He and Harry Blodgett, who was also reelected to the board, were both longtime veterans of public affairs in Temple and would continue their steady influence on the town for another year. I wrote their names in my notebook for Mrs. Stolt.

The voters also took up the election of a new school committee. I didn't know the particular duties of a school committee, but I knew Mrs. Stolt would likely have a great interest in who served on one.

Someone nominated Old Carr to the committee. At that point, he stood up: the same cantankerous and gruff Old Carr who lived next door to me, kept a well-to-do garden, grumbled at cow turds in the road, carped at loud noise, and yelled at my sisters and me when rocks sailed over the fence and landed on his roof; the same Old Carr who, when Pa was away, sent us thoughtful Christmas gifts and wrote Pa letters about Temple doings. He would accept the job of school committee member if he were elected, he said, but only if the voters understood that he wanted a first-rate school in which school kids behaved and learned straightforward stuff like reading and conduct.

"I'm not satisfied," he growled. "Them kids are at the schoolhouse breakin' windahs with baseballs, drawin' pitchahs, and memorizin' multiplication tables. That's not learnin'. I want them to learn behavior and to mind their manners and to respect older folks, not just sit there all day and listen, then on the way home forget what they heard and start yellin' and bangin' and throwin' things around again."

Good gosh, I thought, he's talking about me, and I slumped in my seat. I was afraid of him and kept away from his place except when Ma wanted me to take a pound of butter to Mrs. Carr. I didn't know Mrs. Carr, didn't know she existed until I first took butter to her. She was pleasant to me, but while I was there, I didn't take my eyes off Mr. Carr and was well-mannered toward him—yes sir, no sir, I will, sir. It was a good thing I was, too; in town meeting Old Carr stood up and scolded me. And not just me. Bent forward, leaning on his cane, his lower jaw jutted forward as if a precursor to his words, he went on to reprimand the rest of the kids—and Mrs. Stolt too.

"They don't learn nothin', not a one of 'em. What they need is a good old-fashioned schoolmarm who'll make 'em toe the line, learn readin' and writin' and 'rithmetic, not a lot of nonsense. I know if I was teachin', I'd pound some sense into 'em, and I wouldn't start with their brains neither,"—he whacked his cane on the floor—"but I'd work up to 'em."

This is going to be huge stuff to report to Mrs. Stolt, I thought, and I wondered who would dare do it. But, of course, I reasoned, Leo would. Leo would tell her anything—and then laugh. I made a note in my notebook. Old Carr had worked hard for a better town, and folks respected him, but surely his election to the school committee foretold ill for a peaceful classroom. If he got his way, I thought, learning would be disrupted and a satisfying school day would be scarce.

Toward the end of the meeting, the discussion leader brought up an item to erect a monument to the veterans of the war. Although the war wasn't over, the end would likely come before the next town meeting. Someone asked if names would be engraved on it and was told yes, that was the purpose, an honor roll of those from Temple who had served in the armed forces during the war. I smiled, sat up on the edge of my chair, and listened carefully. If they build a monument, I thought, Pa's name will be on it.

No money, however, was included in the next year's budget for an honor roll. Someone asked how much the monument would cost and how would we pay for it. Mark Mosher, as was his custom when it was time for well-deserved spending in Temple, stood and said a monument was little enough for our boys, and that we should set aside one hundred fifty dollars to put it up. I liked what he said, and so did the voters, and the money was added to the town's budget for the next year.

Though my town meeting notes were brief, I captured the essence of budgets and expenses and committees and town doings—mainly roads and schools. Conservative and independent townsfolk did not waver from applying just enough government to provide serviceable roads and furnish a basic education for those who lived in Temple. And in addition, the town honored its soldiers. I made my report to Mrs. Stolt the next day, and she expressed pleasure at what I had learned. Thankfully, she did not catch the concern I felt about Old Carr being on the school committee and went on teaching in her proven manner. Town meeting, for me, had offered a brief respite from the dreary winter school term, but at our place on Cowturd Lane, it had not interfered with either our daily tedium or our persistent blahs.

Ma's days that winter seemed lifeless. She did not go to town meeting. She wore a housedress and stayed home and ironed clothes. She seemed unwilling to be out with other folks in general and Pa's family, who played a sizable role in town affairs, in particular. She would see us off to school and wait for us to come home. At lunchtime, she would send me to the store for a can of soup and a loaf of bread rather than walk there herself. She was sad and listless, moody and quiet. She brooded deeply over her circumstances and yearned to be elsewhere. She shunned events and avoided interruption in her humdrum routine, except when sudden happenings she could not duck came her way.

Early one morning, soon after town meeting, we gather in the kitchen. In a scene that is much the same every morning, Nancy places breakfast dishes on the oilcloth, I look for my boots or a sweater or a schoolbook, and Patty dresses for school in the warmth of the woodfire.

Someone asks, "Can we eat now, Mommy?"

"In a minute," Ma answers.

Dawn begins to stream in the kitchen window, and soon sunlight reaches the treetops at the edge of the pasture. A dusty overhead light bulb casts its last shadow of the night behind two unwashed glasses and one empty beer bottle sitting on the kitchen counter. We wait for breakfast close to the Glenwood and anticipate the promised warmth of daylight.

Ma hears it first. A thump.

She puts a finger to her lips, "Shhsss."

Then, more thumps, and rattles and grunts.

"Did you hear that?" she asks.

We look at each other. I heard it but wish I hadn't.

Ma opens the door to the shed. Not five feet away with both front feet up on the steps into the kitchen and looking at her is the hog.

Behind him, what was once a nest of tin pails rolls around the shed floor. Behind the pails, the open gate of the hog's winter quarters swings free.

"Oh my God! The pig! The pig is loose! Shoo, shoo." Ma does the only thing she knows how to do. She slams the door. "How are we ever going to get him back in his pen? He's too big. What will we ever do?"

Pa had bartered for the pig when he was home on furlough. A baby Chester White with droopy ears and a tightly spiraled tail, he'd weighed barely fifteen pounds when Pa brought him home. "Here, this is yours, Johnny. Feed him every day. He'll grow," he had said, and put the little pig in the outside pen.

I fed the pig faithfully each night, a sloppy concoction of some kind of grain mixed with cooked food scraps and milk. In November, we had moved him inside to a makeshift pen in a corner of the woodshed. He gained more than a pound every day and grew into a hog—and more. Ma deemed him a menace and had grown wary of sharing the same house with him.

Ma was nervous about all the animals in our barn. She felt exposed to the constant likelihood that something would go wrong: Ted Campbell wouldn't show up to milk the cows, a cow would be sick, the fickle chickens would escape, or the hog would break out of his pen and injure someone. The fearsome hog, now two hundred pounds heavier than when Pa had carted him home, weighed two times more than Ma, and she fussed that she couldn't manage him. She had written to Pa that the little pig was now a big hog and getting bigger. She wrote again that she feared she couldn't move him to his outside pen come spring.

Now, paralyzed with fright, she stands here and listens to him grunt and snort, kick empty pails around the shed, and threaten to charge into her kitchen. "You kids get on your way to school," she says. "I'll figure out something."

Nancy and Patty reject any kinship to the hog and won't go near it.

But since Pa brought it home for me to care for, I feel a responsibility. I need to show Pa I can look after it.

"Let me help," I say to Ma. I go outside, dash around the shed and the barn in the snow, and make sure all the doors are closed and latched. Back in the kitchen, I take broom in hand and face the shed door.

"Be careful," Ma says, and she opens the door.

I step into the shed and swing the broom. "Shoo. Shoo. Get back in your pen, you dumb pig." But he has other ideas and grunts instead into the barn where the cows dwell and gnaw their cud and the heifer munches hay. Fearful of upsetting the cows, I retreat to the kitchen, make the hog a breakfast, and leave it in his pen with the gate open. Broom in hand again, I circle the barn in the snow, enter the back door, and chase him toward the shed. "Shoo. Shoo," I shout. The hog understands me, but he prefers freedom to food and is willing to challenge me for it. I shy away from his belligerent mood and retreat to the kitchen. I am no match for that wallowing mass of pork chops and ham. I go to school. Ma calls Eddie for help.

After school, I tackle my barn chores, including slopping mush to the hog, which, thanks to Eddie, is now securely penned. I am in the shed when Ma opens the door.

"I'll feed the pig tonight," she says.

"No, Mommy. I'll do it. I want to do it. And I'll make sure his pen is closed when I'm done."

"Not just closed," she says, "but latched, too."

"Yes," I tell her. "I will." But, I think, if I provoke him he's hefty enough to wallow through that flimsy slabwood pen any place he chooses.

The hog watches me fill the woodbox, a job Pa has forever reminded me to do, even while he's soldiering. I never get a break from it, and I burden myself with finishing it first every afternoon just to have it done. On the other hand, I have fun tending the calf. When I feed her, she nuzzles me, and I hug her. I spread dry chaff for her to sleep on and hang around and chat a minute. I feed the chickens cracked corn, but they don't know me or thank me or care that I exist. I feed them quickly and carefully, not to rattle them. Otherwise they will flutter, and I'm not keen on commotion when I work with Pa's livestock.

I make the hog wait. Even though I don't admit it to Ma, I am fearful of its power. But more compelling to me than my fear is Pa's expectation that I will care for it. I don't open the gate, not this night. I pour his slop over the slabwood fence into his feedbox and back away without speaking. My hog problems were over a few days later when Ma traded the grunter to Eddie for a cord of firewood—we didn't fatten ourselves on bacon and ham, but we were warm.

The commotion over the hog was only a brief interruption in Ma's gloomy existence. She measured the length of that lonesome winter by the intervals between Pa's letters to her, which arrived more and more infrequently. She knew he wouldn't be home until Germany was thoroughly beaten on the battlefield, and probably not for some time after that. She was alone and frightened, and his infrequent letters offered only momentary solace. Scared he would not come home at all and fretful he would hear some fallacious gossip about her doings, Ma kept out of sight of the townsfolk, but isolation darkened her days. And her gloom foreshadowed troubling times ahead.

Chapter Eighteen
THE BIG PUSH

We're making history here right now.
—Pa, March 1945

T he Allied forces gathered at the Roer River. They came from Britain and France, Holland and Belgium. They came on foot. They came in trucks and half-tracks and armored personnel carriers and railroad cars. They came to the Roer's west bank, to Julich and Linnich and Posterholt, to Hilfarth and Hulhoven and Heinsberg. First to arrive was the 102nd Infantry Division, which for two months had battled its way to the river from Holland, then in December captured Linnich inside the German border and dug in. Next, the 29th Division came to the river in a motor march after von Rundstedt's attack in the Ardennes and kept pressure on the Siegfried Line while the Allies fought the Germans in the bulge.

More troops came: The 84th Infantry and the 30th Infantry, Old Hickory, came in trucks and personnel carriers from the Battle of the Bulge; the 35th Division, the Santa Fe, arrived by train from the Vosges; and last, from the snow-covered hills of Alsace-Lorraine, the 8th Armored Division, the Thundering Herd, came in half-tracks and trucks in the rain and joined the earlier comers at the river. Six divisions—five infantry and one armored—stretched fifty kilometers along the west bank of the Roer River in the north of Germany near the border with Holland. Behind them four more divisions—two infantry and two armored—stood in reserve. Altogether they composed the U.S. Ninth Army of 150,000 soldiers. Across the Roer to the east lay the fertile river valleys and flatlands of the North German Plain. Berlin was five hundred kilometers distant. The Ninth would soon invade the enemy's heartland.

Under the command of Lieutenant General William Simpson, the U.S. Ninth Army kept fit and trained and waited for the order to cross the Roer River. They drilled in rubber rafts for an infantry assault. They practiced driving tanks and trucks and half-tracks on dryland treadways. They attached bulldozer blades to M4 Sherman tanks and assembled materials to build bridges and lobbed artillery shells across the Roer. And when they were ready, they moved into the line and kept a vigil on the river.

Pa, after the long motor march from Port sur Seille, spent a hapless first day in Mheer. An hour after dawn, Frank found him in his sleeping bag on a pile of straw. "Jeezus, El. Wake up."

"Huh? Whatizit?"

"Every goddam truck we put in the orchard last night is stuck in mud, all of 'em. The rain took the frost out, an' they sunk in the goo an' won't move. You better get your ass up and get out there."

"Damn, Frank. I need some coffee and scrambled eggs. You gathered eggs yet this morning?"

"I ain't kiddin', El. Come see."

"Frank, it's raining like hell. We can't go out there."

"C'mon, we need ya."

Pa pulled on combat boots, slid an olive-drab poncho over his head, and joined the battery. All day, they used half-tracks and winches to wrench the supply trucks out of the miry orchard onto solid ground. In the afternoon, the rain stopped, and they took off their ponchos and

field jackets and worked faster. Pa could hear the distant rumble of artillery fire and the hoarse moan of half-tracks and trucks moving troops
and supplies to the front, and once came the harsh drone of a missile
overhead. He looked up. "What the hell . . . ?"

"Jeezus, get down!" someone yelled. "It's an 88!" Pa shuddered at the
notion of the gruesome German 88-mm artillery piece.

"No. That ain't a 88," someone else said. "I've heard a 88, and that
ain't it."

"Look! There it is. Up yonder. See it?"

Pa looked, and an unmanned German V-1 rocket droned westerly
at four hundred miles an hour, a one-ton warhead in its nose. There
soon came another, then another.

"Where they headed?"

"Goddam if I know. Antwerp pro'bly, maybe London. Who
knows?"

Pa watched and listened. "They told us," he muttered to no one in
particular, "that the engine shut down before it dove to the ground." He
listened carefully until the last one had droned out of earshot.

In the days that followed, the weather cleared and turned warm.
Soon the division loaded onto trucks and moved into the line on Ninth
Army's left flank. They convoyed to the front under threatening skies,
and a short, heavy rain fell. The mud-covered road was heavy with traffic, and the convoy moved slowly, following the directions of MPs at
road junctions and passing stockpiles of rations, gasoline cans, and
stores of ammunition. The sounds of war came closer.

At the front, the British 7th Armored Division, the famous "Desert
Rats" of the North African campaign, sat packed and loaded and ready
to move out. The 8th Armored Division moved into their place in the
line near Posterholt and took up positions northerly for four kilometers
and faced the Roer River to the east. The British Second Army sat on
their left, the U.S. 35th Division on their right. Farther north, left of
the British Second, the Canadian First Army took position on the

River Maas. British Field Marshall Bernard L. Montgomery, who had aggravated American generals with his immodest tendency toward self-glorification, commanded the three armies poised there—the 21st Army Group—and would issue the order to attack across the river.

Pa called it the start of the big push, but in February 1945 the attack was known officially as Operation Grenade. In preparation, the 405th Armored Field Artillery Battalion emplaced its gun batteries at Heinsberg, five kilometers south of Posterholt overlooking the Roer, and from under camouflage netting supported on wooden poles lobbed artillery shells into Germany. Pa's battery quartered in abandoned houses in Saffelen, Germany, six kilometers back from the river. In night convoys, he trucked ammunition over the scarred and rutted road from the Sittard supply depot in Holland to the firing batteries at Heinsberg.

A truck in the convoy detonated a land mine, and combat engineers probed with bayonets and magnetic detectors and disarmed the mines they found. The engineers repaired failed sections of roadway, constructed short bypasses, and patrolled the road constantly to keep it in passable condition. As Pa drove in the darkness, the rumble of artillery echoed in the German night, and he could see the flash of the howitzers as they launched artillery shells over the river. To him, Ninth Army must have seemed invincible, and he likely wondered how far the big push would take him.

For ten nights, the 405th fired their howitzers across the river and punished German defenders on the opposite side. Considered the workhorse gun of the Allied ground war in Europe, the 105-mm self-propelled howitzer could shell enemy positions up to ten kilometers distant, or, in close-up warfare, fire directly at the enemy on the front lines. At Heinsberg, the howitzer's long-range firepower kept the Germans under cover at night and thwarted attempts to reinforce their front.

In Saffelen, when Pa's battery was not hauling ammunition and supplies to the firing stations, soldiers rested and attended to their circumstances. They foraged for wine and potatoes and turnips in the cellars of deserted houses. They killed a cow with an M-1 carbine, wrung the necks of chickens, and ate hot meals from a field kitchen fitted to the back of a supply truck. Pa rummaged the village for souvenirs but kept to roads and streets declared free of mines and avoided poking around in yards and houses and places where retreating Germans had likely planted booby traps. He hid from the Luftwaffe's "Bed Check Charlie," who made daily reconnaissance flights over the town, and noted V-1 rockets as they streaked across the sky toward Antwerp or London. He focused on their harsh drone, familiar to him as a meter of relative safety, until it had passed overhead and disappeared westward. One day a V-1 engine stopped in flight above the town.

"Duck!" someone shouted. "It's coming at us!"

"Holy shit!" They took to the cellar. The V-1 veered, plummeted nose first, and struck outside the town, scattering debris into nearby streets.

He drove to the front at night; he slept—and played poker—during the day. "You know," he said to the cardplayers, "we gotta get the hell out of this town. They've figured out where we are. I don't need to be a goddam kraut target."

"You still in, El. How many cards?"

"What's the bet? Two what? Is it reichsmarks or what? Gimme three."

"Three it is."

"Just this one time . . . Just this once," Pa muttered. He dropped two marks onto the tabletop and looked at his cards. "Damn!"

"Another hand, El?"

"Not me. I gotta save some money to send my boy. He's got a money collection I been sending him." And Captain Brockenboug from battalion headquarters wants to go up to the lines. Says he needs to go to the observation post. I gotta go find a jeep and take him."

Pa drove Brockenboug over the rutty road to Heinsberg. The wheels splashed mud and spattered the windshield, and Pa drove slower.

At the firing stations, Brockenbourg watched the 405th's batteries launch shells eastward over the flat, featureless terrain across the river. "What the hell are we firing at anyway?" he yelled.

"Numbers on a map, I think, sir."

"Let's go to the OP."

Pa drove into Heinsberg where they climbed to the top floor of a cut-stone building and found a forward observer surrounded by maps, radios, and binoculars.

The observer saluted. "We're firing at coordinates, sir. Can't see well enough to know what's over there, but I get reports of troops movin' and tanks comin' up to the line and bunkers bein' built, and we fire at 'em." He dragged on a cigarette with his hand cupped around the hot ash. "I couldn't tell you who we're hurtin'. I just send the stuff where somebody wants it."

"Thanks. Let's go, Private. See if we can find a bridge."

Pa drove upstream ten kilometers to a slight rise behind Hilfarth where Captain Brockenboug stood up in the jeep and looked through binoculars into the village.

"Bridge looks okay to me," he told Pa. "But we should capture the sonofabitch before they blow it."

Pa turned the jeep and drove downstream. The road was narrow and muddy, and fallow fields bordered both sides. He drove to Posterholt on the Dutch border five kilometers north of Heinsberg. The Germans had destroyed the bridge, and Brockenboug searched for roads and crossing sites suited for assault boats and pontoon bridges. The land was low and wooded and saturated, and he took note of the troubles the division would find if they approached the river in force.

At normal flow, the Roer below Duren was a placid river fifty or so meters wide and not a formidable barrier to an attacking army. In the

Ninth Army sector, however, it had overflowed its channel—more than four hundred meters in some places—and saturated the soft, loamy land. Below the Dutch border, forests lined the river.

The ground conditions alarmed Brockenboug. "I tell you, Private, the assault will destroy these goddam roads. They'll be impassable to the artillery train and the reserve units and the service companies behind the attacking divisions. If the krauts fight back, we could get bogged down right here."

They went back to the observation tower at Heinsberg, and Captain Brockenboug scanned the river valley with his binoculars. He then looked at Pa. "That's all. Let's go home. We'll be ready when the water goes down."

Soon word passed that the assault across the river was delayed. The Germans had captured the Roer River dams upstream at Schwammenauel, destroyed the control valves, flooded the river plain in front of Montgomery's 21st Army Group, and forced a postponement. Montgomery would wait for the floodwaters to recede.

While Pa waited, he wrote home. He told us that he was somewhere in Germany and there was no need for us to worry. He did not report his doings, what town he was in, or where he was headed. In a letter to Grandma, who had longed to visit Europe before the war broke out, he listed where he had been; such touristy places as London, Rheims, Metz, Nancy, and Leige would have likely kindled a bit of envy in her had circumstances been more peaceful. Except that he wrote that he was in Germany, he could as well have been down the road and I wouldn't have known the difference from reading his letters to Ma or me. Later he would write that he was in the U.S. Ninth Army, but by that time the doings of the Ninth would be so well known to anyone reading *The Franklin Journal* or *Lewiston Evening Journal* that I could have written to *him* the places they had fought.

In Saffelen one night, Pa was writing a letter to me when he heard a German 88 scream over his head and explode behind the town.

"What the hell," he muttered, and then he heard another screaming his way. "Jeezus, what time is it?" He looked at his watch, 8:00 P.M.

"What the hell is goin' on?" he yelled.

The sergeant called them out. "We gotta get to the front and load out the surplus ammo stockpiled there. The Krauts are throwing stuff at us from across the river, and their patrols have penetrated the front. The sonsabitches might attack us."

Pa drove to Heinsberg in a convoy of six trucks. At the firing stations four hundred meters from the river, the artillery batteries fired 105-mm shells at the enemy. Pa could hear mortars coughing and the snap of small-arms fire nearer the river. The men worked fast, anxious that they were under attack. When the trucks were loaded, they moved out in the darkness and at dawn pulled into the Sittard supply depot. The German threat was put down, and later the sergeant ordered them to resume night deliveries.

Following the German uprising, Pa's Service Battery moved to Susteren, Holland, a one-church village in the flatlands farther to the rear near the German border. Pa quartered in a Dutch home where buzz bombs and 88s didn't drop into the backyard and where a friendly Dutch couple offered a hot shower, served warm food, and furnished a soft bed where he could sleep without being awakened by "Bed Check Charlie." There he finished the suspended letter to me. He tucked in some German money for my collection and, of course, reminded me to keep the woodbox filled. By then the front had stabilized, and after Pa had posted the letter, he resumed ammunition deliveries to the firing batteries.

The attack by Field Marshall Montgomery's 21st Army Group—Operation Grenade—kicked off at 2:45 A.M. on February 23. Ninth Army's big guns fired first and threw the greatest concentration of artillery fire yet seen in the war across the Roer. At 3:30 A.M., infantry crossed the muddy, swirling river in rubber rafts and established a bridgehead. Combat engineers, working under a cover of smoke, floated a steel footway on pontoons and infantry streamed across the river and reinforced the bridgehead. On the opening day, armored battalions on the west bank fired tank guns, rockets, and heavy mortars to back up the infantry, and two thousand artillery pieces lobbed forty thousand tons of explosives into the German defenses. Army aircraft flew bombing and strafing missions, and later that night, M4 Sherman tanks crossed on pontoon treadway bridges, and the Ninth Army rolled into Germany.

All through the assault, the 405th Armored Field Artillery fired their howitzers from the Heinsberg firing stations. The day before, Pa had trucked shells from the Sittard supply depot until midnight, and he began again at dawn on the day of the assault. The ammunition trucks labored under heavy loads and turned the Sittard-to-Heinsberg Road into muddy goo; combat engineers were constantly called upon to bulldoze the glop aside and smooth out the road. When the barrage ended and tanks were crossing the river, Pa returned to Susteren. Frank was there. "Hey, Frank," he called out. "This is it, isn't it?"

"I guess ta hell." Frank took a cigarette from a pack of Lucky Strikes, offered one to Pa, and lit them both.

"You know what I did?" Pa asked.

"Yeah, I do. You hauled ammo all day like me. This one is big. Maybe we'll end it right here."

"No, I mean what else."

"What?"

"Two days ago, I went to Maastricht to pick up a load of wine. Took it to the brass at HQ."

Frank dragged on the Lucky Strike. "You get any for us?"

"Yessir. I got a few bottles."

"Where are they?"

"I'll tell you something else, too, Frank. When we get into Germany, there's going to be wine in every cellar—if the infantry don't get it all before we get there."

"Where's the bottles you brought back, El? I could use a little right now."

"I'll get you one, but I can't drink now. I gotta drive to B Battery with a load of smoke shells, then go on guard duty when I get back."

Meanwhile, at St. Odilienberg on the left flank of the 8th Armored Division, Combat Command R faced a pocket of German troops on the near side of the river. Orders came down for CCR to go on alert. The 405th Field Artillery turned the Heinsberg howitzers north toward CCR's front, and the tanks and infantry of CCR went on alert and sent out combat reconnaissance patrols. The patrols detected considerable German activity, and orders came to strike the enemy and clear out the area west of the river.

At 5:45 A.M. on the morning of February 26, the 405th shelled enemy positions in front of St. Odilienberg for fifteen minutes. The infantry struck immediately and encountered small-arms fire but kept to the shelter of M4 Sherman tanks. Near the town of Spielmanshof a heavily mined antitank ditch stopped the advance, and they came under artillery fire from across the river. They called the 405th to fire on the artillery bunkers across the Roer and to cover the ditch with a smoke screen. While tank cannons blasted Spielmanshof, the infantry, enveloped in smoke, crossed the antitank ditch on a thirty-foot horizontal ladder and gained the town, but there they came under mortar fire.

The 405th shelled the mortar positions and also laid a five-minute barrage on an enemy machine gun in the Heide woods on the infantry's left flank. Then, while the Shermans fired on the machine gun, the infantry attacked the woods and pushed the enemy out. But artillery and mortar fire from enemy bunkers across the Roer continued to pound their position, and shattered treetops fell into their midst. They called for smoke and artillery fire, dug in deep, and held their ground while the 405th shelled the bunkers overnight.

The next morning, Combat Command R cleared out the remaining opposition on the near side of the Roer and was replaced by the

35th Division's 15th Cavalry Group. But victory was not without a price. Combat Command R had suffered sixty-two casualties, and two tanks were knocked out of the fight.

During the battle, Pa trucked ammunition to the firing batteries at Heinsberg, but his range of knowledge was limited to what he could see. He hauled load after load, likely unaware of whether the shells were launched over the river to support the big push or were aimed at the machine guns and mortars on CCR's front at St. Odilienberg.

I was home reading the newspaper. I didn't know Pa's doings, but I likely knew more than he did of the Ninth Army's coordinated assault against the Germans across the Roer. The *Lewiston Evening Journal* reported the progress every day. I knew he was in it—somewhere—but I would need to wait for him to come home to tell me his stories.

Orders came late on February 27 for 8th Armored Division to move up. The 35th Division had captured the stone bridge at Hilfarth intact, and they held it for the northern flank of Ninth Army to cross the Roer. At 4:00 A.M., the 405th left Heinsberg for Hilfarth in a column of tanks, half-track personnel carriers, self-propelled artillery, supply trucks, and a host of jeeps, command cars, ambulances, and maintenance vehicles.

Pa carried artillery rounds wedged between sandbagged walls, a sleeping bag, K rations, and a few bottles of Maastricht wine in his duffel. The heavy traffic had turned the road to mire. He drove through deep mud-ruts and across hastily built corduroy patches; mud obscured his headlights and smeared his windshield. He slowed to a crawl and likely recalled mud season in Temple when he had put his truck away and waited for solid roads. But this, he thought, is the big push. To wait longer would allow the Germans to bolster their defense and dig in hard. At Hilfarth, MPs directed the column onto the main street where they waited to cross the bridge into Huckelhoven.

Once across the Roer, CCR turned north and charged toward their objective, the road junction at Wegberg, seven kilometers away. They advanced steadily in a pounding rain, and Pa drove through the rubble of firefights in towns where tanks and infantry had battled the Germans earlier in the day. As darkness fell, he stopped by the roadside five kilometers short of Wegberg, ate K rations, and went to sleep in the truck. Overnight CCR's tanks secured Wegberg, and at dawn, the column continued the advance. At Wegberg, Pa ate hot food from a field kitchen, then pressed forward again.

Past Wegberg, Combat Command R pursued the fleeing German soldiers toward Lobberich, twelve kilometers farther north. Word came from Ninth Army HQ restricting CCR to one narrow, unpaved roadway. Tankdozers cleared away haphazard wooden barriers and fallen-tree traps, and the column kept moving. The countryside was bruised and dented, and Pa passed disabled vehicles, empty bunkers, and abandoned barbed-wire entanglements of the Siegfried Line. Evidence of the Nazi Party—posters, banners, and pictures of Adolph Hitler—was prominent in the villages. They moved through Richelrath and Dulken and Boisheim, where buildings had been destroyed by advancing armor and explosions had filled the streets with rubble. Bewildered civilians appeared from the cellars of their shattered houses to watch. "Look. Are they waving to us?" Pa asked codriver Pechie.

"Could be," Pechie said. "I suppose some of 'em are glad to see us." Pechie waved to a woman who fluttered a white handkerchief. "It's been a long five years for them. But they know it's over now—for them anyway—and mebbe they can start livin' again."

"Gawd! I've never seen anything like this," Pa said. "Don't the krauts know what's happening to their people? Why the hell don't they just quit?"

"They don't care about their people."

Combat Command R rolled on like a freight train. At Lobberich, new orders came down: capture Grefrath, turn east, push hard for Moers, and secure the railroad bridge over the Rhine opposite Duisberg.

Grefrath fell in one day, and CCR's tanks turned east. While Pa slept overnight in his truck at Dulken, combat engineers built a pontoon treadway over the Neirs Canal four kilometers away. At dawn, CCR pressed forward and captured St. Hubert and Schrephuysen, and raced for Moers thirty kilometers away on the Rhine. Outside St. Hubert, the column came under attack by Luftwaffe Messerschmitts, and two half-tracks were destroyed. But Combat Command R pushed ahead relentlessly, and soon resistance collapsed. The German army ran for the safety of the great river. In Schrephuysen, the CCR commander, Colonel Wallace, predicted they would be on the Rhine that night, but in Vinnbruck, fifteen kilometers from the river, CCR halted, pinched out of its zone by the 35th and 84th Divisions. The command lacked room to advance, and orders came down to withdraw to reserve at Grefrath. Their dash to the Rhine was over.

In Temple, no one had heard from Pa for more than two weeks. When his last letter arrived—the letter to me the Germans had interrupted with a volley of artillery fire—the account of Ninth Army's crushing attack across the Roer River had been headlines in the *Lewiston Evening Journal* for several days. There had been no mention of the 8th Armored Division, but I knew from Pa's letter that he was there somewhere. He must be, I thought. Why else would he be in Germany? I was disappointed that he couldn't write me about his doings, and I wondered if I would ever know his place in the attack I read about daily, something I could point to that would validate my lofty feelings of his role in the war. I asked myself, is he in the middle of it; or is he on the outside? Surely, I thought, he will recount the battle to me when the war is over and he is home. I hoped silently for his safe return.

In time, after the Ninth Army had disappeared from the headlines, a letter came for Ma. Pa was healthy and having a rest period. He wrote that he had received a letter from Elmer, his poker-playing pal from Temple, that recounted Elmer's, as well as Vilio's, doings in Antwerp—

firing antiaircraft shells at German V-1 buzz bombs flying into the city—and expressed surprise that Pa was invading Germany. Pa was proud, he wrote to Ma, to serve in such a first-rate outfit as the 8th Armored Division. They were making history, he told her, and said he looked forward to the war's end coming soon.

Pa's letter expressed optimism. He was obviously in good spirits. I imagined he was buoyed by the success of the big push to the Rhine. Maybe the 8th Armored Division had shown itself well against the defending German army in its homeland, and Pa, being part of it, had swelled with confidence. I wished the *Lewiston Evening Journal* had reported where 8th Armored had fought, but I had to go on unknowing. Yet, they were at the Rhine, so they must be good fighters. Only a few days before, they had been behind the Roer. Pa will surely tell me what a juggernaut of an outfit he was in.

Pa's battery had withdrawn to Grefrath. Pa met Frank there, the first time since they crossed the Roer. "El, I remember what you said in Holland. When we goin' to check out a wine cellar?"

"Right now, buddy, right now. Let's go see what we can find."

Pa drove to the edge of town and pulled up in front of an abandoned brick villa with a wide front porch and a glassy sunroom.

"This place looks empty," he said. "And I bet there's plenty of wine in the cellar."

They filled two boxes, held them carefully with both hands, quick-stepped to the back of the truck, and slid the booty under the canvas. They went back twice.

The battery drank German wine that day. Combat Command R had pounded and chased the German army for most of a week. They had suffered one hundred fifty casualties and captured more than a thousand prisoners. Frank, halfway through a bottle of Rheinhessen Riesling, looked around at the noisy soldiers.

"So whaddaya think, El? We've been here two months and we're still okay. Think we'll make it?"

"We were lucky, Frank. We took casualties every day on the push to here. Our number didn't come up"

"Think it will?"

"No. . . . No, I don't. I think it'll be rough across the river, but I think we'll make it. In France, I didn't know. But now I've seen it, I think we can make it. Just do your job."

"Well, I ain't thinkin' about goin' home, not yet. I'm just gonna work it one day at a time."

"Just don't volunteer for anything, Frank. Sarge will volunteer you if he needs you."

"This Riesling's good, El. Can't get stuff like this in Philly. I oughta ship some home. My dad would like it."

"I'll tell you something, Frank. I never drank much wine. A lot of other stuff, but not wine. Back in Temple, this stuff wouldn't hold a candle to Howard Mitchell's hard cider. I've got fifty gallons of the best damn stuff you ever tasted in an oak barrel in my cellar. You gotta come up there and try it. Bring your dad, too. There'll be plenty."

They fell asleep, each grasping a half-empty bottle of Rheinhessen.

While Pa and Frank walked guard, patrolled the Grefrath streets on bicycles, and caught up on rest, the 35th Division and Combat Command B of the 8th Armored fought a fierce tank battle for the ancient riverfront city of Rheinberg on the northern flank of Ninth Army's zone. On the Lintfort–Rheinberg road, a flat, straight thoroughfare between two echelons of tall poplars in an open field, CCB's tanks drove northeasterly against German panzers in some of the most brutal fighting of the push to the Rhine. After four days, the Germans retreated across the river at the medieval river-port city of Wesel and blew the bridge. But the punishing battle for Rheinberg, which cost CCB two hundred casualties and thirty-nine tanks, had proven beyond any doubt that the German army, thought by some to have lost their will to fight, retained considerable life. The Nazis would not give up their homeland easily.

Two weeks after crossing the Roer, Operation Grenade concluded with 21st Army Group occupying a broad front on the west bank of the Rhine. After ten days of battling an enemy who enjoyed no natural defenses to hide behind, Ninth Army had reached the river, but was denied a bridge; the last one at Oberkassel had been blown in their faces. Word came from Field Marshall Montgomery to wait while he planned an assault against the far side. And the disorganized but still vital German army prepared its defense.

Chapter Nineteen
TARMO

The war had been both a catalyst of unity and a disrupter of community ties.
—Doris Kearns Goodwin, *No Ordinary Time*

S eclusion levied a huge toll on Ma's undertakings that winter. By the time of my tenth birthday in February, she had become dormant. She put off her daily chores, dispatched Nancy or me to the store for food and mail, and neglected housecleaning projects. She took no comfort in hobbies, crafts, quilt-making, or the like. And filled as she was with geography, social studies, and reading when she substituted for a day at the Village School, she found no other pleasure in books or writing—except to Pa. She called on no one and received few visitors. She felt deliberately and undeservedly slighted, particularly by Pa's kin, but she dared not assert herself. So she acquiesced to idleness, persuaded by the risk of exposing her behavior to the judgment of Pa's family, and virtually hid herself in a murky existence. She sat in her upstairs bedroom window and watched the comings and goings in the village, kept an ear to Gabriel Heater and Fibber McGee yelling out of the Emerson, and worried and waited for the war to end.

Trouble, I thought, loitered in the shadows of Ma's vague existence. Her aversion to Temple without Pa so depressed her that I feared she had abandoned faith and her misery would turn into transgression. She took to drink more, and for the wrong reasons. On weekends, she would ask Eddie to bring her a couple of quarts of ale, or Marguerite to bring a pint on the mail stage, and she would sip it alone. Her past drinking had been for the excitement and joy of being with Pa or their friends. But now, for the most part, she drank alone, though occasionally strangers, men in uniform, would come to the house and sit at the kitchen table late into the evening and drink a quart or two with her. Whenever they came, Nancy and Patty and I would disappear and play a game or go to bed. I became troubled, anxious that Ma's faithfulness to Pa and her loyalty to the care of his place were wearing down. I didn't like to see her friendly with folks I didn't know and whom she didn't identify, and whenever they called on her, I was relieved to see them go.

"Oh, pshaw," Ma would say. "It's just friends. I'm not doing anything. Don't worry."

But I did worry, and for good reason. Though unrelated to Pa's kin, or, I thought, to Ma's transgressions, trouble soon arrived, brought home by our dog, Cappy.

One winter afternoon as I am tossing firewood into the woodbox, Cappy, his bushy tail tucked between his legs, slinks into the barn; his shaggy head hangs, and his eyes beg for help. I drop on my knees and rub him behind his ears. "What's the matter, Cappy? Don't you feel good?" I ask. And then I see red blots in the snow behind him, and I rush to the kitchen. "Mommy! Mommy! Come quick!"

Ma helps Cappy into the kitchen, lays him on the linoleum, and feels his stomach with her hand. "He has a wound underneath of some kind," she says.

"How bad is it, Mommy? Can you fix it?" I'm sick with worry. Ma isn't good at this.

She reaches underneath with a handkerchief and pulls it back stained with red. "I can't tell what it is or how deep it is, but there's a lot of blood. Something has happened."

"What can we do, Mommy? We have to do something?"

"I'll call Eddie."

I let out a breath. Eddie will know what to do.

Before the war, Pa brought Cappy home in a cardboard box, and he grew up our friend and companion. We named him Captain for Uncle Bill, Ma's brother-in-law, a captain in the Army Air Force. We had not met him, but Ma would say, "Maybe that's Uncle Bill," and point at every airplane, rare as they were, that flew over our house toward Greenland or Labrador or England. We thought Captain a fitting name for our adventurous pet. Cappy loved us, and we him. He tumbled with us on the lawn and ran with us in the fields and lanes and rode with us in the rumble seat and walked with us to the general store. He depended on us.

Now Ma is worried, I am sick, Nancy is scared, and Patty is crying. Cappy hurts. He oozes blood onto an old blanket while Eddie drives to a veterinarian in Farmington.

"What happen to Cappy?" Eddie asks.

I tell Eddie over and over I don't know what happened; I don't know how it happened; I don't know anyone who would harm Cappy.

"Don' worry," he says. "He gonna be alright."

The veterinarian probes Cappy's body and says he feels a piece of metal that might be a bullet. "I'll have to put him to sleep to get that out," he says. "I better keep him here a day or two."

Cappy was home in two days, but he rested a long time before he romped in the snow or walked to the store with me or Patty.

I wondered why someone had shot him. Cappy liked everyone and didn't trouble anyone. He didn't bark at night and keep Old Carr or Mrs. Mosher awake. He didn't raid folks' garbage or chase their cats. He didn't threaten their kids. Most folks Ma talked to seemed to think shooting Cappy a terrible thing—"How could anyone do that?" they would say. But no one knew how it happened. Someone said Cappy had chased deer, but Mr. Bailey, who had been a selectman, told Ma that Cappy was not the guilty one, that another dog had chased deer.

But someone, for some reason, had shot Cappy; the person and the reason were a mystery to me, and Ma, too.

I supposed someone could have disliked us—Ma, my sisters, and me—could have despised us so much they had shot our dog at the slightest aggravation. I was so hurt by that notion that I dared not show myself to the Temple public, and for many days I stayed inside and moped about the house. But what *really* happened? I still don't know. I suspect Ma knew more than she admitted about the circumstances and the name of the coward who delivered the hateful message via the bullet in Cappy. It was her nature to withhold hurtful information, and she kept that knowledge to herself, while her misery held fast.

In March, an uncommonly warm stretch of weather arrived. The pasture snow settled and turned sooty, sap dripped out of wind-broken branches on our front-lawn maples, and Temple's roads rutted deep under the weight of cars and trucks and wagon wheels. It was the kind of March weather that filled us with hope—hope that winter had ended. But soon the mercury plunged, and hope disappeared. Arctic air swept in over Mount Blue. Icicles hung from the maples like daggers. The ruts and potholes and hoof prints froze solid in the roads. Then rain came.

Now the rain turns to sleet, the wind rattles it against the kitchen window, and Ma looks into an empty cupboard for something for supper and asks me to go to the store.

"I need a can of stew for supper," she says, "and a loaf of bread. And see if there's any mail."

"Mother, it's miserable outside," I plead. "It's getting dark. Can't it wait?"

"No," she answers. "There might be a letter from your father. Put on your boots and bundle up."

"How do I pay?" I ask.

"Your grandfather will be there. Tell him to put it on the slip."

I tighten my coat, snug a cap down over my ears, pull mittens onto my hands, and step into the lonely half-light of nightfall, just me and the wind and the sleet. I grumble at my misery, but Ma wants stew. I shield my face against the flying ice and shiver and stumble, sometimes backward to the general store.

The usual lingerers lounge around the woodstove. In the dim light, I see Alex Goldsmith, here early to listen to the talk; Kike Knowles clenches a pipe tight in his teeth while he tells a story; John Hill sits on a wooden soda-bottle case; Harold Staples, who Grandpa C.F. says is the second best checker player in Temple, leans sideways with his elbow against a shelf; Fred Vining, who sports a bushy mustache, waits for a chance to tell his favorite deer story; barrel-chested Matti Sade, a Finn who has walked a mile here from his home on the hill behind the village, sits quietly beside the stove; and tonight I see a soldier standing here, Tarmo Sade, home on leave from the war.

Tarmo was born in a logging camp in north Temple in the shadow of Mount Blue. His parents, Matti and Aino, and a dozen or so other Finnish couples, had immigrated to Temple thirty years earlier during a political upheaval in Finland. They came as loggers and labored in the Temple forests, raised families and kept family farms, built Finnish steam bathhouses, and trekked into the village in winter on homemade cross-country skis. They welcomed Temple folks to their homes, their bathhouses, and their kitchen tables, where they served hard cider and hardtack bread. They learned English in Grandma Luna's Americanization School in Brackley Hall, and some became American citizens. Tarmo attended the Village

Tarmo Sade in his summer uniform at an army training camp somewhere in the U.S. c. 1943.

School, then the high school in Farmington until the woods beckoned him back to his birthplace.

He was one of the soldiers and sailors from Temple who, by 1945, had gone to war and were scattered around the world from the Philippines to the Rhine River in Germany. I was awestruck by these men who left Temple for only God knew where; who came home dressed in khaki tunics, gold insignia, and impeccably creased khaki trousers; who greeted their friends, posed for a picture, walked to the general store, and told their stories; and who, after a few days home, left again to make history. When I saw them, I felt in the company of men who embraced and practiced the principles of America—freedom, the flag, and faith in God—that I had learned in the Village School. Men who proudly and honorably went into the darkness of the unknown to defend those principles and who, I felt, would survive and win the war.

Now, on a wretched March evening, Tarmo stands by the wood-stove in the general store. He is erect and fit, an oak of a man, resplendent in his uniform decorated with battle ribbons and sergeant's stripes and the colorful patches of General Patton's U.S. Third Army. I look up at him, spellbound by his presence, and listen to his stories.

An infantry sergeant, Tarmo has campaigned with the 4th Armored Division since landing in France a month after D-Day, June 1944. By December, he had battled to the German border, the Siegfried Line, when General Patton boldly turned the 4th Armored Division north toward the Battle of the Bulge, where they cracked the German siege of Bastogne and drove the Nazis back into Germany.

He tells them what it was like. "For seventy days, I'm on the line," Tarmo says. "In the morning, the lieutenant shows me on a map what he wants." Tarmo pauses. "Every day for seventy days, we go out and fight for a spot on his map and try to stay alive another day. We fight in cold and in snow. At Bastogne, all but four men in my outfit are killed." He pauses again. And then he refers to the medal on his chest, the Silver Star. "But I tell you the truth . . . I am scared . . . I have never been so scared. And then I get a medal. Sheee-it."

Outside, sleet ricochets off the tin roof and wind pounds against the door, but inside, in the dim light and tobacco-smoke haze around the woodstove, it is ghostly quiet, Tarmo's low, soft voice almost a whisper. These men, loggers and farmers bound to this dark and desolate corner of the world, men who have not been more than a few miles away from Temple in their lifetimes, neither speak nor move but quietly listen to Tarmo's stories.

I stare at him. Is this what Pa will look like when he comes home, I ask myself. Medals pinned to his chest? Stories about being on the line? About battling his way into Germany with the 8th Armored Division? Will Pa stand here and tell *his* stories, too?

After a few minutes, Tarmo notices the quiet, the near reverence, of the men listening to his tales, and he hesitates. "But I tell you," he says. "I want you to know this. I have been to New York and London and Paris. I have crossed oceans and seen great armies in battle. I have been to ancient cities and seen famous castles and cathedrals. I have been to many places. But I tell you, there is no place like home, no place like here. This is the best place; this is where I want to be, with Matti and Aino," as he called them, "and my friends."

Tarmo has finished his stories, and one by one the men button their coats tight, nod to him, and go out into the winter night, into the darkness and the frozen ruts under their feet and the ice-filled wind in their faces.

I ask Grandpa C.F. for stew and bread, and I tell him Ma said to put it on the slip. He puts them in a bag, and I tighten my coat and go out. As I hike across the bridge toward home, I wonder if Pa is on the line.

Ma is glad to see me home. "Was there any mail?" she asks.

"I forgot," I say.

In the days that followed, Ma, pleased at the news that Tarmo was home from the war, if only for a short time, smiled more and showed more life around the house. Pa had grown up with Tarmo and his Finnish sidekicks, and Ma and Pa had found lasting friendships in Temple's Finnish population. In Pa's absence, the Finns had kept their loyalty to Ma and their interest in Pa's doings, and Ma likewise mixed with them. She was welcome in Finnish homes to talk or share a letter or to bathe in a Finnish steam bath on Saturday. The Finns borrowed from her, as she did from them, and seldom did Aino or Naimi walk by our house on their way to the general store and not stop to sit with Ma a few minutes.

Tarmo, while home on leave, came to visit Ma and sat at the kitchen table and drank a quart with her. She willingly accepted him in. She listened to his stories and shared with him her difficulties in Temple, and she didn't feel threatened or judged.

One day soon, Ma tells us we are invited to a party. "It's for Tarmo," she says. "His friends are giving him a party on Saturday. You will like it. Robert will be there. And Miriam."

Ma drives us to the party in the roadster, an uncommonly brave act for her who fears driving so much she would walk four miles to Lowell's Market in West Farmington to buy a pot roast rather than drive there. She believes the roadster was built to confound her. If she attempts to set it in motion, a tire will go flat or a spring leaf will break or the radiator will boil. Or, as is most embarrassing, she will jerk the roadster along and stall it in the road. But for the party, she powers it— in first gear without shifting—up to the Salo farm on the hill beyond our house. Nothing happens, and Ma relaxes. She says she can coast the roadster home.

The festivity is a gathering of Finns. They sit at wooden tables or stand in little knots and prate in Finnish, talk to Ma in the English they remember from Grandma Luna's school, and greet and applaud Tarmo for his doings in the war. They crowd the kitchen and nibble hardtack bread and smoked fish and jerked beef. They sip homemade beer and hard cider, and host John Salo quickly tops off yawning glasses with his best down-cellar reserve. But the partying is not for kids, and I'm bored in only a few minutes here.

Robert talks to me. A Finn, Robert graduated from the Village School last year and is now in high school. He has walked here alone from his home a half a mile down the hill.

"Do you still play the hand-cranked Victrola I sold your Mom?" he asks me.

"Yes," I say.

"I'm taking music in high school," he says. "I play violin. I might play in an orchestra some day."

I'm not sure what an orchestra actually is, but I don't ask him what it is because I think I should know. "That's good," I say.

Miriam lives here with her parents, who farm this hillside when they're not pouring glasses of homemade beer and hard cider for their Finnish friends, and she walks the mile to the sixth grade each day. Miriam knows the right answers to Mrs. Stolt's questions. She would know what an orchestra is. And when she sits in the seventh and eighth grade rows, she will know the answers to Mrs. Stolt's arithmetic questions, and Mrs. Stolt won't need to answer my raised hand.

Miriam points to a plate with a stack of dried meat on it. "Do you like jerked beef, John?"

I take a tasty-looking morsel and bite into it. I put the rest in my pocket and look for a piece of cheese and some hardtack bread.

Someone brings out a cake with frosted curlicues and a huge flaming candle, probably borrowed from the kitchen table, in the center. The Finns cheer, and Tarmo cuts the cake into slanted pieces, trying to avoid the "Welcome Home Tarmo" that is lettered on the icing. Folks eat cake, fill their glasses again and again, laugh and shout to each other in Finnish, and shimmy a schottische dance. This is not like a May Basket party where kids sit in a circle and play spin the bottle and eat candy and go home early. I look for Ma.

But we are the last to leave. The sky has been long dark, and Ma says she doesn't want to drive. Tarmo takes us home in the roadster, coasting down the hill without starting the engine. He drives into the barn and comes inside.

The next morning, Tarmo is still here, asleep with Ma in her room. I am dazed at the sight, and a lump comes into my throat. I creep downstairs and into the back pasture and wait for an hour on the crusty snow by the old shed, alone in the early sun. I am disheartened, and I think and wish and hope a long time. I try to tell myself I have nothing to worry about, but I know I do. I am afraid of hurt and shame. I am afraid of what might be next, that Ma's discontent will soon erupt, and that she will leave Temple and either take us with her or leave us here. Both are disagreeable. I am afraid of rancor, that Pa and Ma will eventually quarrel and clash. I wait by the shed until I see Tarmo stride up the hill toward home.

Back in the kitchen, Ma is making breakfast. I don't tell her what I saw or how I feel or where I've been. I don't tell her, or anyone, anything. Instead, I wait for what will come next.

In a few weeks, the ground began to show through the dirty snow, and I asked Ma if we were going to plant a Victory Garden.

"No, we are not," she said. "Your Aunt Marion won't help, and a garden is too much work for me alone. Besides, we're leaving as soon as school ends, and we won't be here to tend a garden or pick vegetables."

I knew this was coming: I knew she would leave. She would take us with her, she said, and we would wait for Pa in Kennebunk. I didn't want to leave Temple, but I knew that unless Ma's spirits somehow picked up or Pa came home, we could not stay. Understandably, Ma was sick of her circumstances; she could take no more misery. I would go to Kennebunk with her, but I would long for the freedom of the fields and the lanes and the stream, the summer games in the schoolyard, the sights of soldiers coming and going. And I would miss Grandpa C.F.

Grandpa C.F. struggled single-handedly to lift our spirits that winter. He came regularly to sit at the kitchen table and talk with Ma. They shared letters from Pa, and he listened while Ma let out her frustrations and expressed her fears. He played Go Fish with us and threw jar rubbers at a numbered pegboard with us. He hugged us and heartened us and shared tears with us. He was gentle and patient, and he listened when we spoke. Grandpa's support cheered us in those dark days. I loved the old man.

One Sunday in May, after the snow has melted and the stream has shrunk to normal, he takes me fishing. We go to the place where the stream tumbles over the remnants of the so-called lower dam, where once, in the town's more heady days, it flowed through a waterwheel and powered a sawmill. Upstream, white water spills across a rotten log and over a jagged ledge, then ripples by my feet. Farther up, beyond the old millpond, the stream ducks under the village bridge, then, where Old Carr's barn stands high on the bank, it disappears from sight around a bend to the upper dam, where moments earlier it had plunged off the intervale.

Grandpa C.F. tells me that Temple Stream has a rich heritage. Its water once powered profitable sawmills in the village, turned another waterwheel at Gleason's sawmill two miles upstream, and a mile farther up, turned still another saw. In winter, Grandpa C.F. says, the frozen stream was cut into blocks, stored under sawdust in a stream-bank icehouse, and used to cool iceboxes in summer. Teamsters watered their teams in the stream, and the teams, pulling dump wagons, took gravel from the stream to construct Temple's early roads. Farmers cut hayfields along both banks. And at Mitchell's cider mill, where apples were chopped by a two-cylinder Ford engine and pressed by strong-backed men lusting for a barrel of apple juice to ferment, the stream washed away the apple pulp.

Much of a Temple boyhood was indistinguishable from the stream. We swam naked in its intervale pools on summer afternoons and skated on the millpond during winter. We floated on homemade rafts and skied on its frozen, snow-covered surface on long, skinny skis made by the Finns. We crossed it in adventurous ways: jumping from rock to rock, balancing on the bridge rail, and tiptoeing over the decaying remnants of the upper dam. I harbored a pet duck in the millpond. In the fall, we watched wild animals come to its banks and drink, and in the spring, we fished for trout that fed in its pools and eddies. Grandpa C.F. knew where to find them.

Downstream from where we stand, a canopy of tree branches shades the stream as far as I can see. Grandpa C.F. says fish linger in these shady pools. He dresses his hook with one of Ma's garden worms, steps into the stream, and casts his line into an eddy. In a few seconds, he yanks out a small, wiggly trout, removes it from the hook, stuffs it in a brown paper bag, and tucks the bag inside his rolled-down rubber wader. "There's fish here," he says, clenching his pipe tightly in his mouth. "Here. You better try it." He removes a worm from a Prince Albert tobacco can and carefully shows me how to thread it onto my hook. I toss it in the stream and wait. He moves to another pool and catches two more, a larger one and another small one. The small one goes into the bag in his wader, and the bigger one he hangs on a forked stick for me to carry.

We move downstream. Grandpa C.F. catches more small fish, and two more full-sized ones at Wright Dam. I catch two small trout. Grandpa C.F. smiles, tells me what nice fish they are, and puts them into the bag in his wader. I'm puzzled, so I ask, "Why do you put the fish in your boot, Grandpa?"

"They'll stay cooler there," he says, "and keep better."

"Well," I ask. "Why are the bigger ones on this stick?"

He smiles again. "So you can take them home and show your sisters what a good fisherman you are."

I did take them home, and Ma asked me to clean them, as I had seen Pa do, for the supper table.

In spite of Grandpa's attempts to raise her spirits, Ma packed for the move to Kennebunk. We would go to her parents and wait there for Pa. I didn't want to go, but Ma said I could go to the beach and would make new friends. I might just as well see the beach, I thought, but I didn't want Pa to come home to Kennebunk. I wanted him to come home to Temple and tell his stories in the general store. But there was no changing Ma's mind, and I turned down a chance to deliver *Grit* to folks in the village and told Mrs. Mosher I wouldn't be able to mow her lawn that summer. I would be away, plagued by puritanical grandparents and strange surroundings.

Chapter Twenty

THE RUHR

We have come to the hour for which we were born.
—New York Times, 1944

F or more than two weeks in March, the U.S. Ninth Army sat on the west bank of the Rhine River and waited for Field Marshall Montgomery to prepare his plan. Although eclipsed by widely publicized Rhine crossings upstream at Remagen and Wiesbaden, Montgomery's push in the north of Germany had been selected by General Eisenhower as the priority river crossing that would carry the Allied juggernaut deep into Germany, capture Berlin, and squeeze the German army into submission. Still, Montgomery failed to act with any sense of urgency. General Simpson and his ten divisions of armor and infantry sat and fumed, but to no avail. While the enemy constructed breastworks and bunkers and moved panzer units up to the river, Montgomery thoroughly and meticulously devised his assault on the far side.

Orders were passed down: The 405th Armored Field Artillery would go on alert and prepare to take up firing positions at Rheinberg. Pa moved to Lintfort, four kilometers west of Rheinberg, and kept his duffel packed. He trucked clothing and equipment to the river. He shuttled infantry to the front, and he hauled their duffel bags over the battle-scarred road to Grefrath for temporary storage. At night, with blue tissue covering his headlights, he rehearsed motor-march and practiced a river crossing on treadways. And he, like the others, waited for Montgomery's order.

In Temple, I also waited. News of the Ninth Army had disappeared from *The Franklin Journal.* The paper pictured German prisoners captured in earlier fighting and reported on the difficulty troops would find crossing the treacherous and bridgeless Rhine River, but nowhere was the Ninth reported to be in action. I appealed to Ma for news. "Mommy, has Auntie May heard from Daddy? What's he doing now?"

"She gets a letter once in a while, I guess, but they don't say much."

"What's he doing? Where is he?"

"I suppose he's resting while they get ready to cross the Rhine River. He's probably sunning himself on some beach there and eyeing German girls in scanty bathing suits."

Ma dwelt on the worst. Knowing that Ninth Army was not engaged in daily battling, she had stopped fearing Pa would be killed and instead was skeptical of his behavior. She alleged he was goofing off—ogling German women or gambling away his money. In the past, she had overcome her doubts and preserved his loyalty with packages of whiskey or by posting him scarce cash to gamble with. But sending him Rheinhessen or reichsmarks was impossible, and she reeked of pessimism. In spite of her misgivings, however, I knew Pa was engulfed in history. I wished I knew his doings.

Along the Rhine, Pa was not sunbathing. Word had come from Montgomery that his painstakingly precise plan for the river crossing was ready, and the 405th Armored Field Artillery, enveloped in a cloud of fog and artificial smoke, moved into camouflaged firing positions at Rheinberg.

Pa drove to the Lintfort supply depot for a load of ammunition. Frank was there, and they talked while they worked. "Did you get the word?" Pa asked. "We're going—and damned soon. The infantry, the

30th Division they say, will cross in assault boats at night and force a bridgehead. We'll fire all the night before and all day. The word is that 8th Armored will be the first armor to go, probably the next day. That's us, Frank."

"You hear we're goin' first?"

"Yeah. We are. I know it. And there's brass all over the place here," Pa chattered. "This has gotta be the final push. We'll get the sons-abitches for good this time. There'll be no gettin' away. And if the bastards keep backing up, the Russians will get 'em. We'll capture their whole goddam army—and little Adolph too." Pa likely recalled the 1943 matchstick poker game with Elmer and Vilio and realized that of the three, he has the best chance, the only chance "to get little Adolph."

"Goddam right," Frank replied. "And they got it comin' to 'em."

"Hubba hubba! We got any Rheinhessen left?"

For three days, in a convoy of supply trucks, Pa shuttled ordnance fifteen kilometers from Lintfort to the firing batteries on the Rhine. He passed disabled tanks and ravaged half-tracks and the echelons of shattered poplars standing in silent tribute to the fierce tank battle of a few days past. He drove at night under blackout lights, kept to the straight and narrow road, and avoided land mines left by the Germans. Messerschmitts dropped flares and made strafing passes on the convoy. On the third day, March 22, word was passed to suspend trucking at midnight and wait for orders.

The following afternoon, Montgomery telephoned Simpson on the Rhine and ordered him to go that night. The 21st Army Group—First Canadian and Second British Armies on the left of Wesel and U.S. Ninth Army on the right—would launch the final push. The four-hundred-meter-wide Rhine River flowed deep and steady in front of Ninth Army: the 30th Infantry was poised on the river's near shore; German panzer troops were entrenched on the far side.

At midnight, Pa heard the far-off thunder of artillery. An hour later, the Ninth's howitzers opened fire and poured in more than one thousand shells per minute, the most intense artillery barrage in history. Soon word came back that the 30th Infantry had pushed their assault boats into the great river. At 1 A.M., Pa was on the Lintfort-Rheinberg road with ammunition, and he shuttled loads of artillery shells, rockets, and smoke rounds to the firing stations all that day. At daylight, British and American paratroopers filled the sky over Diersfordter, beyond the Rhine, and British fighter planes flew cover for American bombers while they dropped supplies to the assault troops. Pa viewed history being produced outside his windshield and, while the world watched, likely imagined himself an actor in a classic drama. When darkness fell, he returned to his quarters at Lintfort and looked for Frank.

"Hey, Frank, I saw Eisenhower."

"You what?"

"I saw General Eisenhower. He was at the front, wearing his Ike jacket and a helmet with five stars on it."

"What in hell was he doing there? I thought the brass stayed out of range until we had the place secure."

"Not Ike. He's prob'ly trying to keep Monty in line. There's lots of brass up front. This one will wrap it up. They want to be part of it, to be able to say they were here. I carried a load back to the railhead in the back of my truck. They'll catch a train back to HQ."

"But what the hell is Eisenhower's game?"

"I tell ya, Frank, he doesn't want Monty to steal the limelight. It's the Americans who are carrying this fight to the kraut barstards, and Ike wants to make sure the press gets it right. Monty's not here: he and Churchill are off someplace having tea. But Ike is here, and he and Simpson climbed up into a church tower at Rheinberg last night and watched the shelling we gave those bastards. Jeezus, what a sight that musta been. Two thousand guns in Ninth Army, one goin' off every second—better'n fireworks at the Farmington Fair. Another thing, Frank. You better be ready. We're crossin' damned quick. I can feel it."

The order came down the next night, March 26, to cross the river.

The hour had come for 8th Armored. Pa left Lintfort at 2:00 A.M. in a column of tanks, artillery, half-tracks, trucks, ambulances, maintenance vehicles, jeeps, and command cars. Like an iron snake stretched over several kilometers, the 8th Armored slithered along the Lintfort–Rheinberg road toward the river directly ahead of it. In the past two days, while the 30th Infantry held their precious bridgehead and 105-mm howitzers launched deadly shrapnel into German lines, combat engineers had thrown twelve pontoon bridges across the great river. The 8th Armored Division would cross at Rheinberg.

Pa was on the bridge at 4:00 A.M., under enemy fire, leaning forward in his six-by-six, squinting at the truck ahead through the smoke and fog. Codriver Pechie sat quiet, watchful. Searchlights bored upward into the night, and tracers arced across the dark sky. German 88s shrieked toward the bridge from twenty kilometers away and exploded huge geysers from the river. Debris and bodies floated against the bridge. The convoy moved slowly, and Pa focused on threading his truck over the treadways in the smoke and mist. He wanted off the bridge. In five or so minutes, he reached the far shore.

On the shore, shattered pillboxes smoldered in the darkness, and bodies of German soldiers lay broken on the roadside. Patches of woods were shredded, and dead cattle lay in the meadows. Pa heard the thunder of big guns ahead in the distance and the roar of aircraft overhead. The gruesome 88s screamed and slammed into the water behind him. The column continued eastward, with the last vehicle off the bridge at noon. They stopped at Bruckhausen, two kilometers beyond the river, and the 8th Armored's Combat Command R organized for the push east.

I am in Temple and see it in *The Franklin Journal*, "Ninth Army Cracks Eight Miles Across the Rhine," the headline shouts.

I show Ma the paper. "Does this mean Daddy's back in action?"

"Yes," she replies. "Maybe it does. We'll look in the Lewiston paper tonight when it comes."

I read more. They crossed the Rhine at night and met up with what the paper calls "stiff German resistance." I think Pa must be in the battle.

Ma looks up from her ironing. "I wonder if he had time to write us before he moved," she says. And, as an afterthought, adds, "It would be nice if we got another letter soon. But I bet he didn't write."

The Franklin Journal doesn't have battle details. Is Pa okay, I wonder? Is he still alive? I put those worrying thoughts aside. I refuse to think of him wounded or killed in battle, only that he will come home wearing medals and tell his stories in the general store. Perhaps he is earning medals right now.

East of the Rhine, the 8th Armored Division quickly passed through the 30th Infantry, and Combat Command R struck northeasterly toward Dorsten. Pa left Bruckhausen with a loaded ammunition truck on the only road eastward, a narrow, straight, unpaved forest lane. Oak and linden lined the roadside and arched overhead, and he drove slowly in their shadow and kept an interval between him and the truck in front.

Ahead, a fierce German defense of Dorsten by the elite 116th Panzer Division stalled CCR's attack, and the M4 Shermans came to a halt. Pa, in danger of coming under fire, returned to Bruckhausen, and only later that night could he shuttle ammunition up to CCR's embattled tanks and 105-mm howitzers. Dorsten fell the following day, and Combat Command R continued east. They seized a crossing over the Rhein–Herne Canal, advanced through Schoven, routed the now bruised 116th Panzer Division at Zweckel, and captured Buer Hassel against artillery so solidly entrenched that German soldiers had disguised them with flowerbeds and shrubbery.

Pa came under frequent attack as he ferried ammunition on the battlefield east of the Rhine. Eastward out of Dorsten, the Luftwaffe strafed the attacking column, and Pa was forced to take cover under his truck and stay the night at the front, where he listened to Nazi shells crack into the treetops. In Gladbeck, the Luftwaffe flew reconnaissance over the embattled city, and Pa found cover in the cellar of a damaged building, where he listened hard for the shriek of incoming German 88s. At the crucial battle for Zweckel, when the ammunition convoy came within range of the enemy's cannons, they slowed and waited until the panzers had pulled back.

The fall of Zweckel and near destruction of the 116th Panzer Division loosened the German resistance in front of Combat Command R. In the morning darkness of March 31, they pushed three kilometers farther east and struck the enemy at Langenbochum. Pa took ammunition up to the battle and returned to Kirchellen for a second load. On the abandoned battlefields at Buer Hassel and Schoven and Zweckel, he passed dead German soldiers still in trenches and prisoners marching westward. Kirchellen's streets were clogged as the supply column moved up. At dusk, Pa again loaded his truck at the ammunition depot in Kirchellen and waited for orders.

Pa had been in combat since the 405th Field Artillery Battalion had opened fire across the Rhine eleven days earlier. He had slept in the truck when he could, eaten K rations out of an unclean mess kit, and taken his turn at sentry duty. German artillery had assailed him, and the Luftwaffe had strafed his convoy. In four days, after crossing the Rhine, 8th Armored Division's Combat Command R had pushed twenty-five kilometers into Germany against a brutal defense. Langenbochum fell, and the 75th Infantry Division relieved CCR at the front. The 405th moved back to Kirchellen. Two weeks had passed since Pa had written home.

In Temple, Nancy, Patty, and I sit at the supper table. Ma reads the evening paper, every word of the front-page war news. Outside, darkness has overtaken the village, and the air is freezing. A wood fire in the cookstove warms us. Ma is fraught with worry: she hasn't heard from Pa since before the Ninth Army crossed the Rhine nearly two weeks ago. She looks for news that he is okay, but the newspaper reports only the death and destruction being wrought on Germany.

She reads aloud that only General Simpson's Ninth Army, fighting grimly into the Ruhr, is meeting stiff German resistance. "Does this mean," she asks, "that the Germans are putting all their strength against just the Ninth Army? Why don't they spread it around? What are all the other armies doing? Why is your father the only one they're shooting at?"

"Mommy, let me see. Look," I say, "it says here the decisive battle that broke the Ninth Army loose was fought by 8th Armored Division at Zweckel. They attacked the 116th Panzer Division and forced them to turn and run." The Ninth, I explain to her, is the greatest threat to the evil Nazis; the Ninth is headed for Berlin; the Ninth is the most hated by Hitler, and Hitler is fighting hardest to stop the Ninth; the Ninth will win the war over Germany.

"I know," she answers. "But when will we . . . ?" Her voice goes silent.

I worry, too. I don't want to, but I can't help it. I think to myself, what if? "Mommy," I ask. "What would we do if he didn't come home?"

Nancy, who hardly knows Pa, is worried, too. "Yes, Mommy, what would we do?"

"I don't know. I suppose we would . . . we would . . . but . . . I don't want to talk about it now." And then she says, "He'll be back. We'll get a letter soon. You just wait."

The letter, written more than a week earlier, came in a few days. Pa, as he customarily did, simply wrote that he was in the best of health, would be starting the final push soon, and not to worry. The letter was no great news to me, and for sure it didn't answer Ma's questions.

"He said he was okay," Ma exclaimed. "But that was before he crossed the river. We still don't know what's happened to him since then."

Nancy, my commonsense sister, interrupted her. "Mommy, it takes more than a week for a letter to get here. Don't worry. He'll rest again soon, and we'll get another letter."

But the 8th Armored Division, though relieved by the 75th

Infantry, would get no rest. Orders came to join with the 2nd Armored Division in Selm, then push easterly along the north side of the Ruhr to the vicinity of Lippstadt. There, they were to seize Paderborn, a major road junction, and prepare for a thrust farther to the east.

Pa hears the news and looks for Frank. "Frank! Whaddaya make of the news?"

"What's that, El?"

"We're moving up. No break. We're heading east—right now. General Simpson wants us and 2nd Armored in Paderborn tomorrow. Chrissakes, that's a hundred miles from here."

"So? He just wants to get this goddam war over with."

"That's what I'm tellin' ya. The boys say he wants us in Berlin! It's only another hundred miles. We're spearheadin' this thing."

Seen from its perimeter, the great cities of the Ruhr—Duisberg, Oberhausen, Essen, Gelsenkirchen, and Dortmund—were seemingly one. As Pa drove easterly to Selm along the Ruhr's north edge, he glimpsed a wide cityscape of factories, foundries, and steel mills, all fueled by the immense coal deposits of the Ruhr Valley. Visible to the distant horizon, coal-burning smokestacks discharged their black, ash-laden smoke upward in spiral columns, and an orange cloud hung over the valley like sea smoke. Under the cloud, the industrial heart of Germany produced weapons for war. Without the Ruhr, Germany could not fight.

The road to Selm bustled with activity. Bridges over the Wesel–Datteln and the Dortman–Ems Canals and the Lippe River had been destroyed, and Pa crossed on pontoon treadway bridges built by combat engineers. MPs slowed the convoy while they passed thousands of German prisoners being marched to the rear in long columns on each side of the road, a beaten lot with overcoats slung on their shoulders and visored caps low over their eyes. In Recklinghausen and Datteln, which Pa noted in his diary were "level with the ground," tank dozers cleared debris from bombed-out streets.

At Selm, orders were waiting for 8th Armored Division to advance on Paderborn, one hundred kilometers east, and Combat Commands A and B moved out immediately: CCA for Paderborn and CCB toward Delbruck. Combat Command R was held at Selm in reserve. The next day, April 2, vigorous German fighting at Neuhaus stopped the attack on Paderborn, and CCR was ordered into the battle.

Pa, his truck loaded with ammunition, drove eastward out of Selm in a motor-march, following a thin line of flat country roads he had penciled on a German road map. He passed rambling stone farmhouses and roomy barns and truncated cone silos. Cows and beef cattle grazed in wet meadows. Farmers tilled and planted fields, and women spaded gardens. Children played on village roadsides, and women walked to market. There was no evidence of war. For seventy kilometers, Pa drove through the seeming calm of a stormy battleground, sipped wine and cognac, and cached a bottle of champagne under the seat. By the time he reached Delbruck at nearly midnight, he hadn't eaten anything but K rations all day, and he was hungry. The night was cold; he slept fitfully in the truck.

At dawn, CCR attacked southeast out of Delbruck, seized Elsen, and advanced on Neuhaus. But they would not reach it. At 9:00 A.M., Colonel Wallace received orders to turn CCR southwest away from Paderborn toward Lippstadt and attack westward on the south edge of the Ruhr to entrap twenty German divisions in the Ruhr industrial pocket. There would be no dash to Berlin for the 8th Armored Division.

Pa convoyed overnight twenty-five kilometers from Delbruck to Lippstadt. The convoy passed through Wadersloh, where Service Battery had billeted, and the soldiers picked up their duffel bags. Snipers harassed them at Anneppen; they slowed, detoured, and were further delayed, reaching Lippstadt at twilight. The city, scene of a day-long CCR fight with German panzer troops, was burning, and eight German tanks smoldered in the square.

Pa quartered in a cellar and, as Combat Command R attacked south, ferried artillery shells from the Beckum supply depot to the mobile 105-mm howitzers supporting the CCR advance. On the first day, they reached the Paderborn–Soest road.

The following day, April 5, the weather turned hot and humid in the Ruhr Valley, and Pa trucked ammunition westward as Combat Command R battled forward. At the Weslarn–Lohne road northeast of Soest, Combat Command B passed through CCR, and CCR withdrew to reserve in Lippstadt. Pa saw Frank there.

"Didja hear the news?" Frank asked. "The goddam colonel got captured last night."

"I haven't heard nothin'," Pa replied. "I been on the road for two days."

"Yeah, well listen to this. Colonel Wallace tells his jeep driver, some unlucky sonofabitch of a private, that he wants to go to Horne to see Colonel Brooke from CCA. Trouble was, CCA didn't take Horne yesterday, they stopped short; the krauts were still there and snatched Wallace and his driver. They musta thought we were givin' them a present."

"How do you know they got him. They could be hiding out someplace."

"Well, when Wallace didn't show back at HQ, a patrol went out and grabbed a kraut soldier. He said he'd seen 'em. Described Wallace and his driver to a tee. They got 'em alright."

"Frank, ole buddy, aren't we lucky we don't have a soft job drivin' some colonel around? Except for the blisters and callouses you get on your ass drivin' a goddam deuce and a half full of explodin' ammo over some shell-holed road, you don't live half as dangerous as some big bird out in front tryin' to find something to shoot at."

Frank recalled the battle at Dorsten. "You forget," he said. "We been cut off, too, and spent a couple nights at the front. It could happen again."

"Wallace is a good man. He treated us right," Pa said. "I hope he's okay."

"He'll be okay."

"I gotta drive Captain Givens on a recon somewhere tomorrow," Pa said. "I hope to hell he knows where our lines are, or I might meet Colonel Wallace firsthand and see for myself if he's okay."

Pa drove Captain Givens of the 405th westerly beyond Horne and Soest deep into the lush valley of the Mohne and Ruhr Rivers, and Givens looked for a crossing site where Combat Command R could establish a bridgehead.

The wide valley allowed views of fifty kilometers or more to the south and west. Whitewashed cut-stone farmhouses and barns dotted the countryside. Fields of sugar beets touched the barnyards, and yellowed grain stretched to the horizon. The soil was rich and the fields lush. Pa later called the Ruhr Valley the most beautiful country he had seen. He drove as far west as Delecke, where Captain Givens noted a bridge over the Mohne River.

Orders came for Combat Command R to attack west out of Soest, and they moved up. At dawn on April 8, the 405th Armored Field Artillery fired on German positions west of Soest, and CCR tanks established a defensive bridgehead on their left flank across the Mohne River bridge at Delecke. They attacked westward. Pa stuffed his sleeping bag into his duffel, loaded his truck with ammunition, and drove to Soest. The Paderborn–Soest highway—said to be the ancient Hellweg built by the Romans—lay flat and straight and macadamized. Pa moved into a roomy farmhouse nearby bombed-out Soest, and later that night trucked ammunition up to the front. Combat Command R had pushed westward twelve kilometers against enemy 88-mm artillery fire and panzers and overrun Niederense and Hoingen. They had captured more than two hundred Germans, a Tiger tank, and three 88-mm guns. Lacking daylight, they had stopped at the Werl–Wickede road.

For the next five days, Combat Command R attacked westerly against German heavy artillery, mortars, and tanks and drove the enemy deep into the Ruhr. Pa moved up to Werl, and as CCR's tanks and artillery rolled up the German resistance, he brought ammunition to the howitzers at night, each night farther west. Although often pummeled by German artillery fire from south of the Mohne and Ruhr Rivers, bruised by the retreating enemy's armor, and harassed by land mines and booby traps, the 105s and M4 tanks pushed on against the German resistance. In their wake, Pa shuttled artillery shells past a destroyed German army and through a tableau of ruin that was once Germany.

The attack rolled on. South of Unna on the Ruhr River, Combat Command R joined with the 95th Infantry and closed the ring around German Army Group B. In five days of battling panzer troops, the 8th Armored Division had advanced fifty kilometers into the Ruhr against vigorous resistance. They had put down a desperate, last-ditch counter-attack at Dortmund and secured the trap around Army Group B, capturing more than 325,000 German soldiers and their commander, Field Marshall Walther Model. But they were bloodied as well. Combat Command R had lost some two hundred men killed or wounded, eleven M4 Sherman tanks, and nine half-tracks.

Pa, as he shuttled ammunition to the front, witnessed the end of the two-month-long ground campaign against the Ruhr pocket. He met long columns of German prisoners streaming to the rear and huddled on open flatbed trailers and under the canvases of converted supply trucks. They carried satchels and leather bags over their shoulders. Teenagers and younger men sported grins on their faces, and battle veterans showed defiance in their eyes.

He came upon thousands of shabby and pitiable slave laborers pouring out of the Ruhr's labor camps and trudging east toward home—Poland, Russia, Czechoslovakia, Holland, and Belgium. Crowds of liberated and displaced refugees peopled the roadside. They sat wearily in fields; slept on the ground; killed cows, pigs, and chickens, and built fires, and ate the roasted meat with their fingers. They walked with all of their worldly goods wrapped in a rag or tucked in a pushcart, their destinations hundreds of kilometers distant. For as long as five years, they had been forced to labor in the war-machine factories of the Ruhr.

"Jeezus, Pechie," Pa exclaimed to his codriver, "I've never seen anything like it. I can't imagine how the krauts must have treated these people."

Pa would bear forever the memory of that sight. In later years, when he mentioned the war to a relative or friend, it was the Ruhr that first came to his mind. He would recall the downtrodden and dispossessed slave laborers who boasted wide smiles and waved to him in his U.S. Army truck. And he would well up and go silent, unable to put the scene into words.

Orders came for the 8th Armored Division to proceed east again to Wolfenbuettel, north of the Harz Mountains, and wait for orders. Pa was at the fuel dump in Werl loading gasoline onto his truck when he heard that President Roosevelt had died. For him, it was sobering news; his first thought, perhaps, was how the conduct of the war would be affected. God forbid that Roosevelt's death would upset the momentum. The war had progressed quickly and as planned in the past few weeks, and the end seemed imminent. He finished loading gasoline, took on some artillery rounds at the ammunition dump, and waited for word to move.

Early the next day, the 405th Armored Field Artillery Battalion motor-marched eastward out of Werl. At Paderborn, Luftwaffe fighter planes harassed the convoy, and they turned northward into the dark forest. They drove late into the night, through Hamelin, haunt of the fabled Pied Piper, and arrived at the Wolfenbuettel assembly area around one o'clock in the morning. There, orders awaited them to immediately attach to Combat Command B and shield the right flank of XIX Corps, exposed by 2nd Armored's thrust to the Elbe River. An hour later, they left for Halberstadt, eighty kilometers east, where Pa pulled into a lumber yard outside the city and slept a fitful three hours in a drying shed.

He woke early and ate hot food from the battalion's field kitchen, his first in ten days. He was in eastern Germany, eighty kilometers from Magdeburg on the Elbe River. The sky had cleared, and the sun warmed his back. The men talked of Berlin. Will the Americans get there first, or will the Russians beat them to it? News came that 2nd Armored was in trouble, driven out of their bridgehead south of Magdeburg and forced to retreat back across the Elbe. Maybe, Pa thought, they will join 2nd Armored for the final blow. After breakfast, he greased his truck and waited for an order.

In Halberstadt, the 405th established camouflaged firing stations on the right flank of XIX Corps and supported the reconnaissance activities of Combat Command B to the southeast with both long-range and direct fire. Pa delivered a load of ammunition to the firing batteries, then headed for the supply depot at Oschersleben to reload. As he drove closer to Magdeburg on the Elbe River, German fighter planes harassed the convoy but soon left without inflicting damage. The Oschersleben supply depot, a scant thirty kilometers from Magdeburg and the Elbe, would be Pa's closest approach to Berlin during the war. The 2nd Armored Division would sit and wait on the autobahn in Magdeburg for General Eisenhower to order an advance. But the order would not come.

After a few days of reconnaissance and patrol activity, CCB and the 405th Armored Field Artillery reverted to the 8th Armored Division, and orders came to attack Blankenburg in the Harz Mountains to the south. Considered to be part of the fabled National Redoubt of Germany, the Harz Mountains rose more than three thousand feet, and their forests hid the residue of German troops west of the Elbe. The 2nd Armored Division, in their rush eastward toward Berlin, had bypassed the Redoubt, and the 8th Armored took on the mop up of the beleaguered remnants of the German 11th Panzer Army.

Combat Commands A and B attacked Blankenburg from opposite directions, CCA from the west and CCB from the east over the Langerstein–Heimburg road. Combat Command R was held in reserve. CCB's leading tanks quickly took Heimburg against sporadic resistance and displayed their firepower outside of Westerhausen and Blankenburg while a squadron of P-47s strafed the towns' defenses. Colonel Burba, CCB commanding officer, ordered his troops to take a K-ration break while he dispatched a surrender ultimatum. The show of strength intimidated the burgomasters, and they surrendered the German defenders in both towns.

Pa put wooden benches in the back of his truck and shuttled several loads of German prisoners—the battered remnants of the 116th Panzer Division that 8th Armored had beaten up at Dorsten and routed out of Zweckel—twenty kilometers to confinement in Halberstadt.

The capture of Blankenburg and the mop up of Michaelstein in the mountains to the south signaled the end of the war for the 8th Armored Division. Pa returned to Halberstadt and stowed his duffel in his truck. He then looked up Frank.

"You busy, Frank?"

"No. What's up?"

"I need some help. Come with me."

Pa drove to a damaged warehouse at the rail yard. They lifted a supply of canned fruits and vegetables and meats and thirty cases of cognac and wine into the back of his truck.

"I'm not sure where we're headed," he told Frank, "but wherever it is we should eat better than we have been."

The next day, April 21, Pa and Service Battery 405th Armored Field Artillery motored west out of the Harz Mountains for Osterwick, where they found a wine cellar and drank all night. They drank Schnapps and Rheinhessen and pilsner and several brands of cognac. They cheered the end of fighting—three months of combat since their initiation in the snowy hills of Alsace–Lorraine—and moaned their failure to mount an attack on Berlin. And when they were sober, they readied to move again.

They traveled southwest in half-tracks and supply trucks converted to troop carriers. Pa drove through the Harz Mountains, cleared of German troops, to Gottingen and beyond. Farmhands worked fields, and Pa sipped wine and waved to them out of the side window. In a small village west of Gottingen, they billeted in half-timbered houses. Spring had come; green filled the fields, and flowers bloomed in the square. They were safe now, out of artillery range and beyond the ability of the Luftwaffe to strike their convoy.

Pa spent two rainy days there, and he ate and drank from the booty he had lifted from the Halberstadt warehouse. He trucked a load of German prisoners from CCR's headquarters at Clausthal–Zellerfeld in the Harz Mountains to the railhead in Kassel. On the road, he passed refugees and slave laborers walking out of Germany and likely felt he should stop and offer them a ride. In Clausthal–Zellerfeld, he saw General Simpson, commander of U.S. Ninth Army, and he recalled the rumor that Simpson had been ordered to prepare the Ninth for more war—in the Pacific. But when word came to move, Pa drove twelve kilometers to Gottingen, where he would join with the Military Government Army of Occupation and adapt to not being shot at.

Chapter Twenty-one
KENNEBUNK 1945

Now the Lord had said unto Abram, get thee out of thy coun-
try, and from thy kindred, and from thy father's house, unto a
land that I will shew thee.

—Genesis 12:1

Ma was desperate to get away from Temple. Although she had promised Pa that she would stay and manage our place while he went to war, Germany had surrendered in May. The war in Europe was over, and she had, she said, fulfilled her promise. One and one-half years had passed since he left; she had confronted two winters without him, the first the most severe in memory. He had left her to search for firewood, to cope with his animals and his hard-to-heat house, to cultivate his gardens, to countenance his drinking pals, and to stomach his carping and galling sister and mother. Ma was sick of it. The town, she said—I suspect she meant Pa's family less Grandpa C.F.—could keep on hoeing their sustenance gardens, splitting their wood into neat piles, and taking their pleasure from the misery of family farming, but she could take no more. Victimized by self-deception, she knew we were living a failure and that life in Temple without Pa was impossible. Hope had stopped. We were leaving.

She said we were moving to the home of our grandparents in Kennebunk, a town of upscale and stylish people who enjoyed the good life a hundred miles away from Temple, where the ocean kept winters warm and summers cool. She needed to help Grammy Watson care for Grampa, she told us, and that we would wait there for Pa because he would be home by the end of summer. But I knew that Grampa, who had been sick and in the hospital, had recovered and was at work again. Grammy didn't need help, I thought; Ma did. But she also said that she could not face Temple any longer without Pa, and I believed her.

In spite of Ma's hopelessness, I was heartbroken that she was taking us away. I was happy in Temple, where I had good friends and could explore the paths and pastures with them, and where I could watch men work and overcome their flaws and make a life. In summer, I could swim in the stream, go fishing with Grandpa C.F., and mow lawns for money. I had thought that Pa's fighting the war and our running the home place would bring respect to our family. Pa would appreciate us more, and we would grow closer to him. We had struggled while he was gone, but we had managed. And now, when our suffering was almost over, we give up, leave, run away.

On the day after I finish fifth grade at the Village School, Fern comes to drive us to the train station. She helps Ma pack some boxes and offers advice. "El wants you to stay here, Clarice. Stay. Don't upset him like this."

But Ma, her mind made up, slams a suitcase shut and says, "He won't have points enough to come home for five or six months, Fern. I don't want to live with my parents, but I can't live here alone that long. I'm going, and that's it."

"But what are your parents going to say about your smokin' or drinkin' a stubby of beer once in a while?"

"I don't care. If I have to live in a tent on the beach, I will," Ma says.

There is no talk, and we fill the roadster quickly. We need to catch the Portland train at the West Farmington station. Nancy and I squeeze into the rumble seat, smothered by suitcases and boxes and bags, and Patty stuffs herself into the front seat between Fern and Ma and holds the last suitcase on her lap. I wonder what we will do with all of this stuff in Kennebunk when Pa comes home. I wonder, too, if he even knows we're going to Kennebunk.

As Fern starts the roadster down our lane toward the bridge, I turn my head and look back. Cappy is chasing us in the dust. "Mommy! It's Cappy! He wants to come."

"He can't come. There's no room," she answers.

"But he'll die," I plead. "He can't live alone." I am frantic. How could we leave Cappy here alone? I lean forward, "Mommy. Can't we take him with us?"

"He'll be okay. He'll be here when we get back." Ma sounds so sure.

Nancy shrugs and says Ma probably knows best, but I don't agree. Folks in town will know that we just drove off and left him. But Nancy trusts Ma and says Ma will care for us. She says we will make new friends and that Ma will be happy away from Pa's godawful relatives.

To our relief the train was not crowded. Ma piled her suitcases and boxes on an empty seat and sat down behind Nancy and me. I looked out the window and wondered when I would see home again.

We started up with a jerk and then another, then moved slowly and smoothly, gathering speed. The woods and fields drifted by quietly, and a stream meandered along beside me. The train crossed an unpaved road where a car, the driver's arm out the window, waited for us to pass. Soon we slowed and stopped at a station. Outside my window, a dingy freight yard looked lifeless and desolate. A man with a satchel came into our car and sat next to the aisle. He looked like a doctor, maybe on his way to visit a patient in the next town. We began to move again. The stream, still next to my window, reminded me of home. Ma leaned over the back of my seat and put her hand on my shoulder. "Are you all right?" She asked.

"I don't know," I answered. "I think so."

"Are you unhappy . . . or worried?"

"Yes. A little bit. But I'll be okay." I held my chin in my palms and stared out the window. The train passed another village without stopping, and I heard Ma, behind me, say, "You'll be fine. I know."

In Portland, we changed to a train for Boston. A porter helped Ma put our boxes into a wire rack at the front of the car. The train eased out of the station and rolled along the waterfront, where seagulls floated on the summer breeze. Then a man wearing a blue coat and a round cap with gold insignia walked up the aisle holding onto the seatbacks and asked Ma for our tickets. He wanted to know if we were going to our grandparents for a visit, and she said yes, maybe even for the summer. He smiled and told us that grandparents are fun and they love kids and for us to eat plenty of ice cream while we're there. We smiled back. He didn't know our grandparents.

The train stopped twice before it slowed for the station at Kennebunk. Passengers began to stir and gather their belongings. As we stopped, Ma pointed out the window to Grammy and Grampa standing on the station platform and waved to them. "There they are," she announced. "They see us. Wave to them." I could see them standing passively on the platform and, in spite of my misgiving, they looked harmless there. I raised my hand and waved. They didn't see me.

I did not know Grammy and Grampa Watson very well. I couldn't remember them being in Temple. Nor could I remember ever feeling welcome in Kennebunk. I had been to Kennebunk other summers but only briefly, and they had seemed to take no notice of me except to ask Ma how I was doing in school. They were from England and had come to Kennebunk when Ma was four years old. Now they attended Sunday church and prayer meetings at the Kennebunk Baptist Church where Grampa, a lay minister, occasionally preached to the congregation. A quiet and gentle person, perhaps even shy, he had not hugged us, played games with us, or busied us in conversation during our past visits. He avoided showing friendliness or affection, or any sentiment whatsoever. On the other hand, Grammy had been stern and inflexible. She had instructed Ma to keep us quiet, wash our faces, and make us behave, and had refused to upset her daily regimen or change her mind on our account. I suspected it would be the same this time.

Grammy and Grampa lived their orderly lives in a three-story house on Fletcher Street with neighbors—in houses filled with people, dogs, cats, bicycles, and cars—on both sides, across the street, and in the back on Storer Street. Grampa kept his front yard closely clipped and manicured and his six-cylinder Chevrolet sedan out of sight in a garage at the end of his stone-covered driveway. We were told not to go to either place. Cars and trucks whizzed by in front and in back and kept us out of the streets and awake at night. Grammy's tiny backyard had flowers and shrubs, a picnic table, two wooden lawn chairs, a circular clothesline that she could hang clothes on without moving her feet, and barely room for us to toss a ball or kick a can. My sisters and I were assigned to this little patch of cluttered green behind the house.

Grammy and Grampa's luxurious house was, I thought, built for lazy people. We crammed our stuff into the upstairs where we enjoyed our own bathroom—a white-enameled interior privy like Aunt Marion's that splashed hot water out of sparkling faucets into a shiny sink, sluiced gallons of water down an enameled one-holer, and sported a jumbo-sized glossy wash tub that eliminated any need to go to the neighbors for a hot bath. Ma could smoke in the back bedroom out of Grammy's sight.

Downstairs, a gas cooking stove abolished any need to fill a wood-box, and an Easy Spindrier washer had done away with wrinkled shirts and broken buttons. We ate in a separate dining room, snacked at another table in the kitchen, and rocked in a chair on the front porch. Grammy and Grampa Watson displayed accoutrements and trappings I hadn't seen in Temple, except at Aunt Marion's, and here, too, it seemed as though luxury made people demanding and self-interested. In spite of Grammy's soft chairs and soft beds, she ran our lives as if she were some snooty empress.

She treated us like dirt. In the dining room at noon on the first day, soup bowls and sandwich plates waited poised on the table. Grammy eyed us up and down and, like some sergeant at Fort Bragg, issued orders to Ma.

"Can't you keep those kids clean, Clarice? Look at Johnny. Dad will be home for lunch in seven minutes."

Ma nodded me upstairs. "He washes his own hands and face, Mom. I don't do it for him."

"And make sure he has shoes on, too. Doesn't he wear shoes at home?"

The first day on Fletcher Street, I learned that Grammy served meals by the clock and to be ready. Grampa, who worked at the post office, arrived home at 12:10 for lunch, which had been prepared and waited for him on the table. When he came through the door, we were ready and seated at the table. We ate lunch in virtual silence, and at 12:50 Grampa left for another afternoon of stamping letters, and I let out a sigh of relief.

We didn't eat supper at Grammy's; we ate dinner. More accurately, we attended what seemed to me a ceremony. Forty-five minutes after Grampa arrived home from work, the ceremony began. Grammy insisted that Ma scrub our hands and faces, comb our hair, dress us in clean clothes, and command us to sit quietly and wait. Promptly at 6:00 P.M. with food steaming out of flowered, egg-shaped bowls on the white tablecloth, we put our hands in our laps and listened to Grampa pray. He then served each of us portions from the oval bowls—meat, potatoes, and vegetables—with silver, curlicue-handled utensils; normal behavior, I supposed, for upscale and stylish people, but unheard of at our house in Temple.

Neither Grammy nor Grampa knew how to do anything wrong. Conversation was proper, deliberate, and forced. They spoke to us indirectly by addressing Ma: "Johnny is too quiet," or "Johnny doesn't eat all of his squash," or "You should get Patty some new clothes," or "Nancy is old enough to have a Bible."

Ma would nod, and we would try not to disrupt dinner by smiling or speaking without permission. It was the same ceremony every day. I moved as little as possible and spoke only when spoken to.

Mornings and afternoons we played games in the backyard. Grammy didn't have toys, Ma said, so we played hide-and-seek, hop-scotch, and kick-the-can, and made too much noise, as though we were still in Temple. Grammy, afraid we would bend the grass, or startle other kids yelling in their own backyards, would say to Ma, "Clarice, tell them to stop."

Then Ma would bring us a snack to eat at the picnic table and whisper to us that the noise bothered Grammy and to play quietly, but I didn't know how to play quietly and neither did Nancy or Patty. So Grampa found a teepee-shaped canvas tent in the garage and put it up for us. We played and ate snacks in the tent, where sounds were muffled, and wondered what kids do in the other backyards and why Grammy couldn't be like Ma and just leave us alone. But she couldn't and kept yelling at Ma, "Clarice, tell them to stop." And at the end of each day, she told Ma to make us pick up our playthings and put them away, so the backyard would be clean and neat and presentable to the neighbors. We put the tin cans in the teepee and tried to straighten up the bent grass.

Eventually, we met the other kids in the neighborhood and played dodgeball and kickball in their yards, where no one seemed to mind. We yelled all afternoon, and kids went home when they were tired or when their mothers blew a whistle to beckon them. The neighbors' kids had their own whistle code, like a telephone number; one long and two shorts, or two longs, or three shorts and a long. When they heard their whistle code, they went home. At suppertime, what Grammy called dinnertime, the neighborhood sounded like a bad piccolo lesson.

But Grammy said Ma didn't need a whistle. "Clarice, you better get your kids. It's time for them to be here." Then Ma would tramp around the backyards until she spied us and summon us back to Fletcher Street.

But we were not always in someone else's backyard. Twice each week that summer, a yellow bus, the words Kennebunk School Department painted on its sides, took Kennebunk kids to the beach, three miles away. Ma said we should go to the beach. Furthermore, she told us, we would like Kennebunk Beach, where she had played as a child. I had never been on a school bus or a beach, but on a summer Tuesday I followed my sisters down Fletcher and across Main to Park Street School where I boarded the bus. I was nervous and sat alone and worried. I feared that the bus driver wouldn't know where to take us, that the beach would be too crowded and I wouldn't find a place to sit, that I wouldn't like it, that I'd be lonely, and that I wouldn't know when and where to get on the bus to come home. Nancy and Patty had friends on the bus, and they talked. I could hear them, but it was too noisy to make out the words. I listened to everything and heard nothing and looked out the window of the bus.

The bus passed an empty railroad station. It passed a housing development on a small hill above a marsh filled with boggy grass where gulls and herons and stark white egrets searched for fish. The bus stopped, then crossed a highway where a gasoline station and a roadside lunch stand kept tourists supplied with fuel, red hot dogs, and Orange Crush. Inside the bus, the kids grew noisy, so noisy I couldn't think. Everyone was talking at once. The boy next to me was wearing a baseball cap and a T-shirt with something printed on it. I wanted to tell him I had never been to a beach or seen the ocean. Maybe, I thought, he would say something that would tell me what to expect. I tried to speak to him, but nothing came out. I looked out the window again.

The bus turned onto Beach Street. One side of the street was filled with sprawling summerhouses with wraparound, columned porches and clipped hedges, and the other with a sand beach that fronted the ocean. It seemed as though the world ended there where the sand met the water. Beyond looked like vast space, in which the line between the ocean and sky was invisible. I was dizzied by that space and felt so exposed I feared the earth could topple into it. Then, far out on the water beneath the sky, I watched a ship transect my view from right to left, and I squared myself to the world.

On the beach, hundreds of people lay on blankets or sat on chairs under beach umbrellas while kids dug holes in the sand with miniature shovels. Boys slapped a ball back and forth over a net, kids played tag in the surf, and mothers walked along the water looking for scallop shells and starfish. I walked to the water's edge, listened to the ocean's din, watched the waves break and fall, and searched for ships. I waded in the water and squinted my eyes along the beach for where Nancy and Patty had spread a blanket.

I ran there to sit with them, and sand flew up on me and stuck. Sand covered my legs, invaded my swimsuit, and clung to my hands and face as though I was coated with glue. I tried to wash the sand off in the surf, but I seemed to rub on more glue. I stayed there at the ocean's edge until the yellow bus came to get us, but I knew that I wanted to come back and listen to the ocean bellow and growl and shout. I also wanted, after having watched some of Kennebunk's kids toss a ball around and chatter on a blanket and gossip and giggle on the bus, to make some friends.

In a town where ten-year-old boys played ballgames and went to parties and boasted to each other about what they had seen and done with girls their age, I was nobody. The only girls I knew were my sisters' friends, and they scarcely knew my name, or I theirs. I was uncomfortable and self-conscious, and I felt inferior. After listening to some of Kennebunk's ten-year-old Casanovas boast of their experiences, I knew I should overcome those shortcomings.

Louise, an outsized blonde with long hair, a suntanned face, and a constant smile, lived next door to us on Fletcher Street. Sometimes she played games with my sisters in Grammy's backyard, but to me she was mostly a stranger. On hot days, she invited Nancy to her house to cool off in her basement playroom. One day I went with Nancy to Louise's basement, and we lounged on the sofa, slurped Popsicles, and listened to Vaughan Monroe on Louise's record player. Louise and Nancy prattled on about movie stars and music and boys and grandmas, but I listened to Louise. She sounded interested in boys, and I thought I liked her a bit. Suddenly she spoke to me.

"John," she said. "Would you like to hear our player piano?"

Why me? I thought. I don't know a player piano from a ukulele. "Sure," I said.

"Me, too," Nancy said, sounding every bit as though she listened to a player piano daily. "I love player piano."

We watched and listened to the piano play "Chattanooga Choo Choo" and "Moonlight Serenade" and then, as I started to leave, I spoke to Louise in what I hoped was a friendlier way than I had spoken to other girls my age. "I liked listening to the music, Louise," I said. "I left my records and a Victrola in Temple. Grammy doesn't let us listen to music at her house, anyway."

"Why don't you come over with Nancy again sometime," she said.

Louise and her younger sister, whom Patty found to be playful and good-natured company and who once brought Patty a Popsicle, were the only kids in the neighborhood who came to our backyard. They came to play kick-the-can on Grammy's fenced-in patch of bent-over grass and to play house and tell stories in the tent. When Louise was in Grammy's backyard, she fixed imaginary tea and cookies for me to share with her, showed me a constant smile, and chose to be my partner in the games. As the summer passed, she became my secret passion. I fantasized that I lived with her, kept house with her, undressed in the same room with her, and lay on the same bed with her, her long blonde hair hanging in my face.

One day my passionate musings took a turn toward reality. Alone with me inside the tent, Louise dared me to undress. Shamelessly, we agreed to undress together. Piece by piece, shirt for shirt, and shorts for shorts, we looked at each other across the tent. I paled. She was flat; her chest looked like mine. My fantasy chilled, and at that moment the truth ended my imaginary affair with Louise. She returned to her player piano and Nancy's prattle, and I to kick-the-can, reading Big Little Books, and waiting for Pa to come home and tell me his stories.

After two months away from Temple, I missed the laid-back freedom of its fields and lanes more than ever. I did not belong in Kennebunk. I was a country boy with a country clock who wanted to eat when I was hungry and to fish when they were hungry. I needed the space and freedom I had so loved in Temple. I needed Pa to come home. I hadn't received a letter from him for a time, and I didn't know where he was or when I would see him. So I conformed to Grammy's rules—played quietly, dressed for dinner, and arrived at meals on time—and waited.

Grammy and Grampa treated me cordially, but I never really knew whether they liked me or not. And I didn't look for clues. Instead, in their presence I kept to myself and read almost constantly. But one evening Grampa asked me, "Do you know what you want to be, John, when you grow up?"

I looked up from *The Adventures of Dick Tracy* and said, "No, I don't know." I hoped he would accept my answer and not lecture me, often a feature of a visit from Grampa. But I knew Grammy had seen in me signs of what she called "a bump on a log," a loner who drifted without any sense of direction, and I suspected she had ordered Grampa to direct me. Although I had tried to not stir them up, Grampa had likely agreed that he should straighten out what Grammy called my tendency to drift off center.

"Well," he asked, "shouldn't you be reading *The Adventures of Tom Sawyer* or *Lassie Come Home* or something more useful than stories about Dick Tracy or Prairie Bob, or whatever they're called? Something that will help you make up your mind?"

"I do," I said. "I read in school. I read *The Adventures of Tom Sawyer* and *Huckleberry Finn* and *Peck's Bad Boy and His Pa* and books my teacher says to read. In summer, I read adventure stories, the Hardy Boys' books and Nancy Drew." He should know I don't read just *The Adventures of Dick Tracy*. I suspected he was getting around to a lecture on the Bible. I had read church-school stories all summer and stories from the Bible he carried around with him all day on Sundays. I had read more church stories than I had adventure books. If he had been watching, he would know.

Every week that summer, I spent six days on summer vacation and one day in school—church school. Although Ma had joined the Baptist Church in Temple, she and Pa had not attended, nor had they sent us to the church school there or the vacation bible school in the summer, and we were unfamiliar with church doings. Contrary to our experience, Grammy and Grampa did not miss a Sunday in church, and they took Ma with them and told her to take us to the basement church school. There I studied the stories of Abraham and Lot—who were also called on to move from their home to a far place—David and Goliath, and the prophets Amos and Jeremiah. Once my teacher asked me whether Abraham had heard God's promise with his ears, and I answered yes but only partly with his ears, and the kid beside me laughed. I thought, Why not? If Abraham listened to God with his whole being, why wouldn't that include his ears? But no, she said, God doesn't speak in words. And so I learned in the Kennebunk Baptist Church School not to listen with my ears and to covenant, to forgive, and to pray. And I prayed for Pa to come home and for the end of the basement church school, and I listened with my whole being for God's message to go back to Temple.

Grammy and Grampa were the first deeply religious people I knew. They were stern, no fun, sit-in-a-chair-all-day-Sunday Baptists, and after church, we sat with them and read the Bible and church books and classics. I sat with my feet off the floor in an overstuffed parlor chair, a church-school book on my lap, and listened to the grandfather clock in the front hall tick and tock. No newspapers, no comics, no Big

Little Books. Reading stopped at 2:00 P.M. for Sunday dinner, and we ate and talked for two hours. Grampa expected each of us to describe church, to speak out about what we learned or observed, and to tell if we had come away from church with any spiritual feelings. More reading followed dinner. Grampa listened to a radio minister, then went to bed. No backyard games. No playing cards or Parcheesi or eating popcorn. Sundays were puritanical. We were hermits.

I was struck that summer by the lack of visitors to Grammy's. No friends or acquaintances came to see her, nor did she visit anyone. The neighbors did not knock to borrow a cup of sugar or leave a loaf of homemade rye bread or anything else, and she did not chat or gossip with them over the side-yard fences. She and Grampa lived solitary lives. The folks who did come to her house that summer came to see Nancy or Patty or me.

John Cannon, a boy I had met at church school and who lived nearby on Storer Street, came one day to see me. I knew him as an honest and upright boy who went to Cub Scouts, played a musical instrument in his parlor, and whose parents likely lived the stylish Kennebunk life—his father was a doctor. I greeted him warmly when he turned into the front yard and eased his bike to a stop.

"I'm trying to sell my bike," he said, and he reached out with one hand to straighten the wire basket sitting askew on the handlebars. "Want to buy it?"

I looked at his bicycle. It showed scratches and dents and smooth tires, and it lacked handlebar grips. The blue paint had mostly worn off, and the chain guard looked loose. He had likely dragged the brakes and tossed the bike on the ground whenever he got off, but I ignored its condition. "How much?" I asked.

"Ten dollars, if you have it."

"I don't have it."

"How much do you have?"

Upstairs in my room I kept a brown envelope of cash, my pay for selling *Grit* in Temple and mowing lawns for Mrs. Mosher and Aunt Marion last summer. I decided the bicycle was more valuable to me than the envelope. "I have a little bit over six dollars," I answered.

"That's enough."

"John, I've never been on a bike. Can I try it out?"

Nervous, I swung one leg over the three-cornered cushion seat, kept one foot on the ground, gripped both handlebars, and pushed a pedal with the other foot. As the bike moved forward, I instinctively guided it and balanced it using the handlebars. Shaky at first, I followed the Fletcher Street sidewalk, turned right on Mechanic and crossed over to Storer, and turned right again. By that time, I felt certain I could control the bike, and I left the sidewalk for the street. Kids were playing in a grassy yard on Storer, and to get their attention I pedaled as fast I could, my face pushing the rush of air aside, then coasted to the intersection with Fletcher. I turned right again, coasted as slowly as I could without falling, then pedaled faster and coasted again. I braked to a stop in Grammy's yard. I told John to wait while I went upstairs to get the envelope. I gave him the money, and he walked home. I was broke, and I thought surely Ma would have a list of questions for me to answer.

At the end of summer, I longed to see Pa, longed to hear his stories. But we heard no word that he was coming home soon. Ma, who had lingered in Kennebunk beyond her promise, was not making any move to go back to Temple. School would soon begin, and I knew if she lingered much longer, I would ride my bicycle down Fletcher Street, instead of Cowturd Lane, to the schoolhouse.

Chapter Twenty-two
ARMY OF OCCUPATION

*Practically every battalion and many individual companies
opened their own clubs.*
—Captain Charles R. Leach,
In Tornado's Wake: A History of the 8th Armored Division

T he university dominated Gottingen. Founded in 1734, the
University of Gottingen grew to world prominence in the
arts, mathematics, and philology. Its renowned physics institute had
produced a lengthy portfolio of Nobel prize winners from among the
world's leading physicists, In 1945, American scientific curiosity in
Germany focused on Gottingen. The atomic scientist Werner
Heisenberg, perhaps the world's most eminent theoretical physicist,
had remained in Germany during the war—some thought in
Gottingen—which led the U.S. Office of Strategic Services to fear the
physics institute was producing an atomic bomb. It was here in 1945
that the OSS sent American spies to determine what German scien-
tists knew about nuclear fission. When Pa and the 405th Armored
Field Artillery Battalion arrived in Gottingen near the end of April, the
spies had come and gone away empty-handed, and the Military
Government Army of Occupation controlled the city.

Drab and colorless, its Renaissance architecture unappreciated by contemporary Germany, Gottingen reminded Pa of a Grade-B black-and-white movie. The shadows of ancient blackened cathedrals ominously shaded the white facade of the institute. Unkempt medieval buildings lined the city's debris-filled streets. Dirt and grime on benches, fountains, awnings, and the statue of the little Goose Girl in the central market square discolored the city. Laboratory technicians, professors, doctors, and nurses in white frocks mixed with soldiers in army olive drab. In Gottingen, the soldiers of the 405th, no longer a target for German guns, looked for decent living conditions and opportunities to add some pleasure to their lives.

They moved into the abandoned Krone Hotel and spent the first night in sleeping bags on the lobby floor. They cleared out debris, swept floors, repaired what furniture they could, and stole enough more to make it livable. They rebuilt the bar and furnished the lounge. Pa, on sentry duty at a Warehausenstrasse warehouse, found a distillery and after he was relieved went for Frank and a truck. An hour later, they returned to the Krone with canned sauerkraut, sauerbraten, and four hundred bottles of red wine, cognac, and schnapps. They were noncombatants now, and felt they had earned a chance to relax.

As the war came to an end, they felt it unpatriotic not to celebrate. They drank heavily and partied in the lounge with WACs and nurses who also had been exposed to German guns. They celebrated reports of Hitler's death. Pa found no relief in the news. Instead, he felt it to be anticlimactic, overshadowed by the devastating tragedy Hitler had brought to the German nation. But he felt compelled, as his pals Elmer and Vilio would have wanted, to celebrate little Adolph's demise. The battalion's soldiers also celebrated the first reports of the German surrender, which turned out to be false. They celebrated again when the Germans signed the surrender at Rheims, and a third time at the Berlin signing. They celebrated an additional day, too, officially called V-E (Victory in Europe) Day, to be sure they didn't miss the moment the war in Europe ended.

They celebrated General Devine's promotion to major general. They celebrated distribution of the whiskey ration. They celebrated fixing a flat tire. They celebrated for no reason at all. Frank and Pa made several more visits to the distillery on Warehausenstrasse to keep the Krone stocked with red wine and cognac. After a time, they were fulfilled and went back to soldiering.

First, the 8th Armored Division paraded its strength in Gottingen city and honored its commander, Major General John Devine. The soldiers had come together on maneuvers in Louisiana more than a year previous and had arrived in Gottingen after three months of combat in France, the Ardennes, and northen Germany. They had suffered 310 soldiers killed in action —two in the 405th Armored Field Artillery Battalion—and 2,626 had sustained battle wounds. More than three hundred were decorated for bravery, and several units received Meritorious Service Awards, including Pa's battery, Service Battery 405th Armored Field Artillery.

Pa and a self-propelled 105-mm howitzer, the workhorse gun of the ground war in Europe, in Gottingen, Germany. May 1945.

Pa held two jobs for the Army of Occupation, security duty and trucking. He walked a post on Warehausenstrasse to prevent theft of food, dry goods, and liquor stored in sheet metal warehouses there. He carried a rifle and a walkie-talkie, and he likely avoided using each. He patrolled the grounds and corridors of Gottingen Hospital and checked passes at the hospital entry checkpoint. He carried a pistol and mingled with German-speaking doctors and nurses as well as American soldiers and German prisoners of war recovering from wounds and sickness.

He drove his supply truck to Grefrath and picked up duffel bags he had stored there in March. He passed over 8th Armored's former battlegrounds at Soest and Gladbeck and crossed the Rhine River twice at Duisberg, the artillery barrages now silent and the great river peacefully wedged between two banks of destruction. He hauled salvaged clothing to Hildeshiem, German ammunition to a warehouse in Gottingen, U.S. ammunition to an ammo dump in Munster, and food to the prison camps. From the windows of his truck he watched the German people emerge from their cellars, till their fields, repair their buildings, and restart their lives.

He put benches in his truck and, in convoys, distributed people throughout Germany. More languages were likely spoken under the canvas of his six-by-six than in most eastern U.S. liberal arts colleges. Pa spent long, tiring hours moving people over the roads of central Germany. He suffered fatigue from the enormity of the country's chaos and anguished over the conditions of its displaced people.

He was involved in three accidents. On the road from Hildeshiem, his truck struck an eight-year-old German boy on a bicycle. Codriver Pechie called for an ambulance, but the boy died from the injuries. Pa, although not driving, was extremely troubled by the tragedy. For weeks, the sight of the boy lying in the road beside the crumpled bicycle haunted him. War had not hardened him for such a sight, and he stopped drinking and stayed mostly to himself, though he talked to Frank about the boy. And he probably talked about me.

Later, on the road to Munster with a load of French slave laborers, he hit a German soldier. The soldier survived the injuries, and Pa did not show the remorse he had for the boy, perhaps because the man survived or because he was a soldier. Pa likely put the incident quickly out of his mind.

Finally, Pa wrecked a jeep on Hospital Street in Gottingen, and the MPs, who were also the local police officials, pinched him for speeding and fined him fifteen dollars. Frank, when he heard the news, found Pa on his bunk, sipping a bottle of Rheinhessen red. "You okay, El? What the hell was the hurry?"

"I'm okay, Frank. Lucky as hell though."

"You should be as lucky at poker. You coulda got killed. Or busted."

"Busted from what? Besides, I haven't been playing poker. Haven't been going to the club either. I'm tired and I've been busy . . . busy doing things."

Frank reaches for the Rheinhessen. "Things?"

"Yeah, things. I need to relax. For one thing, I went fishing yesterday. In the Leine, with hand grenades. Scooped up the fish with a helmet. Works slick as hell. Before that I went to see the Bible. Have you seen the Bible?"

"What Bible?"

"At the library. Five-hundred-year-old Bible. Printed by Gutenberg, or something like that, in German or Latin, I don't know. I couldn't read it. They said it was insured for eight million bucks. Whaddaya think of that?"

"I think it coulda been in English and you still couldn't read it."

"I've been *places* too. Why are you giving me such a hard time, Frank?"

"I ain't givin' you a hard time, El. I'm just trying to keep you out of any more trouble until you can get home. Places? What places?"

"I went out to the airstrip and hitched a ride on a C-47 to look around. We went all over, as far as Berlin. Took about three hours before we got back. Jeezus, you shoulda seen the damage. Saul was stove all to hell. Hamm stove up, too. Kassel level with the ground, the whole city. Frank, you've never seen anything like it. Everywhere we went, it was the same. Paderborn. Berlin. I didn't see a building in Berlin that hadn't been hit."

The next day, orders came to pack their duffels. Rumors circulated that the division was moving to Czechoslovakia. The 8th Armored Division, and Pa, was back in General Patton's U.S. Third Army.

The division formed a convoy and left Gottingen on June 4. At Weimar, they pulled off the autobahn and bivouacked, and Pa and Frank shared a pup tent. On the grassy shoulder of the highway, they ate K rations, drank Rheinhessen, and ate oatmeal cookies from Aunt Marion's shiny kitchen.

"Frank," Pa asks, "when do you think you'll go home?"

"Don't know, El. I only got about fifty points. I don't get bonus points for kids and a wife, like you do. I got no medals, no nothing. I just get two points a month. Keerist, I might be in the army a long time."

Pa had known since he was drafted he would be in until he had earned eighty-five points. He figured it would take two years, and he would probably stay in Germany after the war, perhaps even for six months. "Maybe," he says, "but my points don't add up to eighty-five yet. I don't know why they want to keep an old fart like me in the army anyway. I came for the war, but now it's over—and they're sending me farther away. My pals in Temple went in before I did, and they're on their way home already. All the liquor will be gone and women used up and worn out by the time I get there. Where we headed for this time? I heard it was Czechoslovakia. What the hell are we gonna do there?"

The next morning, back on the autobahn, they turned southerly through Triptis, Hirschberg, and Munchberg, towns and villages spared the destruction of the industrial and contested regions of Germany farther north. They traveled slowly, and after turning off at Bayreuth and heading eastward for Czechoslovakia, they slowed even more. They passed horse-drawn wagons full of belongings and thousands of German and Czech refugees on foot and on bicycles, carrying suitcases and bags, headed for home. They slowed for U.S. Army truck convoys taking German prisoners of war to distribution centers in central Germany.

Frustrated at the lack of progress, General Devine called a halt on the Czech border at Neustadt. Pa encamped in a hay field, ate cold K rations, and looked at a Czechoslovakian language primer. He thought Czech the toughest language he'd yet seen. He slept fitfully and hoped when they arrived they'd be billeted in private homes with spongy beds.

In Czechoslovakia, they moved into a lavish, thousand-bed summer resort high on the Bohemian plateau southeast of Pilsen. The battalion settled into the Villa Anna, stocked the bar with the wine and cognac they had brought from Warehausenstrasse, arranged a schedule of baseball games, and worked on learning enough of the Czech language to say hello to women in nearby Letney. Pilsen, the home of Bohemia's pilsner-style golden lager, would, they thought, be a suitable place to wait and rest.

Service Battery 405th Armored Field Artillery Battalion poses in Pilsen, Czechoslovakia, in June 1945. Pa is seated in the front row ninth from the left.

While headquarters units of 8th Armored arranged to feed, identify, and prepare thirty-five thousand German prisoners for relocation,
Pa rested. He bet on Service Battery in baseball games, hiked the villa's
trails, swam in the pool, posed for a Service Battery picture, and wrote
home.

Ma read to Nancy and Patty and me from his letter. He wanted to
come home, he wrote. It was beautiful at the villa, but he was bored.
The artillery had no work. Other artillery outfits assigned there had left
for home after two weeks, and he hoped the same would happen to the
405th. He complained that he couldn't fraternize with the Czechs; he
had been able to learn just a few Czech words. He sounded unhappy,
and I wondered, if he doesn't have anything to do, why doesn't the army
send him home so he can tell me his stories?

Pa's Czech dialogue was suitable enough in the villa's ballroom, however, to persuade a young woman to dance. He simply smiled, as he had
done in Temple or Chesterville so many times, and pointed to the dance
floor. But he didn't know the dance step and he turned the wrong way
or trampled on her feet until she quit and danced with another soldier.

Frank smiled and shook his head. "She doesn't understand what you
want, El," he whispered. "Try a little body language next time."

Pa and Frank attended classes on Pacific warfare. Frank feared they
would be transferred to the island war.

"No one wants to go there, Frank," Pa told him, "except the officers,
and then just those who don't have the infantry badge or the Bronze
Star or some other decoration. They want to get close enough to the
front to get their chest decorated without getting a hole in it, and the
Pacific war is the only one they've got now. I doubt if we'll be going.
Besides, we're too old for those Oriental women."

Pa continued to dabble away the time. He drove to Pilsen for beer,
shot craps in the villa, went to the circus in the next town, Klatovy, and
practiced motor marches over local roads. He attended USO shows,
watched American movies, and drank golden pilsner in the bars in

Pilsen. At the end of June, the battalion transferred to nearby Polen and moved into private homes. With the passing of another month, Pa earned two more points—eight left to go—toward his trip home. He wrote Ma that he wished he were in Temple.

Three weeks later, the battalion moved again, three hundred kilometers to Nussdorf, Germany, sixty kilometers south of Munich. An ammo truck exploded on the way, killing two men in the convoy. The injured were taken to the Munich hospital where German doctors stopped the bleeding and bandaged the wounds. Still nagged by the shadow of death, Pa grieved for his buddies and brooded over the futility of dying so near the end. His thoughts surely shifted to Temple, to the security of the fields and lanes and logging roads. Would Temple be the same when he returned? Would he be the same?

In Nussdorf, at the foot of the snowcapped Bavarian Alps, Headquarters issued Pa an armored command car. An open four-seater with a convertible-canvas top, side curtains, and running boards, it carried a spare ration of gas and had been used for ground reconnaissance and to transport high-ranking officers to frontline strategy meetings. Afternoons, Pa drove the command car to a country house on the edge of Miesbach, where he picked up officers and their staff and drove them to Munich or Rosenheim to see a movie or a show at the USO. Dressed in an olive-drab uniform and shined combat boots, he would salute the colonel or major and ask, "Where to today, sir?"

"To Munich, private, to a show at the club. Perhaps you'd like to go with us. We plan to stay overnight, probably at the Hotel America, unless we find other quarters."

"Thank you, sir. I'd like that," Pa would say. That summer he saw Bob Hope and George Raft and Billy Rose entertain the troops at the Munich USO and learned the first name of the desk clerk at the Hotel America.

In August, he officially transferred to Headquarters Battery of XX Corps Artillery in Miesbach to drive the command car. The colonel obviously appreciated Pa's willingness to please the officers and keep his mouth shut. He regularly picked up their liquor ration at Bad Tolz, frequently drove the colonel and a few of his staff to see an evening show, and most Sundays woke up with a hangover. The officers liked him.

Pa took considerable pleasure in chauffeuring the colonel and his assorted aides in the imposing command car. He delighted in being able to travel again, and from his rare position of status—still a buck private—he tended carefully to the wants of his newfound friends. He was at their service, but not so dutiful that he neglected to take part in their doings, since they included him as one of them as well.

During a break in the Munich delights, he drove them to Berchtesgarden on the Austrian border, to Hitler's mountaintop retreat, a place smelling of Nazi lust, where Hitler and his warlords—Himmler, Goebbels, and Goering—had plotted conquest and destruction. At the end of a long tunnel bored into the Bavarian Alps, Hitler's private elevator lifted Pa to the Fuehrer's Eagle's Nest where he swaggered and swelled and lauded his role in the demise of the Nazi regime. Later, a C-47 flew him, the colonel, and the headquarters staff to Paris. There, precursors to the flood of postwar tourists, they strolled the Champs-Elysees, gazed up at the towering Arc de Triomphe, rode the elevator to the top of the Eiffel Tower, and, as Pa described it, got awful drunk.

The colonel arranged a three-day pass for him to a summer resort at Priem on the Chiemsee east of Munich. There Pa sailed and cruised and fished and refreshed himself swimming in the Bavarian water. He boated to Herron Island and toured the grand castle of Ludwig II, one of many monumental edifices the crazy king of Bavaria had erected to himself. Shown the lavishly furnished rooms and profusely elegant art and silver and told the construction lasted eight years and consumed $30 million, Pa gasped, "Sure's some joint here!"

He returned to the Miesbach headquarters relaxed, untroubled, and proud of his job. He had made friends in high places, drunk the best cognac, and seen the most engaging sights. He took great pleasure in being what seemed like an American tourist. But nagging at his consciousness was home and friends and the roads and lanes of Temple. His pals waited at the West Farmington Fire Company. Vilio and Elmer, home then, waited on the highest bench of Lauri's Finnish steam bath. The fish waited in the stream. Ma waited in Kennebunk. And I waited, too, for him to tell me stories of how he fought great battles in faraway places and whether he won medals like I had seen on Tarmo's chest.

On September 2, V-J (Victory in Japan) Day, Pa sprawled on a sofa in the parlor of his Miesbach quarters and listened to President Truman and General MacArthur speak to the troops on Armed Forces Radio.

Frank came and sat with him. "How was Munich this time? Did you take the colonel to church, or did he insist on the club?"

"Actually," Pa said, "I met my old sergeant from Fort Bragg and tried to outdrink him. But I think he won."

"You look as if you did."

"Is it true what he told me, Frank, that eighty-pointers over thirty-five years old are eligible for discharge? Have you heard anything? I just picked up two more points the first of the month. Makes eighty-one for me."

"No, I ain't heard it. Besides, why would I listen to it? Or why would anyone? Except for me, you're the only guy in the outfit who's thirty-five years old. Chrissakes, you'll be drawin' social security before you get home if you don't go pretty soon."

A week later, word came for Pa, with his precious eighty-one points, to transfer to the 285th Field Artillery Battalion; the 285th was leaving for home the next day. Pa moved fast. He stood for clothing and equipment inspection. He slid two 9-mm Luger pistols into a pair of wool socks, wrapped the pieces of a 16-gauge Mauser shotgun in an army sweatshirt, and buried the guns in his duffel with the remainder of his clothes. He drove the command car to Nussdorf and picked up mail from Ma and Aunt Marion. Back in Miesbach, he found Frank. "Hubba-hubba, Frank. I got lucky. I'm shippin' out tomorrow, headed for Rheims. I'll be on a boat soon."

"Jeezuss, El. That's good news."

"I just got a letter today from the ole lady askin' me if I'd heard when I was comin' home. She oughta feel better now."

Frank went somber. "Good luck, El. And stay in touch."

"Goddamit, come to Temple after you get home. I'll treat you to a pitcher of hard cider and a Finnish steam bath."

"You bet your ass. I'll let you know." Then they who had shared the perils of a monstrous war and watched over and protected each other since battling the chiggers in Louisiana hugged.

"Stay in touch. And goddamit take care."

For three days, Pa and the 285th convoyed nearly a thousand kilometers through Germany and France to the processing camps at Rheims. They passed through Munich and Stuttgart and the mountainous Black Forest to Strasbourg where they crossed the Rhine River on a temporary bridge put up in March for assaults into Germany. They traveled slowly, twenty-five miles an hour, and kept to the main roads. The soldiers were cheerful and boisterous, and they drank wine and waved to the peasants in the fields. They stopped in Nancy, where Pa recalled being in January's bitter cold, and slept in tents pitched in a muddy field outside of the city. On the third day, the convoy arrived at Mailly-le-Camp, south of Rheims, and billeted in Camp New Orleans, one of seventeen redeployment camps thrown together in the area. Here, they would prepare for the trip back across, the trip home.

Pa spent three weeks in Camp New Orleans. It rained the first two. He and twenty-five thousand other soldiers slept restlessly in tents under wool blankets in the cool and dank French climate. When the rain and wind beat against his tent and the incessant mud clung to his combat boots, Pa recalled the days in England on Windmill Hill, before he had seen war, and wondered how war had changed him, how home would seem.

The army tried to tell him what to expect at home. He listened to lectures on how to become a civilian, how to talk without swearing, how to eat sitting at a table, and how to react to people who didn't understand or appreciate what he had done. He was instructed on the value of life insurance and spent too much time, he thought, enduring physicals. The doctors poked and jabbed and scraped and pinched and told him he was in good shape—and did it all again. He played poker until his money was gone, then watched American movies. He listened to the Tigers play the Cubs in the World Series, and he sweated out the Merchant Marine strike at LeHavre. He thought of maple-lined stone walls, lonely pastures, fattened game birds, and snowy traplines. The war was over. He wanted to go home.

After the fourth game of the World Series, word came to be ready to move. He repacked his duffel and at 1 A.M. rode in the back of a truck to a rail siding where he and hundreds of other homebound soldiers packed into ancient and rusted boxcars and were transported by railroad to St. Valery. Carrying his duffel on his shoulder, Pa hiked the final five kilometers to Camp Lucky Strike, where the USS *West Point* waited at a LeHavre dock for the troops to board. There a sergeant passed the word that a longshoremen's strike in New York had delayed departure, and they wouldn't board the ship for probably a week.

Pa tuned in the World Series again, wrote letters to Ma and Aunt Marion, and waited. He waited in chow lines, in PX lines, in movie lines, and in inspection lines. His impatience grew to frustration. The World Series ended, and he had seen the run of movies at the PX. He wrote Ma that he was at the dock but the ship was late and if the New York longshoremen hadn't stopped work he would have been in Kennebunk.

Chapter Twenty-three
BACK ACROSS

I shall be telling this with a sigh
Somewhere ages and ages hence:
Two roads diverged in a wood; and I . . .
—Robert Frost, *The Road Not Taken*

T o me in Kennebunk, the end of summer proclaimed the end of the year, more so even than when New Year's Eve came to Temple. On Fletcher Street, maple trees hardened off, and leaves fell to the ground. Darkness and cooler days came upon us. Summer friends disappeared, and daily play stopped. The neighborhood backyards went silent, and school,which I had hoped to attend in the more familiar surroundings of the Village School, started in Kennebunk.

Ma enrolled Nancy and me in Park Street School; Nancy in fourth grade, me in sixth. She did not enroll Patty, who had completed kindergarten in Temple the year before, and Ma, I supposed, thought she had learned enough there to forsake the Kennebunk school system altogether. But Park Street School, a homely, two-story brick structure set close to the sidewalk among a settlement of nineteenth-century sea captains' homes on the far side of Main Street, about a half a mile from Grammy and Grampa's, had served Kennebunk kids well for many years. Ma told Nancy and me that we would find satisfaction there as well. I found little comfort in that knowledge, but I went there the first day with a sense of hope.

We lived too close to the school to catch the bus; hence, unless we walked up Storer Street to the last bus stop a quarter of a mile farther away, Nancy and I were forced to walk to school. On our walk, we had to cross Main Street, and Ma—who had lost her trust in me to cross Main Street alone when I had been knocked down by a car earlier that summer—didn't know whether a crossing guard would be stationed there, so she walked with us the first day.

"The streets here aren't like the streets in Temple," she told me.

I soon learn that Park Street School is not like the Village School either. The front walk ends at an imposing set of concrete steps, at the top of which are wide, double front doors. As I climb the steps to the entrance, the second-story windows glare mercilessly down at me like some Frankenstein monster. Inside, I say good-bye to Nancy and climb the stairs to the second floor. The sixth-grade classroom is off the center hallway toward the back. It looks full. More than twenty students sit there, more than in the entire school in Temple. Square-jawed Miss Watham, Park Street's legendary sixth-grade teacher who, Ma had told me, delivered only fully qualified students to the seventh grade, squints at me and beckons with her pointy finger toward an empty desk near the front. "What is your name?" she asks.

I quickly see she is a no-nonsense commander of our classroom, and I will not be whispering to any of my classmates during lessons. "John," I gulp and sag into my seat, hoping she will forget I'm here.

She strides to the blackboard, writes her name in perfect Palmer Method script, and turns to the class. Standing in shoes with heels that make her two inches taller, she looks out over the top of her reading glasses and proclaims, "My name is Belle Watham. You may call me Miss Watham. I am the sixth-grade teacher at Park Street School. In the sixth grade, you will learn language, arithmetic, European geography, ancient history, and spelling. Students in this classroom in the past have mostly mastered these subjects, and I expect you, if you work hard enough, will too."

I learned two things that first day: I had to compete with too many kids to be assured of success, and Miss Watham's strict semblance could likely give rise to an unusual level of worry in a lonely sixth grader. I hadn't been exposed to such ominous classroom power before. I looked for an escape but saw none.

Sixth-grade subjects seemed hard for me to grasp, harder even than when I listened to Mrs. Stolt in Temple, standing two rows away from me, teach sixth-graders Alice and Leo and Myron the particulars of North American geography. Miss Watham taught ancient Greek history and Mediterranean geography. I paid attention and labored over my lessons in the classroom, but after supper, I had to ask Ma to help me learn the dates of the Ottoman Rule and the Byzantine Empire, and what countries bordered the Adriatic Sea. Ma had to look for the answers in my textbook, and I wondered why I had to know such stuff. I didn't care about the Ottomans anyway. And I didn't want to be in Miss Watham's classroom, where the hot sun pounded on me through the glass and twenty-odd other kids knew more than I did and played up to Miss Watham's compassionate side in search of a higher grade. I could handle reading and language and arithmetic, but I couldn't handle the Byzantines. Mrs. Stolt wouldn't have wasted our time on the Byzantines in the Village School. Perhaps I had forgotten how to learn, Nancy said, or maybe my brain was already full.

I knew how to learn. But as much as I wished it were not so, it seemed every day I discovered how ignorant I was. My ignorance was especially evident during the one hour each week Miss Watham took us to the music room. You need to know the scale, she said, and plunked the piano keys and directed us to sing the notes. I went mute, frozen, and managed only to hum each note at the same pitch, so quietly neither Miss Watham nor my classmates could hear me. Each week we practiced the notes and sang the cowboy lament called "Git

Along Little Dogies." I didn't learn the scale or the notes, and I barely learned the words to the dogie song, but eventually I knew them well enough to mime along while my classmates sang the words aloud.

I don't think Miss Watham was conscious of how little I knew, or how much I learned in her class and quickly forgot. She treated me well on my report card, and she would hark back to my presence when Nancy and Patty passed through her class in later years. But my memory of her classroom is limited to a place where I sweated and sweltered in the heat of an Indian summer, and not the Mediterranean geography and ancient Greek history I labored over in September and October 1945. The crux of my learning was centered on the experience and not the subject. And the same was true outside her classroom.

One day a few of my classmates invited me to meet them on Saturday under the Lafayette Elm for touch football. I had seen trees all over town, but I didn't know which ones had names and I would be too embarrassed to wait under the wrong tree, so I asked, "Where is it?"

"Where is it?" They laughed, and one said, "You don't know? Everyone knows the Lafayette. It's the biggest tree in town. On Storer Street, just down from your house on the big, grassy lawn beside the yellow house—the Storer House. Gawd, everyone knows that."

He thought I should know the Marquis de Lafayette had actually slept there. I could feel the crimson creep into my face. "Okay," I said. "I'll be there."

Those who had played together other Octobers dominated the Saturday game. I was not left out, but I wasn't included. I had space to occupy and instructions to follow, and I went straight downfield long or short and turned left or right as they told me. But time and again, I watched the biggest boy throw the ball to a friend, and after an hour in the shadow of the Lafayette Elm, I quit the game and walked back to Grammy's. Lonesome, I needed Pa to come home and take me back to Temple and to Cappy. I needed him to tell me his stories.

I didn't know then that Pa had started for home, but soon a letter came to Fletcher Street. He wrote that he was at the docks in LeHavre and waiting for word to board a ship. Because it has been more than a week since he wrote the letter, I reasoned that maybe he is close or maybe here. "Mommy, is he coming home or going to another army camp? Does he say?"

"He says he's coming to Fort Devens in Massachusetts, then here to Kennebunk. If he left on time, he might be getting close." She stopped, and dreams came into her eyes, dreams of bliss. "Maybe he'll arrive on our anniversary. What a gift that would be!" She stood up, paced to the window and back, and arranged her hair with her hands. She looked for Grammy. She looked at me. "Let's hope," she said.

Unknown to us, while we read the letter, Pa was being tossed around in a seventy-knot gale on the North Atlantic. The USS *West Point*, formerly the luxury liner SS *America*, had left LeHavre four days previously, on October 16, and now steamed at twenty-two knots through rough and rainy weather for Newport News, Virginia. This was its seventh crossing of the Atlantic since V-E Day, and the luxury liner was no longer luxurious. The hull had been painted a drab gray, the promenade deck compartmented with steel partitions, the former ballroom converted to sleeping quarters, and the swimming pool filled with supplies. Pa didn't mind; USS *West Point* was taking him home.

The ship carried eighty-five hundred soldiers, WACs, and army nurses, and they suffered through their worst day at sea since leaving LeHavre. Many confined themselves to compartments and lay on bunks or sat and held buckets between their knees. Pa, who seemed immune to seasickness, enjoyed a second helping of unclaimed beefsteak at dinner in the mess hall, then watched a movie.

After midnight, the skies cleared, the ocean calmed, and the ship reached the halfway mark on its three-thousand-mile voyage. While Pa slept, the ship's crew published the next day's edition of the *West Point*'s daily newspaper, the *Log*. The feature story proclaimed they would arrive in Newport News on schedule.

In Kennebunk, Nancy, who has more courage than I and doesn't mind hearing Ma say no, looks up at her and asks, "Can we go to the movies?" She knows Grammy does not allow movies and Ma will likely deny her request, but she asks anyway because she knows Ma is a softy.

"You know Grammy doesn't approve of your going to the movies," Ma answers. "Besides, it's Sunday."

Nancy persists. "But all the kids are going. We want to go, too. Can we?"

"What is it?" Ma asks.

Aha, I think. She's weakening.

Nancy continues, "*The Three Caballeros*. It's for kids. It has Donald Duck and music and flying on a magic carpet to South America. Can we go? Pleee-ze. It's in color."

"Uhh . . . uhh, I don't know. I wish you could."

"All the kids are going, Mommy," I say. "Everyone's going to the matinee, four o'clock. We can leave after dinner and be home at six-thirty."

Ma is silent. I suppose she is thinking of Pa, afraid he has forgotten their anniversary. But, after a moment, she blurts, "Yes. Yes, you can go. I don't care what Grammy thinks. Leave right after dinner and don't say a word to anyone. I'll take care of Grammy."

In the theater, we munch popcorn and take a musical tour of Latin America. Donald and Panchito and Jose, the cigar-smoking parrot, tie on sombreros and fly to Mexico, where Jose and Panchito sing and dance and Donald chases female birds. Then to Brazil where more of the same goes on. We laugh at their absurd exploits and forget about stuffy Sundays on Fletcher Street. Grammy doesn't know, and anyway Ma said we could come and that she could keep us out of trouble. But somehow it all seems too good to be true—and it is.

I hear a commotion and turn my eyes away from Jose, who is singing a love song and puffing on a smoky cigar, and look toward the aisle. Two people, one with a shaded flashlight, walk the length of the aisle and turn and come back. They look into the row where Nancy, Patty, and I sit. The one with the flashlight is an usher. The other is Grammy. Good God, she's come to get us! I don't believe it. Then she points and speaks.

"I see you sitting there," she growls. "You know you're not supposed to be here. Come with me this minute." The usher, nervous, beckons with his flashlight. Mortified beyond words, we exit as fast as we can.

Outside, Grampa is waiting in the car. On the way home, Grammy sputters to us that we have committed a sinful act and declares that we will be punished next time. I don't speak, nor does Nancy or Patty. At home, Ma is red-eyed and repentant that she had failed us. "I'm sorry," she says.

"It's okay, Mommy," I say.

If the three caballeros had flown their magic carpet over the Atlantic Ocean that Sunday afternoon, we could have looked down on the USS *West Point*, its sweaty compartments full of soldiers and WACs and army nurses, steaming at twenty-two knots for Newport News, Virginia—and home. Pa, out of poker money, rested in his stuffy cubicle where he read in the *Log* that he would arrive in Newport News early Tuesday morning. At 5:00 P.M., he fetched his mess kit from his duffel and endured an hour in the chow line, then watched the evening's feature movie.

Later he lay on his bunk in the darkness and connected images and memories. The barn door in Temple, open and peaceful in the summer sun, would be closed when he arrived, and the house would be cold. The trees he felled in the back pasture on his last leave more than a year ago would be dried and hard, and he would bring them in and fit them to the furnace. Tarmo would come, and they would work together as they had in the past, one splitting, one lugging and stacking. Later, Pa would drive them up to Lauri's in the roadster, passing by brown fields and barns full of hay and dead vines rotting in kitchen gardens. In Lauri's Finnish steam bath, they would sweat out the beer and embellish their exploits in General Patton's U.S. Third Army. His mind drifted . . . one more day, one more night.

Standing with Nancy in front of the Kennebunk Public Library waiting to cross Main Street, I asked her, "Do you have music today?"

"No," she answered. "The fourth grade doesn't have music on Tuesday. We have art."

"Well, I have music this morning, and I dread it. I forget the words, and I don't know anything about sounds or tones or pitch. I just sing along with everyone else, except I'm about half a word behind. I hate it." We cross and walk down the Dane Street sidewalk toward Park Street School. Kids pass us in the gutter. "Besides, I'm tired of the same darn song. You'd think she would have changed it by now."

"She's probably not going to change it until you learn it."

Nancy was so right she could discourage even my most timorous efforts to learn that dogie song. "I suppose if I ever do learn the darned thing, I'll just have to learn another one." I smirked. "Maybe I'll just stick with this one."

"John, you're learning the wrong stuff. Learn that song, and another one, too. Don't figure out how to get out of it, for gosh sakes."

"We're not going to be here all year, are we?"

"I don't know," she answered.

Later, Miss Watham raised her pointy finger in music class and said, "Don't think you can get away without learning this song. You are going to sing it until you know it, no matter how long it takes. You're not going to the seventh grade without knowing the musical scale and how to sing the notes to the dogie song. And after you learn that one, I've another."

Nancy's words came back to me, and I forced myself all of that grueling hour to learn the blasted song. But, as it turned out, I didn't have to know it. By the next Tuesday, I would be gone from Miss Watham's classroom.

On the USS *West Point* Tuesday morning, the bugle call sounded at

3:00 A.M.. Pa was prompt out of his bunk, and his bare feet landed softly on the compartment's steel floor. He jostled for space to shave in front of a mirror and quickly dressed in a clean uniform, garrison cap, and combat boots. He retrieved his mess kit from his duffel and went to the mess hall where he waited in line for a warm mixture of water and dried scrambled eggs and a cup of hot coffee. He ate standing up and sloshed his mess kit in a can of lukewarm dishwater and returned to his compartment, pinned identification and order-of-debarkation tags to his cap, packed the final items in his duffel, and waited.

The USS *West Point* docked at Newport News at 6:30 A.M., just as I was getting out of bed in Kennebunk. An hour later, the first soldier stepped off the ship. As I made my way to Miss Watham's music class, Pa made his way down the narrow gangplank and onto U.S. soil for the first time in a year. No military band greeted him with "When Johnny Comes Marching Home Again," and no Red Cross girls handed him hot coffee and doughnuts. Instead, a line of army trucks waited in the street to take him to Camp Patrick Henry in Norfolk. He and twenty other soldiers threw their duffels into the canvas-covered body of a converted supply truck, climbed in, and sat on wooden benches for the ride across the James River.

At Camp Patrick Henry, Pa spent most of two days standing in line for food, a movie, and lectures describing the proper way to be a civilian. On the second day, he boarded a troop train leaving for Fort Dix, New Jersey, at 6:00 P.M., precisely the time Grampa was repeating the Wednesday dinner grace.

By Saturday, a period of Indian summer had descended on Kennebunk. The warm and gentle morning begged me to be outside, and Grammy sent me to play in the backyard. Restless and by myself, I failed to find entertainment in her sparse patch of faded grass; I just wandered around with my thoughts. I had tried to be an upscale and stylish boy in Kennebunk, but I just couldn't do it. In Temple, I could skip flat rocks on the millpond, explore an abandoned barn, climb the pasture gate and hike out the lane for apples, or scratch a hopscotch game in the dirt. I could pull turnips for Ma, carry water to the calf, or fill the wood box. I could always find something different to do in Temple. Here I'm stuck with a solitary game of kick-the-can.

I gulped a sandwich, then biked to the Lafayette Elm. There, a dozen boys contested the Saturday football game, and I waited for a chance to play, but no chance came. I waited until the sun's rays began to slant through the branches of the giant elm, then I biked up Storer Street looking for a kickball game. No game in sight, I rode back to Grammy's where I found Nancy in the backyard. "Did the mail come yet? Did Mommy hear from Daddy?" I asked.

"No," Nancy answered, "but she thinks he must be off the ship by now and might call us."

"I wish he would hurry up."

No one spoke about Pa at dinner. The conversation was all "What did you do today?" and "Wipe your face" and "Eat your squash" and "You need to go to bed early because tomorrow is church school." Pa is on his way here, and no one seemed interested enough to talk about it.

After we finished eating, I asked, "Is Daddy on his way home? Has his ship landed?" But of course they didn't know. And Ma, although as anxious as I was to see him, didn't want to talk about it. She went upstairs to her room. I found a chair and read late into the evening before Ma told me it was too late for Pa to call and time for me to go to bed. I was certain he would call, and I promised myself to pray in church school tomorrow for him to turn up soon.

After standing in line at Fort Dix for two hours Saturday night, Pa approached the clerk's paper-littered desk. It was 10:00 P.M., 2200 hours in army language. This would be the last day, he thought, that he would need to know army talk. Since arriving at Fort Dix early Thursday morning, he had been counseled by psychologists, examined by physicians, and instructed by sergeants in the ways of civilian life. He had waited all that day in the barracks for his turn to stand in a line that would be his last in the army. The clerk looked up from behind his desk. "Name and serial number, soldier."

"Hodgkins, E. W., three, one, four, zero, zero, zero, four, five, sir."

"You don't need to call me sir, private." He pushed a cluster of papers at Pa. "Here. Sign these, soldier. At the bottom where I've checked."

"What am I signing?

"You're granting the army permission to discharge you. It's your ticket home." Pa handed the papers back. "Thanks," the clerk said, eyeing the bottom of each sheet where Pa had signed, "Now step over into that next line."

Thirty minutes later, Pa had been issued a new dress uniform complete with a garrison cap and an Eisenhower jacket. He stuffed it in his duffel bag and moved to the next line. In another hour, he had received his final pay—in cash—from the U.S. Army, an authorization for free transportation home, and at 11:50 P.M., clutching his discharge tightly in his left hand, Pa heard the clerk behind the desk in front of him issue him his last order, "Move your ass along there, son. You ain't in this man's army no more." Five minutes later, he was in a taxi on his way to the train station in Trenton.

When Pa arrived at the Trenton train station, I had been asleep almost two hours. Six hours later I woke and dressed and sat at the breakfast table.

Ma takes Grammy's serving platters away. "Finish your breakfast, kids. You need to start getting ready."

Then the telephone rings, and Ma is talking, but I can't make out what she's saying. She hangs up and rushes into the dining room, her face red, beaming the contained radiance of a year's anticipation. "Kids, it's your father! He's in Boston! He will be here on the ten o'clock train!"

At last, I think, Pa's home. It's over. I don't have to go to church school today; I don't have to pray for him to get home soon; I don't have to go to Miss Watham's sixth grade tomorrow. I haven't seen him for more than a year, and it has been nearly two since he left home. I wonder what he will be like, whether he will be different, whether I will know him. But in spite of all that, I am sure he will know me and have stories to tell me and will take all of us home to Temple.

We stand at the end of the narrow platform at the Depot Street station and stare down the tracks toward Boston. Grammy and Grampa stand quietly behind us. Ma, who had insisted we come early, stands first on one foot and then the other and looks at her watch every fifteen seconds. Ma sees it first and moves onto the platform trailing the rest of us behind her. The train clanks and stops beside us, and I stop breathing.

Pa steps onto the platform, resplendent in his new uniform, gold badges on the lapels of his Eisenhower jacket, service ribbons and medals pinned to his left breast, the 8th Armored Division patch on his left shoulder, and the "ruptured duck," a patch for service in a foreign war, stitched over his right breast pocket. He drops his duffel onto the platform and hugs and kisses Ma first, hanging onto her, and she onto him for what seems like forever. He gathers Patty in his arms and hugs her and kisses her on the cheek. And then Nancy, too shy to be kissed, hugs him around the neck. He leans over and hugs me, and I, too big to be carried, reach up and try to squeeze him around the shoulders. He nods at Grammy, shakes Grampa's hand, and then turns to retrieve his duffel. I don't recall a word being said.

He talks at dinner and for most of the afternoon, keeping us entertained with an account of his trip home: the truck ride to chaotic and disorganized Camp Patrick Henry, a crowded troop train to Fort Dix where he waited for his discharge, then the wild taxi ride and overnight train to Boston. Listening to him is, for me, the culmination of one of the most uniformly happy days of my life. Pa is home, in his uniform, telling stories. It doesn't matter that they are stories of train rides and sleepless nights. I know they are just a prelude to tales of great armies and crucial battles and decisive victories.

Pa left for Temple the next morning, alone. He boarded the train at Depot Street, and Grandpa C.F. and Grandma and Aunt Marion met him at the West Farmington station. One day later, we said good-bye to Grammy and Grampa Watson, whose goodness that summer I now admit I had overlooked in my own self-serving interests. Pa met us at the train station and took us home in the roadster, where Cappy bounded at us and licked our faces. Everything was as we had left it. Eddie had milked and pastured and fed the cows, fattened a new pig in the outdoor sty, and brought Cappy a full ration of food and water every day. Against my fears, the place had survived our flight to Kennebunk.

The first days in Temple were a series of emotional reunions. Aunt Marion hosted a family welcome-home celebration, complete with cards and cakes and gifts, for Pa and Uncle Austin, who was discharged soon after Pa. Pa absorbed the admiration of his family and their pleasantries graciously, and Ma, yielding softly to his family's sincerity, radiated pride at the attention given him. We walked home from Aunt Marion's and chatted along the lane, relaxed and thankful to be together.

Pa reunited with his friends, and they rejoiced at the sight of him. Tarmo came to the house, and the two former soldiers in General Patton's Third Army hugged each other in the driveway. Elmer walked up from his home in the village and drank beer with Pa in the sun of an Indian summer. Pa drove up to Lauri's where Vilio and Weikko greeted him with laughing faces and teary eyes, and they unwound in the heat of Lauri's Finnish steam bath. Mrs. Mosher, Old Carr, Kike, Fern, and Eddie and Nellie all came and welcomed him home and expressed their gratitude. For days, the house swarmed with people bringing joy and good wishes. But as much as we wanted the attention to continue, the excitement predictably diminished, and we were left to resurrect our lives.

In another story perhaps, or in this one with a firmer beginning, we would go back to our former selves and be happy together ever after, proud of our service and of our sacrifice. In this story, we *were* proud of our service, and we *did* go back to our former selves, and for an instant our life was as I had dreamed it would be. But coming home was difficult for Pa. After his experiences soldiering, he was changed, and home seemed changed to him; home lacked purpose and direction and a place for him to focus. His friends, except for those who also had served, had carried on with their lives and were distant. His trucking business had languished and required more investment and commitment to restore than he could muster. And he and Ma skirmished with each other.

They start with what seems like harmless bickering. Ma, delighting in his presence at home, makes him pot roast or biscuits or custard pie, his favorite desert. At the kitchen table, he shows no appreciation for her thoughtful stab at his happiness and sips from a tumbler of Krueger ale. She serves him, and he tastes the results of her labor.

"What were you doing all the time I was gone?" he says to her. "These are burned, like always. Look!" and he holds up a biscuit. "Haven't you learned how to make biscuits yet?"

Ma, prim in a new housedress, puts a stick in the stove and sits at the opposite end of the table. She dusts flour from her sleeve, grins at him, and then glowers. "Doing?" she answers. "I had to split wood and clean your privy and chase your pig. I didn't have time or enough wood to heat an oven and bake biscuits for myself. I baked these for *you*. We've gone without."

In the dim yellow light of the kitchen table where so many had sat and buoyed up Ma, I become aware of conflict, a rivalry over sacrifice. The sacrifices they each had known were not to be shared but kept and hoarded and used to strike a blow at the other.

He tells Ma, "Gone without! You don't know how easy you've had it. Fern and Eddie waitin' on you all the time, bringin' you all the drink you want, and takin' you dancin'. Don't tell me how rough you had it. You don't know what I've been through, no idea how rough I had it."

"As far as I know, Elliott, you had nothing to worry about with a million soldiers looking after you. I had nobody but Eddie. Your self-righteous family wouldn't lift a finger to help me."

As time goes on, the bickering grows. They suspect each other's faithfulness and accuse each other of wrongdoing. I grow afraid.

Pa goes out a lot, and he comes home late. Ma is in a terrible state, alone, unhappy, fraught with worry, anxious that he doesn't care for her. She sits in the dark of her bedroom window late into the nights, a tumbler within reach on the windowsill, and watches over the village. Across the stream on the road from West Farmington, headlights come into view, and she watches them move through the dark village and turn away from her toward the intervale.

Nancy asks why Pa doesn't come home.

"He'll be here soon," she tells Nancy. "He must have had to get something in town."

I think she actually believes he is on an errand, but she can't sleep. She sits in the chair, the tumbler emptied and refilled, and stares into the darkness. There is nothing there. Another car comes and turns away.

Ma is still on that straight-backed chair when headlights turn across the bridge and weave up our lane. I hear Pa's footsteps heavy on the stairs and the bedroom door pushed shut; muffled voices strain through the house into my room. His behavior hurts Ma, and he drinks too much. And he doesn't care. Neither one respects the hardships the other has suffered.

Frank Pierce, who had spent another year in the army in Germany, came to see Pa as he had promised he would. They drove together over Temple's dusty roads and fished the pond and the stream. They drank hard cider and sat on the topmost seat at Lauri's Finnish steam bath and reminisced. Pa seemed easy and relaxed and showed Frank off to his family and friends, proud that they had warred together. But Pa's cheerful spirit was for Frank to enjoy. When Frank left, Pa became disagreeable again, offensive, and sometimes violent.

Pa had no rules that governed the behavior of a man except those that were not governing—leave life to chance; if it feels good, it's okay; society's rules are for others. I wanted a father who would love me, teach me about life, tell me stories, and come home at night and play a game with me, but what I got was, "Wise up, boy." Ma also yearned for him to love her, and she had let him strip her of her strict upbringing to help him, she thought, find pleasure in her. Now he ridiculed her anxious attempts to satisfy him.

The abuse went on, and for a time Ma endured it. Pa drank most days and gambled away the little money that remained. He criticized Ma intolerably, and he abandoned her bed. He threatened her, even struck her, and his fearsome presence frightened us all. Folks said he was tormented by the war and just needed time to return to normal. He was more likely tormented by peace. He felt forgotten, and his former bond with the town, family, friends, and work was either lost or distant. To start over was more than he could face. At times, he became downcast and heavyhearted and sobbed uncontrollably. He knew that the most fulfilling time he would live—a time of goals and purpose and sacrifice and, especially, pride in himself—was over.

Ma retaliated. She drank heavily, too, and argued with Pa over ownership of drink. They stole liquor from each other, and they watered each other's hidden cache. She tried to reason with him, but in the face of his bullying, the load was too heavy. She withdrew to her bedroom, to the chair in the window, to whiskey, beer, and cigarettes.

Hope stopped. I knew we were living a failure, and I suffered shame, and fright. What would happen? How would we go on? Neither Ma nor Pa could console me. Ma would say, "It will be all right," and I would think of the Christmas chicken Eddie had killed. Pa would say, "It will all come out in the wash," and I wouldn't know what he meant. I—Nancy and Patty, too—was nowhere, lost. By age ten, I had lived a dream, been fulfilled for an instant, and suffered the dream's failure.

In October, two years after Pa had stepped off the train in Kennebunk, he and Ma divorced. On the appointed day, the judge decreed the dissolution of the marriage without the appearance of either one in the courtroom. What had thirteen Octobers before been a marriage of passion was no longer desirable. Soon after the divorce, Ma and Nancy and Patty left for Kennebunk. I couldn't leave Temple, nor had Ma shown any inclination toward my going with her. Predictably, Pa showed no interest in my upbringing or future. I was an orphan. I moved to Aunt Marion's. Although I had often thought her treatment of Ma and Pa to be unjust, her kindness and generosity showed through her criticism of their circumstances, and she welcomed me with warm assurances and oatmeal cookies.

After a week or so in her company, not having seen Pa since Ma left, I walk the quarter-mile road to our place on Cowturd Lane. The October sky is dull, and across the stream the hillsides are turning from red and yellow to ocher and gray. Leaves have dropped on the roadside, and cow turds have dried in the roadway. I smell a wisp of woodsmoke in the air.

Pa is not at the house. I let myself in through the shed to the kitchen. Water drips into the pail in the sink. The worn oilcloth hangs over the edge of the kitchen table. The cookstove is cold. On the parlor desk, Pa has left a month-old, unfinished birthday card and note to his niece. The house is chilled and dark and quiet—deathly quiet. More than four years have passed since Pa and Elmer and Vilio played the matchstick poker game at the kitchen table, two years since the phone rang in Kennebunk to begin the happiest day of my life. Now I am alone with images of the past stuck in my head.

I stand in the stillness: edgy, restless, anxious that I am alone. I sit in the padded parlor chair, worn hard by the years, and pick up a book lying there, then put it aside. Ashes lie cold and damp in the brick fireplace where we had popped corn and played Go Fish with Grandpa C.F., and where Aunt Marion had hung our Christmas stockings on a tension-filled Christmas Eve.

I walk through the house. Upstairs, the straight-backed chair sits askew by the front window in Ma's bedroom. The hole in her bedroom door—splintered by Pa's foot—haunts me, and I turn away. In my room, where night winds had shaken the window and kept me awake, where snow had drifted through cracks onto the sill, where I had huddled in the cold and listened to Ma and Pa yell at each other, nothing remains. It's as though I hadn't existed.

I leave. Out through the barn, by the empty woodbox—Pa is not disposed to filling it himself—past the heifer's stall where Pa had cached whiskey and Ma had found it and watered it; out the back door and down the steps where I had seen Pa, unable to resurrect the good days, sit in the evening and sob.

A few days later, Pa came to Aunt Marion's to tell me he had sold the house and was moving to Farmington, to a room at Uncle Phil's and that he would be back to see me and perhaps we would visit Ma around Christmas.

"You were at the house," he said.

"How do you know?"

"I saw your tracks."

"Why, Daddy? Why did it have to happen?"

"It'll all come out in the wash," he told me.

Someday, I thought, I will know what that means.

I was left in Temple, where I first knew the loneliness of winter twilight and the haven of a warm kitchen stove. Where I first probed curious places and ran in the paths and lanes and explored the rocky stream bank. Where I first came face to face with beauty, a single, pale orchid in a boggy wood. Where I first knew the aura of a star-polished sky, and where I first heard the fierce night wind scream outside my window. And where, for a short time, I honored my father as only a boy can.

Aunt Marion suffered a stroke in 1985. She lived four more years, mostly in Temple until she could no longer manage a house, then she moved to assisted-living quarters in South Windham, Maine, followed

by the Freeport Nursing Home. I was with her at the end. Her func
in Farmington, was standing room only.

I had lived with Aunt Marion and Uncle Lawrence for fourteen
years after Ma's and Pa's divorce. They willingly took me in, provided for
me, and cared for me. They gave me opportunity and encouraged me.
Aunt Marion did not change her character, but she changed my life. She
saw to it that I learned a few human graces; that I understood the value
of achievement, friends, and family; and that I knew the importance of
education. And she became a grandma, of sorts, to Beth's and my children—the same Auntie May who had watched over Nancy, Patty, and
me during our childhoods. I am forever grateful for her kindness.

For months before her death, Ma wheeled around an oxygen bottle,
the final lingering indignity from her life in Temple. She had cast off
alcoholism and found a new life in a Salem, New Hampshire, first-
grade classroom where, during a span of fifteen years, she reacquired a
reputation for scholarly excellence. But the consequences of years of
smoking—a habit learned in Temple—could not be overcome. She
died in 1969.

I saw her last in the General Hospital in Lawrence, Massachusetts,
where she was surrounded by oxygen, IV tubes, bottles of pills, and
glasses of various liquids. Although she was spirited in conversation,
she was gaunt in appearance, and I said my silent goodbyes to a mother
I mostly felt sorry for.

After Temple, Ma and I had kept in touch, and I would visit her on
occasion—Mother's Day, Thanksgiving, Christmas, or when the horses
were running at Rockingham Park. She lived comfortably in Salem,
with Nancy and Patty close by, and seemed well-adjusted to the setting.
Sometimes, when I went there, Pa came along, and later, Beth. At other
times, Ma and her sister, Eileen, came to Yarmouth to visit Beth and
me. But Ma and I were not close. I often wished there had been more
room for me in her life, or her in mine. But I told myself that I understood her circumstances.

I don't think Pa ever knew the level of support Ma gave him during the war in the face of debilitating family humiliation. Her struggle to please him had gone unappreciated, and she died without ever receiving his gratitude. He went with me to her funeral—perhaps to finally say thank you—a quiet affair on a cold, barren November day in Salem.

Pa spent his postwar life battling alcoholic demons. From time to time, he beat them off—he once held a job for a year, and I was heartened—but then they would rise again. He lived his final years on the stream bank in Temple where I would visit him occasionally, anxious as I approached his little trailer that he would be drunk or sick or hurt. Seldom did we do anything together.

Frank Pierce of the 405th Armored Field Artillery Battalion came from Philadelphia to the trailer one day late in Pa's life and tried unsuccessfully to wake him from an alcoholic stupor. It was the last time the two old veterans of the European campaign were together.

In August 1974, I returned from vacation to find that Pa had been admitted to the Veterans Administration Hospital in Togus, Maine. He seemed healthy when I visited, but they were keeping him, he said, to strengthen him. We walked the hospital grounds and talked. Later, I arranged a weekend furlough for him, and he came to Yarmouth to see his grandchildren. Beth made him biscuits and custard pie.

In September, Pa suffered a stroke. I called Nancy and Patty, and we went to Togus together for a final visit. He died on September 30 and was buried on a snowy day at the Maine Veterans Cemetery in Augusta. A soldier folded the flag that draped his coffin, handed it to me, and saluted. He knew not what that flag meant to me, or to Pa.

EPILOGUE

O n a Sunday morning more than half a century after that luckless October in 1947, Beth and I, at the end of a three-day journey from Maine, slowly approach the French village of Port sur Seille. I drive along its main street, which is lined with stone buildings and vegetable gardens and grazing cows, to the far end and park close by a little bridge. I have come here in search of a missing piece of my past—the story my father never told me—and I want to walk the town's streets and look into its yards and feel its spirit.

The sun warms our backs as we walk along the main street, and the odor of cow manure hangs in the air, giving truth to the industry of these people. Fields of hay and barley and oats surround the small collection of rectangular cut-stone farmhouses and barns. A church spire dominates the skyline. Probably two hundred people live here, working the land, tending animals, building families, attending church. But today we walk the street alone. A rooster breaks the silence. At the sound, Beth takes my hand, and I feel a part of this town; a part of its tight cluster of sturdy buildings, its reliance on the land, its grace, its history.

My mind wanders back to when Pa was here with the 405th, roads clogged with blowing snow and soldiers bivouacked in barns. Back to January 1945, when the U.S. 8th Armored Division battled panzers for Butzdorf and Sinz to the north, in Germany, holding the 11th Panzer Division in place while U.S. Third Army turned toward Bastogne and broke the siege at the Battle of the Bulge.

I can see Pa now, tramping the main street, sandbagging his truck, loading it with gasoline or ammunition at the supply depot, and heading for the front. I see him, too, huddled in his sleeping bag in one of these barns, perhaps after a hot meal from a nearby family, perhaps reading a letter from Ma by lamplight. I sift countless thoughts as I walk through this village, a village that has seen the advancing armies of two world wars, but mainly I seek a better understanding of a man I tried—and failed—to know.

Ahead of us now, near the center of the village where the road turns, I see a man standing in the shadow of his house, a can of car polish in one hand, a cloth in the other. Beside him, the gleaming finish of an old French car reflects his robust physique. Behind the Frenchman, beyond a green strip of clipped and manicured grass, stands a two-story cut-stone building decorated with window boxes of showy verbena and bordered by gardens of iris and roses, the only visible color in this farming village. A sign on the building reads Café de la Seille.

He smiles and waves, and I return the wave. "Bonjour, Monsieur," I say.

"Bonjour," he replies.

"Parlez-vous anglais?"

He lowers his head slightly and answers from within his belly. "Non, non." We both laugh.

In twelve seconds, I have used my entire French vocabulary. And now he says he doesn't speak English. I turn to Beth. "What do I do now?"

"I don't know. Try pantomime."

"Pantomime?" I answer. "I don't know pantomime any better than I know French. I thought you knew French, from high school, from your French friends?"

"It's been thirty-five years, and you expect me to remember? What do you want to say?"

"I want to ask him what he remembers. I bet he was here. How do you say father?" I smile at the Frenchman.

Beth thinks. "Some words are almost the same. Try Papa—with plenty of body language."

Pa had died without telling me his story. He did not mention the war to me. I asked once, but he said I was too young to understand. Now, fifty-five years later, on Father's Day 2000, I am old enough. Pa has died, and I have devoured his legacy to me: a diary, some maps, a few letters, memorabilia, and I stand at the site of his first engagement in a long-ago war—a war that was his brush with world history.

I turn back to the Frenchman. He will write to me later that his name is Robert Mesmer, but now we set about understanding each other. I grin, point to myself, and say, "Ameri*cahn*."

"Aaa-a-ah." A broad smile appears, and I extend my hand in greeting.

"My Pah-Pah," I continue. "My Pah-Pah. Port sur Seille 1945." I gesture to the village.

"Aaa-a-ah." He forms his arms and hands as though he is holding a gun, looks at me, and asks, "Boom, boom, boom?"

"Yes!" I reply. "Yes. Yes. Artillery. Cannons."

For the next hour, stimulated by our distant yet common partnership, and fortified with Beth's thirty-five-year-old high-school learning, we communicate in rudimentary French syllables, liberal use of body language, facial expressions, and hand gestures. He shows me his family's café, where, as an eleven-year-old boy, he watched American soldiers convert it to a field hospital. He expresses sorrow at the destruction of the small stone bridge over the Seille and points out the ammunition storage magazine, damaged in both wars and not repaired after the second. He shows me barns where American soldiers slept, the house where he sheltered in the cellar, and the church where his family prayed for liberation. In that hour, we become friends.

When it is time to leave, he asks us to stay and meet his wife. A pleasant and gentle woman, she stands devotedly at his side while he proudly tells her we are Americans. He then kisses Beth on both cheeks and embraces me with the gratitude of generations of French.

The author and Robert Mesmer in Port sur Seille, France, in June 2000.

"Merci. Merci," he says, and we pose for a picture.

"Au revoir," I reply.

We head north into Germany. We follow the Moselle River to Nennig, then drive uphill along the winding main street of Butzdorf, between stone homes and cowbarns and hand-tilled vegetable gardens, to the village square where an elderly woman tends her lettuce patch and a gray-haired man pitches hay onto a tractor-drawn wagon. In another kilometer, we reach the Orscholz high ground, the coveted terrain where German panzer troops stopped the advance of 8th Armored Division tanks in the deep snows and bitter winds of January 1945. We stop, and I look back at the years.

Only during the war years had I honored Pa. The years after the war were self-centered for me and unkind to him. He floundered and failed and eventually died alone. And now, standing on a little dirt road outside Sinz, Germany, I wonder if it could have been different.

Pa and I had a complicated—and sad—relationship. We had been filled with pity and shame and pride, as well as the deep emotions found in our failure to come together as father and son. He was an ambiguous man, but his flaws were real and visible. For much of his life, I failed to understand him, or to even try. I rejected his defects; he hid his righteousness. During the postwar years he did not uphold, nor did I heed, the importance of his life. He avoided being a father; I neglected to be a son. I did not know what it meant to him to have served, the honor he felt in being part of world history: he failed to teach me what being in that war meant to him. But here, in this far-away land, I know his life had direction and purpose, perhaps for the only time, and now, on Father's Day in France and Germany, I search for the stories he never told.

Later, Beth and I search in ancient Heinsberg and on the stone bridge over the Roer River at Hilfarth and in the streets of Grefrath. We seek understanding at Rheinberg and in the swirling waters of the Rhine River. At Bruckhausen, we pause, then turn toward Dorsten and on to Kirchellen and Lippstadt and the Ruhr, and we ponder Pa's time in these hamlets and crossroads on the main street of his life. For whatever else he may have achieved, I'm sure now that his war years counted most.

And as we find our way through that time, I begin to know my father.

★   ★   ★

John Hodgkins was born and grew up in Temple, Maine. A long-time civil engineer for the Maine Department of Transportation and an adjunct professor of engineering at the University of Maine, he received many honors in the field. Now retired, he and his wife Beth live primarily in Yarmouth, Maine, though they maintain ties to Temple and spend a few months each year there, raising Christmas trees and making maple syrup.